Karl Marx
Interviews and Recollections

By the same author

Engels
Karl Marx: Early Texts
Karl Marx: His Life and Thought
Karl Marx: Selected Writings
Marx
Marx before Marxism
Marxism after Marx
Marx's Grundrisse
The Thought of Karl Marx
The Young Hegelians and Karl Marx

KARL MARX

Interviews and Recollections

Edited by
David McLellan

Barnes & Noble Books
Totowa, New Jersey

First published 1981 by
THE MACMILLAN PRESS LTD
London and Basingstoke
Companies and representatives
throughout the world

First published 1981 in the USA by
BARNES & NOBLE BOOKS
81 Adams Drive
Totowa, New Jersey, 07512

MACMILLAN ISBN 0 333 28362 7
BARNES & NOBLE ISBN 0–389–20114–6

Printed in Hong Kong

LC : 81-7970

For Gabrielle

Contents

Preface

I have tried to include in this volume all the important descriptions of Marx by those who knew him personally. As a basis, I have relied on the Moscow *Reminiscences of Marx and Engels* (n.d.). However, the editors of this edition (henceforth *'RME'*) have omitted many passages they considered unfavourable to Marx. These I have consistently restored from the original. About a quarter of the material is published in English for the first time. I have added a minimum of explanatory notes to the text. Proper names are dealt with in the extensive biographical index, not in the notes; the abbreviation *'MWE'* refers to the Marx–Engels *Werke* (Berlin, 1957 ff.).

I am grateful to Nick Caswell and Deborah Derrick for help with the index and to Ivan Poniatowski for help with the original Russian of two excerpts.

13 Ivy Lane, Canterbury
January 1980   D. M.

Acknowledgements

The author and publishers wish to thank the Society of Authors as the literary representatives of the Estate of Sir Compton Mackenzie for permission to reproduce an extract from *My Life and Times; Octave VII: 1931–1938.*

Introduction

The biography of a single individual can in no way be separated from the biographies of previous and contemporary individuals: indeed, it is determined by them.

Karl Marx

Until recently the easily accessible sources on the more private side of Marx's life have presented rather an unbalanced picture; for interest in Marx the man was largely confined to the more orthodox and straightlaced of his followers, who edited their collection of reminiscences accordingly.[1] But now the recent spate of scholarly publications affords a more nuanced picture. The interviews and recollections reprinted below give (together with Marx's voluminous correspondence[2]) the best picture of him as a person. Of course, this picture can be no more than an impression. Many of these reminiscences were written some thirty or even forty years after the event, and here particularly Marx's favourite maxim, *de omnibus dubitandum* (see no. 44 below), is in order. This caution is all the more necessary as the picture of Marx that emerges from the texts below is, at first sight at least, by no means a unified one. Indeed, there seem to be four distinct Marxes. First, there is the absent-minded bohemian intellectual (as in, for example, no. 5 below); then the ruthless, practical schemer bent on wholesale domination (no. 29); then the highly cultured English gentleman with a rather distant air and wry sense of humour (no. 37); and finally the warm-hearted family man, lover of children and animals (no. 23).

These different aspects are explicable partly as successive stages in Marx's life. As a student he was (sometimes at least) a spendthrift who indulged in bouts of duelling and drunkenness, and the same disordered life-style persisted among the *Lumpen*-intellectuals in Paris and the German émigrés in London. It was the abortive revolutions of 1848 and the First International around 1870 that afforded Marx scope for his rather dubious talents as a political organiser. His life took on a distinctly more bourgeois aspect with the secure income of the 1870s and the visits to European spas. Also, of course, many of these observations are reflections of the observers' own propensities: it is Heinzen (no. 5) who sees Marx as a bohemian, Bakunin (no. 29) who sees him as an intriguer, and Grant Duff (no. 37) who sees him as a gentleman like himself.

Yet it is not just a question of a linear evolution. The whole framework of Marx's existence was penetrated by profound structural contradictions. He was a Jew living in a Christian culture. He was a German living in London. He was a socialist living in a bourgeois society.

The extent to which Marx's character was influenced by his Jewishness is difficult to establish. Inevitably his doctrine has been read by some as a secularised form of the Judaeo-Christian tradition.[3] Certainly Marx never attempted to conceal his strongly rabbinical ancestry. But, unlike his daughter Eleanor,[4] he never referred to himself as a Jew either. But the violence of his reaction when his son-in-law Longuet mentioned racial prejudice against Marx in Jenny Marx's family suggests that this was a matter of considerable concern to him.[5] Certainly his Jewishness was quite often referred to in attacks by his political opponents (see, for example, no. 29). It has even been claimed that, by a curious inversion, Marx was himself anti-Semitic.[6] It is true that in some of his early writings the notions of capitalism and Jewishness seem to be conflated and subjected to a common attack; that the *Neue Rheinische Zeitung* of 1848–9 printed, with Marx as editor, several racialist articles; and that Marx referred to Lassalle as a 'Jewish nigger'.[7] But this is not enough to sustain a charge of anti-Semitism: Marx's remarks on Judaism in his early writings are notoriously difficult to decode, and his references to Lassalle formed part of the unfortunate, but common, parlance of the time – he referred to Lafargue, his French mulatto son-in-law, as 'our little nigger'. It is open to speculation whether there is any affinity between Marx's own domestic life-style and that of his ancestors. One of the earliest and most striking commentators on this wrote,

> My mother told us of our great-grandfather whom she had known in her childhood: in the small village in Pomerania sat the white-bearded old man in the back room. Day after day he bent over huge Hebrew folios, while, in the front room, his wife dealt with the farmers, raised the children and organised the material affairs of the family. Why burden oneself with worrying about the upkeep of the family when life is only given us to learn the Talmud? So too Marx, in London in 1850.[8]

What is certain, in any account, is that Marx retained a profound ambivalence to his own Jewishness.

This sense of alienation was increased by the more tangible 'sleepless night of exile' in which Marx spent the greater part of his life. For someone who lived thirty-five years in London, it is curious how distant he remained from his surroundings. His intimate friends – always a very restricted circle – consisted of German émigrés like himself. His contacts with the English, whether social or political, were largely formal. All his daughters, during his lifetime, took up with Frenchmen, and the two who married moved to France. Only Eleanor immersed herself in English affairs – and only after her father's death. Unlike Engels, Marx never completely mastered the English language. He remained a German living in London.

This structural isolation of race and nationality was compounded by Marx's politics. Marx saw himself as committed both to the promotion of socialism and to a bourgeois life-style, and so much of his life was permeated by the painful tension between the two. The financial crises affecting the Marx household are well known. In one of his worst years, 1852, Marx wrote to Engels,

> My wife is ill; little Jenny is ill; Lenchen has a sort of nervous fever; I cannot and could not call the doctor, because I have no money for medicine. For eight to ten days I have fed the family on bread and potatoes, of which it is still questionable whether I can rustle up any today. Naturally this diet was not recommended in present climatic conditions. I did not write any articles for Dana, because I did not have the penny to go and read newspapers. . . .
>
> I had put off to the beginning of September all the creditors, who, as you know, are only paid off in small sums. Now there is a general storm.
>
> I have tried everything, but in vain. . . .
>
> The best and most desirable thing that could happen would be that the landlady should throw me out of the house. At least I should then be quit of the sum of £22. But I can scarcely trust her to be so obliging. Also the baker, the milkman, the man with the tea, the greengrocer, old butcher's bills. How can I get clear of all this hellish muck? Finally in the last eight to ten days, I have borrowed some shillings and pence (this is the most fatal thing, but it was necessary to avoid perishing) from layabouts.[9]

A decade later, after moving from the slums of Dean Street to the Haverstock Hill area, which was being opened up to middle-class housing development, Marx made the following suggestion to Engels as a way of escaping from the nightmare of bourgeois respectability:

> I have at last brought my wife to agree to a suggestion that I made a long time ago and which, with all its inconveniences, is not only

the sole solution, but is also preferable to life of the last three years, particularly the last, as well as restoring our self-esteem.

I will write to all my creditors (with the exception of the landlord) and say that, if they do not leave me in peace, I will declare myself bankrupt. . . . my two eldest daughters will get positions as governesses through the Cunningham family. Lenchen will go into another service and I with my wife and Tussy will go and live in the same City Model Lodging House in which Wolff and his family lived previously.[10]

Although this was more of a cry for help than a serious proposal it does indicate the stark nature of the choices facing Marx.

Marx's self-declared idea of happiness was to fight (see no. 44); and his idea of misery was submission. Struggle was essential to him. Yet his proud assertion of independence from bourgeois society entailed – paradoxically – a continued submission to its pressures. Marx was resolved 'to pursue my aim through thick and thin and not let bourgeois society turn me into a money-making machine'.[11] He complained – with a lot of justification – that 'I have sacrificed my health, my happiness and my family'[12] to the completion of his work. It is arguable that both his work and his family would have benefited had Marx taken steps to obtain a secure job. But this was impossible given his personality: he wistfully recalled his mother saying 'it is a pity that Karl doesn't make some capital instead of just writing about it', but any acceptance of this view would have undermined Marx's conception of himself as necessarily struggling against all the odds.

These difficulties were made all the more acute by Marx's attachment to his family. He could write grimly, 'there is no greater stupidity than for people of general aspirations to marry and so surrender themselves to the small miseries of domestic and private life'.[13] Nevertheless, the relationships in the Marx family seem to have been warm, close-knit and decidedly non-authoritarian. Marx conserved a deep affection for his wife throughout his life. Their relationship survived even the birth, in 1851, to Helene Demuth of Marx's only surviving son, a child known as Frederick Demuth, who was immediately farmed out to foster-parents and had no contact with his mother until after Marx's death.[14] Marx was by nature as over-optimistic about money as he was, on occasion, about revolution. When even this was not enough, he tried to balance Jenny's increasingly pessimistic moods by a silent stoicism. But he could sometimes be very expressive. In 1856 he wrote to her,

But love – not of Feuerbachian man, not of Moleschott's metabolisms, not of the proletariat, but love of one's darling, namely you – makes a man into a man again. In fact there are many women in the world, and some of them are beautiful. But where can I find another face in which every trait, even every wrinkle, brings back the greatest and sweetest memories of my life? Even my infinite sorrows, my irreplaceable losses I can read on your sweet countenance and I kiss my sorrows away when I kiss your sweet face. 'Buried in your arms, awoken by your kisses' – that is, in your arms and by your kisses, and the Brahmins and Pythagoreans can keep their doctrine of reincarnation and Christianity its doctrine of resurrection.[15]

These 'infinite sorrows' that Marx had inflicted on his family imposed on him an immense burden of guilt. This is brought out clearly in a long letter Marx wrote to his prospective son-in-law Lafargue which shows him at his most 'Victorian'. 'To my mind,' he wrote,

true love expresses itself in the lover's restraint, modest bearing, even diffidence regarding the adored one, and certainly not in unconstrained passion and manifestations of premature familiarity. Should you plead in your defence your Creole temperament, it becomes my duty to interpose my sound sense between your temperament and my daughter. If in her presence you are unable to love her in a manner that conforms with the latitude of London, you will have to resign yourself to loving her from a distance. I am sure you take my meaning.[16]

Marx went on to explain that he himself had 'sacrificed all my fortune to the revolutionary struggle'; this he did not regret, but had he to make the choice again he would not have married. 'As far as it is in my power, I intend to save my daughter from the rocks on which her mother's life has been wrecked.'[17] And, indeed, the price of Marx's vocation was high: of his seven children (one died at birth) only two survived him, and both of these committed suicide.

Outside the immediate family circle, there was only one relationship that survived that aggressive side of Marx's temperament that his sisters had so early discerned (see no. 23). For Marx's whole life-style depended on the financial and psychological assistance of Engels. As a salaried employee and then a partner in his father's Manchester cotton-spinning firm, Engels eventually made so much money that he became, by present-day standards, a millionaire. In the 1850s and 1860s sums of money from Engels – sometimes sent in postal-orders, sometimes in £1 or £5 notes cut in half and sent in separate letters – often saved the unworldly Marx from complete disaster. 'Karl was frightfully happy', wrote Jenny on one occasion, 'when he heard the fateful double knock of the postman: "There's

Frederick! two pounds extra! saved!" he cried out.[18] Engels also
acted as Marx's window on the practical world of commerce and
industry. He even accepted paternity of Marx's illegitimate son. This
financial dependence inevitably caused a certain amount of resent-
ment. But the only serious possibility of a breach between Marx and
Engels occurred on the death of Mary Burns, an Irish working girl
who had been living with Engels for the previous fifteen years. On
learning of her death, Marx wrote a letter to Engels which contained
two short sentences on Mary and a lengthy description of his
financial difficulties coupled with a demand for more money. Engels
was incensed, as all his 'philistine' friends had shown him more
sympathy than Marx, and he wrote to tell him so. Marx waited ten
days before replying in a letter containing the following revealing
passage:

> I can now tell you without further ceremony that, in spite of all the
> pressure I have endured in the last weeks, nothing burdens
> me – even relatively speaking – as much as this fear that our
> friendship should now break up. I repeatedly told my wife that
> nothing in the whole mess was important to me compared with the
> fact that, owing to our lousy bourgeois situation and her eccentric
> excitement, I was not in a position to comfort you at such a time
> but only to burden you with my private needs. Consequently
> domestic peace was much disturbed and the poor woman had to
> face the music, although it was no fault of hers, in as much as
> women are accustomed to demand the impossible. Naturally she
> had no idea of what I wrote, but her own reflection could have told
> her what the outcome would be. Women are funny creatures –
> even those endowed with much intelligence.[19]

Behind this lay Jenny's ambivalent attitude to Engels's relationship
to the Marx household and particularly her disapproval of his
irregular menage: Mary was never invited to accompany Engels on
his visits south and never mentioned in Jenny's letters.

The tension between Marx's intellectual vocation and his
bourgeois life-style can be seen most clearly in his financial
arrangements – or lack of them. As a student Marx had been
extravagant, far outspending his father's very generous allowance.
This was not just self-indulgence, for he could be extremely
generous (see, for instance, no. 32). With his settling in London and
the exhaustion of previous funds, a financial crisis was inevitable.
But a close examination of Marx's revenues gives the strong
impression that his difficulties resulted less from real poverty than
from a desire to preserve appearances coupled with an inability to
husband his financial resources. This is certainly what one would

expect from Marx's incapacity to manage the large sums of money that he had previously received and was again to receive in the 1860s. On his arrival in London Marx was quite prepared to rent a flat in Chelsea that was very expensive – more than twice the rent Marx eventually paid for a house when he moved out of Dean Street. In his worst years Marx's income was never less than £200 a year. In the early 1850s the cost of living was in fact falling and £150 was considered quite an adequate income for a lower-middle-class family with three children. Skilled workers earned about £50 a year, and a bank clerk about £75 a year. Freiligrath, whose family circumstances were similar to Marx's, earned less than £200 a year and yet boasted that he had never been without 'the luscious beef steak of exile'.[20]

Apart from his intermittent forays into journalism, and a few meagre advances on books, Marx made only two attempts to earn money. He applied for a job as a railway clerk, but was turned down because of his appalling handwriting. And in the early 1870s he became a partner in a company founded to exploit a new copying machine – but the enterprise soon foundered over quarrels as to who owned the patent. (He also once claimed to have made some money on the Stock Exchange, but this appears to have been mere boastfulness.) The difficulties created by Marx's refusal to turn himself into 'a money-making machine' were heightened by the need he felt to compensate his family for the burdens he had placed upon them. The family had always had one servant (and for a few years there was a second one). The children were sent to private schools and had extra lessons in music and drama. He wrote to Engels in 1855, 'I live too dearly for my circumstances in any case, and this year in addition we have lived better than before. But it is the only way that the children – quite apart from how much they have suffered, and for which they were compensated at least for a short time – can enter into relations and circumstances that can ensure them a future.'[21] His income still had to be supplemented even after Engels had settled a regular £350 a year on him.

Another aspect of Marx's self-imposed struggle was his battle against illness. Although excused Prussian military service on the grounds of a weak chest (it was pleurisy that eventually caused his death), Marx seems to have enjoyed a generally robust constitution, which he gradually sacrificed to what he took to be the necessities of his work. In the Preface to *Capital*, Marx referred to 'an illness of many years duration which again and again interrupted my work'.[22] In fact Marx seems to have suffered from several illnesses, and his correspondence is strikingly full of references to their nature and possible cure. He had constant eye irritations and his haemorrhoids were directly related to his studying. He also suffered from a liver complaint – which was thought to have been the cause of his father's death. But what plagued him most were his boils, which continually reappeared; they usually started in the autumn and came to full bloom (so to speak) in January. There were times when Marx's body was so covered with them that he could only stand upright or lie on his side on the sofa. He took lots of advice, seldom followed it very long, and after some years claimed to know more about boils than any doctor; certainly he pursued widespread researches in the British Museum on the subject. At various times he took such extraordinary medicines as creosote, opium and arsenic (this for years on end), gave up smoking for months and took daily cold baths. He wished that the boils had been given to a good Christian who would have been able to turn his suffering to some account; but at the same time he comforted himself with the idea that the bourgeoisie would have good cause to remember his sufferings from this 'truly proletarian disease'.[23] On extreme occasions he would even operate on himself. 'Today', he wrote to Engels, 'I took a sharp razor (a relic of dear Lupus) and cut the wretch in my own person.' He was proud to think that 'I am one of the best subjects to be operated upon. I always recognise what is necessary.'[24] When the boils approached his penis, he lightened the occasion by copying out and sending to Engels specimens of sixteenth-century French pornographic verse – a field in which he considered himself 'well-read'. Marx admitted to Engels in 1866 that 'the doctors are quite right that it is too much night work which is the chief cause of my relapses. But I cannot convey to the gentlemen – it would be completely pointless anyway – the causes that *compel* me to this extravagance.'[25]

Although it is not true that Marx died at his desk (he died in his armchair), it is symbolically appropriate – as is, too, the fact that he died intestate and stateless, only a fragment of his work completed. Given his unremitting struggle with his domestic circumstances, with his lack of finance, and finally with the imperatives of his own body, it is also fitting that he should have felt that the myth which most closely conveyed the key to his life was that of Prometheus, who brought men the secret of fire – and remained, as a punishment, chained to a rock and devoured alive.

NOTES

1. See *Reminiscences of Marx and Engels* (Moscow, n.d.). Hereafter cited as *RME*.
2. For an excellent selective edition, see S. Padover (ed.), *The Letters of Karl Marx* (New York, 1979).

3. Two accounts which stress Marx's Jewishness, from contrasting perspectives, are (for the positive) A. Massiczek, *Der menschliche Mensch. Karl Marx' judische Humanismus* (Vienna, 1968), and (for the negative) A. Kunzli, *Karl Marx. Eine Psychographie* (Vienna, 1968). There is an informed and well-balanced discussion in J. Carlebach, *Karl Marx and the Radical Critique of Judaism* (London, 1978).
4. See Y. Kapp, *Eleanor Marx*, vol. II: *The Crowded Years* (London, 1976) pp. 510 ff.
5. Cf. K. Marx and F. Engels, *Werke* (Berlin, 1957ff.) vol. XXX, p. 259. This edition is referred to hereafter as *MEW*.
6. See, for example, E. Silberner, 'Was Marx an Anti-Semite?', *Historia Judaica*, XI (1949) 3 ff.
7. *MEW*, vol. XXX, p. 259.
8. E. Lesser, 'Karl Marx als Jude', *Der Jude*, VIII (1924) pt 3.
9. *MEW*, vol. XXVIII, pp. 128 f.
10. Ibid., vol. XXX, p. 315.
11. Ibid., vol. XXIX, p. 570.
12. Ibid., vol. XXXI, p. 542.
13. Ibid., vol. XXIX, p. 285.
14. See further Y. Kapp, *Eleanor Marx*, vol. I: *Family Life 1855–1883* (London, 1972) pp. 289 ff. For a view claiming that the paternity remains a mystery, see F. Raddatz, *Karl Marx. A Political Biography* (Boston, Mass., 1979) pp. 125 ff.
15. *MEW*, vol. XXIX, pp. 535 f.
16. Ibid., vol. XXXI, p. 518.
17. Ibid., vol. XXXI, p. 519.
18. Ibid., vol. XXVIII, p. 656.
19. Ibid., vol. XXX, p. 319.
20. Quoted in F. Mehring, *Karl Marx* (London, 1936) p. 227.
21. *MEW*, vol. XXXI, p. 131.
22. K. Marx, *Capital* (London, 1956) vol. I, p. 7.
23. *MEW*, vol. XXXII, p. 573.
24. Ibid., vol. XXXI, p. 182.
25. Ibid., vol. XXXI, p. 174.

Chronological Table

1818   Birth
1824   Baptism
1830   Entered grammar school
1835   Began at University of Bonn
1836   Began at University of Berlin
1838   Death of Heinrich Marx
1841   Obtained doctorate; moved to Bonn
1842   Death of Baron von Westphalen; moved to Cologne as editor of *Rheinische Zeitung*
1843   Marriage; left for Paris (Oct)
1844   Birth of Jenny (May); met Engels (Sep)
1845   Moved to Brussels (Feb); visited England (July); birth of Laura
1846   Set up correspondence committee (Jan); quarrelled with Weitling (Mar); birth of Edgar (Dec)
1847   Joined Communist League (Jan)
1848   Moved to Paris (Mar) and Cologne (June) as editor of *Neue Rheinische Zeitung*
1849   Left for Paris (May) and London (Aug); birth of Guido (Nov)
1850   Death of Guido (Sep); settled in Dean Street (Dec)
1851   Birth of Franziska (Mar); birth of Frederick Demuth (June)
1852   Death of Franziska (Apr); dissolved Communist League (Nov)
1855   Birth of Eleanor (Jan); death of Edgar (Apr)
1856   Death of Baroness von Westphalen (July); moved to Grafton Terrace
1861   Visit to Holland and Germany to see Lassalle (Feb–Apr)
1862   Lassalle visited London (July)
1863   Death of Mary Burns (Jan); death of Marx's mother (Nov); Marx to Trier (Dec)
1864   Moved to Modena Villas (Mar); death of Wolff (May); death of Lassalle (Aug)
1867   Marx to Hamburg for *Capital* (Apr–May)
1868   Marriage of Laura
1869   Retirement of Engels; Marx visited Kugelman (Sep–Oct)
1870   Engels moved to London (Sep)
1872   Marriage of Jenny
1874   Marx to Karlsbad (Aug–Oct)

1875   Marx to Karlsbad (Aug–Sep); moved to Maitland Park Road
1876   Death of Bakunin; Marx to Karlsbad (Aug–Sep)
1877   Marx to Neuenahr (Aug–Sep)
1881   Marx to Argenteuil (Aug–Sep); death of Jenny Marx (Dec)
1882   Marx to Algiers, Monte Carlo, etc. (Feb–June)
1883   Death of Jenny Longuet (Jan); death of Marx (Mar)

1 Eleanor Marx (i)

The following brief note was written as an introduction to the first publication of the only letter from Marx to his father known to have survived. The letter, written in November 1837 and several pages long, vividly describes Marx's intellectual evolution as a student in Berlin.

Karl was a young man of seventeen when he became engaged to Jenny. For them, too, the path of true love was not a smooth one. It is easy to understand that Karl's parents opposed the 'engagement' of a young man of his age.... The earnestness with which Karl assures his father of his love in spite of certain contradictions is explained by the fairly stormy scenes his engagement had caused at home. My father used to say that at that time he had been a really furious Roland. But the question was soon settled and shortly before or after his eighteenth birthday the 'engagement' was formally accepted. Seven years Karl waited for his beautiful Jenny, but 'they seemed but so many days to him, because he loved her so much'.

On 19 June 1843 they were wedded. Having played together as children and become engaged as a young man and girl, the couple went hand in hand through the battle of life.

And what a battle! Years of bitter pressing need and still worse, years of brutal suspicion, infamous calumny and icy indifference. But through all that, in unhappiness and happiness the two lifelong friends and lovers never faltered, never doubted, they were faithful till death. And death has not separated them.

His whole life long Marx did not only love his wife, he was in love with her. Before me is a love letter the passionate youthful ardour of which would make one think it was written by an eighteen-year-old. Marx wrote it in 1856, after Jenny had borne him six children.[1] Called to Trier, by the death of his mother in 1863, he wrote from there that he had made 'daily pilgrimages to the old house of the Westphalens (in Römerstrasse[2]) that interests me more than the whole of Roman antiquity because it reminds me of my happy youth and once enclosed my dearest treasure. Besides, I am asked daily on all sides about the former "most beautiful girl in Trier" and "Queen of the ball". It is damned pleasant for a man when his wife lives on in the imagination of a whole city as a delightful princess.'[3]

Marx was deeply attached to his father. He never tired of telling about him and always carried an old daguerreotype photograph of him. But he would never show the photo to strangers, because, he said, it was so unlike the original. I thought the face was very handsome, the eyes and brow were like those of his son but the features were softer about the mouth and chin; the type was generally definitely Jewish, but beautifully so. When, after the death of his wife, Marx undertook a long, sad journey to recover his health[4] – for he wanted to complete his work – he took with him everywhere the photo of his father, an old photo of my mother on glass (in a case) and a photograph of my sister Jenny. We found them after his death in his breast pocket. Engels laid them in his coffin.

SOURCE: *RME*, pp. 256 f.; from the German original in *Die Neue Zeit*, XVI, pt. 1 (1897–8).

NOTES

1. Repr. in *MEW*, vol. XXIX, pp. 532 ff.
2. In English, 'Street of the Romans'.
3. Reprinted in *MEW*, vol. XXIX, p. 643.
4. From February to October 1882, Marx went to Algeria, the south of France, and Switzerland.

2 Moses Hess

Hess, a very generous and enthusiastic man, describes below the impression made on him by Marx who had just completed his doctorate and was about to embark on a career as a university lecturer. The extract is from a letter written in September 1841 to his friend Berthold Auerbach, who shared Hess's intellectual interests. Hess, known to his friends as 'the communist rabbi', was a close friend and collaborator of Marx at this time.

You will be pleased to meet here a man who has now become one of our friends, although he lives in Bonn, where he will soon be lecturing. . . . He is a phenomenon that made a tremendous impression on me in spite of the strong similarity of our fields. In short you can prepare yourself to meet the greatest – perhaps the only genuine – philosopher of the current generation. When he makes a public appearance, whether in writing or in the lecture hall, he will attract the attention of all Germany. Both from inclination and from philosophical schooling, he goes not only beyond Strauss but also beyond Feuerbach – and that's saying a lot! If I could be in Berlin when he lectures on logic I would be his most assiduous listener. I have always wanted such a man to be my teacher in philosophy. Now

I feel for the first time what a blockhead I am in real philosophy. But patience! I will still get around to learning something! Dr Marx (that is my idol's name) is still a very young man – about twenty-four at the most. He will give mediaeval religion and philosophy their *coup de grâce*; he combines the deepest philosophical seriousness with the most biting wit. Imagine Rousseau, Voltaire, Holbach, Lessing, Heine and Hegel fused into one person – I say fused not juxtaposed – and you have Dr Marx.

SOURCE: trs. by the editor from M. Hess, *Briefwechsel*, ed. E. Silberner (The Hague, 1959) pp. 79 f.

3 Gustav Mevissen

Mevissen was a prominent Rhineland businessman of liberal inclinations and one of the financial backers of the *Rheinische Zeitung*, of which Marx became editor in October 1842.

Karl Marx from Trier was a powerful man of twenty-four whose thick black hair sprung from his cheeks, arms, nose and ears. He was domineering, impetuous, passionate, full of boundless self-confidence, but at the same time deeply earnest and learned, a restless dialectician who with his restless Jewish penetration pushed every proposition of Young Hegelian doctrine to its final conclusion and was already then, by his concentrated study of economics, preparing his conversion to communism. Under Marx's leadership the young newspaper soon began to speak very recklessly.

SOURCE: trs. by the editor from H. von Treitschke, *Deutsche Geschichte im Neunzehnten Jahrhundert* (Leipzig, 1905) vol. v, p. 201.

4 Wilhelm Blos (i)

Blos was social-democratic journalist who made Marx's acquaintance in the 1870s and wrote his reminiscences some forty years later. The story below refers to late 1842, when Marx was editor of the radical *Rheinische Zeitung* – a position he held for six months between his abandonment of a university career and his emigration to Paris and espousal of communism.

Marx told an interesting little story about his battle with the censor. It occurred in the early 1840s, when he was editor of the old *Rheinische Zeitung* in Cologne. The censor was very antipathetic to the paper, because of Marx's notorious article on the provincial diet,[1] and he harassed it whenever and however he could. Marx eventually contrived a means 'to bring this lout to heel'. The proofs had to be brought to the censor in the evening, because the paper appeared in the morning. The censor's red pencil meant that the printers often had to continue their work long into the night.

One evening the censor has been invited, with his wife and nubile daughter, to a grand ball given by the President of the Province. Before leaving he had to finish work on the censorship. But precisely on this evening the proofs did not arrive at the accustomed time. The censor waited and waited, because he could not neglect his official duties and yet he had to put in an appearance at the President's ball – quite apart from the openings this would give his nubile daughter. It was near ten o'clock, the censor was extremely agitated and sent his wife and daughter on in front to the President's house and dispatched his servant to the press to get the proofs. The servant returned with the information that the press was closed. The bewildered censor went in his carriage to Marx's lodgings, which was quite a distance. It was almost eleven o'clock.

After much bell-ringing, Marx stuck his head out of a third-storey window.

'The proofs!' bellowed up the censor.

'Aren't any!' Marx yelled down.

'But – '

'We're not publishing tomorrow!'

Thereupon Marx slammed the window shut. The anger of the censor, thus fooled, made his words stick in his throat. He was more courteous from then on.

SOURCE: trs. by the editor from W. Blos, 'Karl Marx als Mensch', *Die Glocke*, v (1918) 159 ff.

NOTE

1. Marx wrote two articles highly critical of the sixth Rhine Province Assembly. They are reproduced in K. Marx and F. Engels, *Collected Works* (London, 1975) pp. 132 ff. and 224 ff.

5 Karl Heinzen

The following extract is taken from Heinzen's memoirs published in 1874. He was a writer of radical democratic learnings who later emigrated to the United States. Marx vigorously attacked his views in a long 1847 article entitled 'Moralising Criticism and Critical Morality'.

I first got to know Marx in Cologne, where he had been summoned to edit the *Rheinische Zeitung* after he had attracted the notice of the publishers through some of his contributions. At that time I had a lot of respect for his talent and liberalism, and my passion for observation was enthralled by this small, ingenious fellow who was so indifferent and careless about his outward appearance. I was uncommonly interested when I saw him sitting in the inn with his short-sighted eyes fixed on a newspaper and then suddenly going to another table and reaching for papers that were just not available; or when he ran to the censor to protest about the cutting out of an article and then, instead of the article in question, stuffed into his pocket some other newspaper or even a handkerchief and hared off. He won my heart through such inspired absent-mindedness and droll mistakes, just as my mind had been attracted by his articles. I therefore did indeed think very highly of him, and in my virginal literary enthusiasm could have become his best friend had I not discovered that he was an untrustworthy egoist and a lying intriguer whom no meeting of minds or honest goodwill could attach to another – for he merely sought to exploit others and was almost more governed by common envy of others' achievements than by his own ambition.

Among his most attractive qualities in Cologne was his penchant for boozing. One evening this allowed me to get to know this curiosity from a totally novel angle. We had drunk several bottles of wine together and, because he could not take much, I brought him back home in a rather deranged state. At the door of the house, which he opened laboriously with a long key, he pressed me with mysterious hints to enter. Curious to learn what he had to tell me, I entered. As soon as I was in the house, he shut the doors, hid the key and jeered comically at me that I was his prisoner. He asked me to follow him up into his study. On arrival I sat myself down on the sofa to see what on earth this marvellous crank would get up to. He immediately forgot that I was there, sat down astride a chair with his head leaning forward against the back, and began to declaim in a strong singing tone which was half mournful and half mocking, 'Poor lieutenant, poor lieutenant! Poor lieutenant, poor lieutenant!' This lament concerned a Prussian lieutenant whom he 'corrupted' by teaching him the Hegelian philosophy. He had arranged a meeting at his house that evening but his boozing had made him forget both the lieutenant and the Hegelian philosophy. After he had lamented the lieutenant for a while, he started up and suddenly discovered that I was in the room. He came over to me, gave me to understand that he had me in his power, and, with a malice that recalled an imp rather than the intended devil, he began to attack me with threats and cuffs. I begged him to spare me that sort of thing, because it went against the grain to pay him back in the same coin. When he did not stop I gave him a serious warning that I would deal with him in a way which he would certainly feel and when that too did no good I saw myself compelled to dispatch him into the corner of the room. When he got up I said that I found his personality boring and asked him to open the front door. Now it was his turn to be triumphant. 'Go home then, strong man', he mocked, and added a most comical smirk. It was as though he were chanting the words from Faust, 'There is one imprisoned inside. . . .' At least, the sentiment was similar, although his unsuccessful imitation of Mephistopheles made the situation comic in the extreme. In the end I warned him that if he would not open the door for me, then I would get it open myself and he would have to pay for the damage. Since he only answered with mocking sneers, I went down, tore the front door off its lock and called out to him from the street that he should shut the house up to prevent the entry of thieves. Dumb with amazement that I had escaped from his spell, he leaned out of the window and goggled at me with his small eyes like a wet goblin.

SOURCE: trs. by the editor from K. Heinzen, *Erlebtes*, pt 2 (Boston, Mass., 1874) pp. 425 ff.

6 Marcel Herwegh

The extract below was compiled by Marcel Herwegh from correspondence between his parents and published in 1898 as editorial comment to an edition of his father's letters.

Herwegh, a prominent radical poet, and Ruge, a former university teacher who had independent means, had emigrated from Germany to the more congenial intellectual climate of Paris in the summer of 1844.

Concerning his personality, I take the following from the correspondence of George and Emma Herwegh.

Karl Marx had a most expressive physiognomy. His eyes were not large but they were dark and bright; luxuriant black hair overshadowed his forehead. He was superbly suited to play the role of the last of the scholastics. Very learned and a tireless worker, he knew the world more from theory than from life. He was fully aware of his real worth; and, when he bore it in mind, he would be in a good temper and suppressed in his heart the two bad counsels of jealousy and envy – which he could never entirely silence. The sarcasm with which he pitilessly pursued his opponents was not bourgeois sarcasm but sliced cold like the executioner's axe.

In 1843 Karl Marx, Georg Herwegh and Arnold Ruge met together in Paris. The first came from Cologne, the second from Ostend and the third from Dresden in a large omnibus in which, with a great deal of trouble, he had installed his wife, a swarm of children and a large leg of veal.

Scarcely had he arrived when Ruge suggested to Marx and Herwegh that they move in with him and found a sort of phalanstery[1] in which the women would take turns at undertaking the role of Fourière[2] – no pun intended. Frau Herwegh summed up the situation at first glance. How could Frau Ruge, the nice, small Saxon woman, get on with the very intelligent and even more ambitious Frau Marx, whose knowledge was far superior to hers? How could Frau Herwegh, who had only been married so short a time and was the youngest of them, find herself attracted by this communal life? Herwegh and his wife therefore declined the invitation of Ruge who set up house with Marx in the rue Vanneau.

Two weeks later the two families had split up; but Herwegh and his wife remained on the best of terms with Marx and Ruge.

SOURCE: trs. by the editor from *1848: Briefe von und an Herwegh*, ed. M. Herwegh, 2nd edn (Munich, 1898) pp. 328 f.

NOTES

1. The name given by the utopian socialist Charles Fourier to the communes whose establishment he advocated.
2. That is, 'provider'.

7 Arnold Ruge

The two excerpts below are taken from letters written by Ruge to two of his friends in the summer of 1844. Ruge was co-editor, with Marx, of the *Deutsch-französische Jahrbücher*. The project collapsed after the publication of the first issue, owing to lack of support. The split between Marx and Ruge was exacerbated by Marx's espousal of communism and Ruge's disapproval of Marx's bohemian life-style.

My fellow-editor Marx was always struggling with financial embarrassments and unjustifiably expected to be rescued by the enterprise. In addition he has a peculiar personality – perfect as a scholar and author but completely ruinous as a journalist. He reads a lot; he works with unusual intensity and has a critical talent that occasionally degenerates into a wanton dialectic. But he finishes nothing, breaks off everything and plunges himself ever afresh into an endless sea of books. With his scholarly temperament he belongs completely to the German world, but his revolutionary attitudes exclude him from it. I have for long taken a lively interest in him and now the unpleasant fact is that it is precisely this interest that has caused the dissension between us. I was involuntarily reminded of Daumer and his excessive sensitivity; if possible, Marx is even more irritable and hot-tempered, particularly when he has worked himself sick and not gone to bed for three, even four, nights on end. . . .

As soon as the certainty of our failure was established, Marx informed me quite explicitly that he could no longer work with me. Philistine, inhuman and uninspired – that was his opinion of my views on marriage that had come to the fore in an argument over Herwegh – namely, that one should not abandon one's wife after the first year, that it was shabby to give oneself over to an empty sybaritic life, like Herwegh, and to elegant, blasé airs when one had every encouragement to serious co-operation. And now in *Vorwärts*, a journal that has suddenly slipped from Teutonism into communism, Herr Marx demonstrates how right was his judgement, that I do not think socially, have remained wedded to the 'most ordinary political point of view' and, as an author, am a 'literary charlatan'.[1] *Bon*! Marx has the gift of affirming and proving everything, a true Eulenspiegel of the dialectic. No one suspects his sleight-of-hand, since up to the last instant he reserves the freedom to say black just as much as white. At the beginning of our friendship I made the acquaintance of a man in his company whom I still cultivate, a Herr von Ribbentrop, whose every word Marx twisted into its opposite. I reproached him, saying that this was an underhanded and disreputable way of carrying on. 'No,' he said, 'that is the way to handle the fellow.' He wanted thereby to teach him to think. Now I have to endure this schooling, which would be fine if I had the inclination really to get into it. But we already come in for enough criticism here, and Marx, in particular, because of his cynicism and crude arrogance is anathema to the French. His opinion is that the whole culture of present-day France must disappear, and, because at its inception the new humanity can only be crude and inhuman, he immediately adopts these virtues. The French workers are infinitely more humane than this inhuman humanist. . . .

If Marx does not destroy himself through depravity, pride and crazy methods of working and, in his communist ingenuity, lose all sense of simple and noble style, then we can still expect something from his great scholarship and even from his unscruplous dialectic . . . .

Marx wanted to criticise Hegel's Natural Law from a communist point of view, then to write a history of the Convention,[2] and, finally, write a critique of all socialists. He always wants to write on what he has just read, but then he always reads wider and makes new excerpts. I still think it possible that he will produce a really big and truly abstruse book in which he will shove everything he has been piling up.

SOURCES: trs. by the editor from *Arnold Ruges Briefwechsel und Tagebuchblätter aus den Jahren 1825–1880*, ed. P. Nerrlich (Berlin, 1886) p. 343; and J. Schultze, 'Arnold Ruge über Karl Marx', *Tägliche Rundschau*, 22 July 1921.

NOTES

1. The reference is to an article entitled 'The King of Prussia and Social Reform', in which Marx vigorously criticised Ruge's views on reform in Germany from a socialist standpoint.
2. That is, the National Convention which was the seat of governmental power in France from 1792 to 1796.

8 Eleanor Marx (ii)

The following reminiscences, referring to the summer of 1844, were attributed to Eleanor Marx in an anonymous commentary to a letter from Heine to Marx published in 1895. The author of the commentary was probably either Mehring or Kautsky.

There was a time when Heine dropped in on the Marxes day in, day out in order to read out his verses and obtain the verdict of the two young people. Heine and Marx could go through a short poem of eight lines innumerable times, constantly discussing this or that word and working away and polishing until everything was smooth and every trace of work and polish was removed from the poem. But you had also to be very patient, for Heine was obsessively sensitive to any criticism. Occasionally he came literally weeping to Marx when some obscure critic had attacked him in a newspaper. Marx then knew no other remedy than to send him to his wife, whose wit and kindness would soon restore the self-doubting poet to reason.

But Heine did not always come to seek help – sometimes he brought it. One occasion was particularly well remembered in the Marx family.

Little Jenny Marx, a baby a few months old, was attacked one day by strong cramps which threatened to kill the child. Marx, his wife and their faithful helper and friend Helene Demuth were standing round the child in a complete quandary. Then Heine arrived, had a look and said, 'The child must have a bath.' With his own hands he prepared the bath, put the child in and saved, so Marx said, Jenny's life.

The picture of Heine as a practical child-minder must surprise many.

Marx was a great admirer of Heine's. He loved the poet as much as his works and looked as generously as possible on his political weaknesses. Poets, he explained, were queer fish and they must be allowed to go their own ways. They should not be assessed by the measure of ordinary or even extraordinary men.

SOURCE: trs. by the editor from 'Berichte über Heines Verhältnis zu Marx', *Die Neue Zeit*, XIV, pt 1 (1895–6).

9 Mikhail Bakunin (i)

This reminiscence, written in 1871, refers to the meetings of Marx and Bakunin in Paris in 1844.

Marx was then much more advanced than I was, and he still remains today incomparably more advanced than I – as far as learning is concerned. I knew nothing at that time of political economy, I still had not got rid of metaphysical abstractions, and my socialism was only instinctive. He, although younger than I, was already an atheist, an instructed materialist, and a conscious socialist. It was precisely at this time that he elaborated the first bases of his system as it is today. We saw each other pretty often, for I greatly respected him for his learning and for his passionate and serious devotion – though it was always mingled with personal vanity – to the cause of the proletariat, and I eagerly sought his conversation, which was always instructive and witty, when it was not inspired by petty hate, which alas! was only too often the case. There was, however, never any frank intimacy between us – our temperaments did not permit. He called me a sentimental idealist, and he was right; I called him vain, perfidious and sly, and I was right too.

SOURCE: K. Kenafick, *Michael Bakunin and Karl Marx* (Melbourne, 1948) pp. 25 f.

10 Pavel Annenkov

This glimpse into Marx's first essay into practical politics was written a generation later by a well-to-do and liberally-minded Russian tourist whom Marx had got to know in Paris. Soon after his arrival in Brussels Marx had started to establish a Communist Correspondence Committee, which was to give rise to the Communist League and be the embryo of all subsequent Communist Internationals. It was designed as an instrument to harmonise and co-ordinate communist theory and practice in the European capitals. The dispute described below occurred early in 1846 at one of the first meetings of the Brussels branch. Marx's antagonist, Wilhelm Weitling, was the illegitimate son of a French officer and a German laundry-woman, and earned his living as a journeyman tailor while absorbing the writings of the

French socialists. His messianic demands for immediate revolution had earned him a large following among German emigrant workers.

Marx himself was the type of man who is made up of energy, will and unshakable conviction. He was most remarkable in his appearance. He had a shock of deep black hair and hairy hands and his coat was buttoned wrong; but he looked like a man with the right and power to demand respect, no matter how he appeared before you and no matter what he did. His movements were clumsy but confident and self-reliant, his ways defied the usual conventions in human relations, but they were dignified and somewhat disdainful; his sharp metallic voice was wonderfully adapted to the radical judgements that he passed on persons and things. He always spoke in imperative words that would brook no contradiction and were made all the sharper by the almost painful impression of the tone which ran through everything he said. This tone expressed the firm conviction of his mission to dominate men's minds and prescribe them their laws. Before me stood the embodiment of a democratic dictator such as one might imagine in a day dream. He was a most striking contrast to the type of man I had recently left in Russia.

At our very first meeting Marx invited me to a conference he was to have at his house next day with Weitling, who had left a fairly large group of supporters in Germany. The conference was intended to determine, if possible, a common line of action for the leaders of the working-class movement. I eagerly accepted the invitation.

The tailor–agitator Weitling was a handsome fair-headed young man in a coat of elegant cut, a coquettishly trimmed small beard, more like a commercial traveller than the stern, embittered worker that I had expected to meet. We introduced ourselves to each other rather casually, with a touch of elaborate courtesy on Weitling's side, however, and took our places at the small green table. Marx sat at one end of it with a pencil in his hand and his leonine head bent over a sheet of paper, while Engels, his inseparable fellow-worker and comrade in propaganda, tall and erect and as dignified and serious as an Englishman, made the opening speech. He spoke of the necessity for people, who have devoted themselves to transforming labour, of explaining their views to one another and agreeing on a single common doctrine that could be a banner for all their followers who lacked the time and opportunity to study theory. Engels had not finished his speech when Marx raised his head, turned to Weitling and said, 'Tell us, Weitling, you who have made such a noise in Germany with your preaching: on what grounds do you justify your activity and what do you intend to base it on in the future?'

I remember quite well the form of the blunt question, because it was the beginning of a heated discussion, which, as we shall see, was very brief. Weitling apparently wanted to keep the conference within the bounds of commonplace liberal talk. With a serious, somewhat worried face he started to explain that his aim was not to create new economic theories but to adopt those that were most appropriate, as experience in France had shown, to open the eyes of the workers to the horrors of their condition and all the injustices which it had become the motto of the rulers and societies to inflict on them, and to teach them never more to believe any promises of the latter, but to rely only upon themselves, and to organise in democratic and communist associations. He spoke for a long time, but to my astonishment and in contrast to Engels, confusedly and not too well from the literary point of view, often repeating and correcting himself and arriving with difficulty at his conclusions, which either came too late or preceded his propositions. He now had quite different listeners from those who generally surrounded him at his work or read his newspaper and printed pamphlets on the contemporary economic system: he therefore lost his ease of thought and speech. Weitling would probably have gone on talking had not Marx interrupted him with an angry frown and started his reply.

His sarcastic speech boiled down to this: to rouse the population without giving them any firm, well-thought-out reasons for their activity would be simply deceiving them. The rousing of fantastic hopes just spoken of, Marx continued, leads only to the final ruin and not to the saving of the sufferers. To call to the workers without any strictly scientific ideas or constructive doctrine, especially in Germany, was equivalent to vain dishonest play at preaching which assumes an inspired prophet on the one side and on the other only gaping asses. . . . People without constructive doctrine cannot do anything and have indeed done nothing so far except make a noise, rouse dangerous flares and bring about the ruin of the cause they had undertaken. Weitling's pale cheeks coloured and he regained his liveliness and ease of speech. In a voice trembling with agitation he started trying to prove that a man who had rallied hundreds of people under the same banner in the name of justice, solidarity and mutual brotherly assistance could not be called a completely vain and useless man; he, Weitling, consoled himself for the attacks of today by remembering the hundreds of letters and declarations of gratitude that he had received from all parts of his native land and by the thought that his modest spade-work was perhaps of greater weight for the common cause than criticism and armchair analysis of doctrines far from the world of the suffering and afflicted people.

At the last words Marx finally lost control of himself and thumped so hard with his fist on the table that the lamp on it rang and shook. He jumped up saying 'Ignorance never yet helped anybody!' We followed his example and left the table. The sitting ended, and as Marx paced up and down the room, extraordinarily irritated and angry, I hurriedly took leave of him and his interlocutors and went home, amazed at all I had seen and heard.

SOURCE: *RME*, pp. 270 ff. (with restoration of omission, trs. by the editor); from the Russian original in *Vestnik Evropy*, Apr 1880.

11 Friedrich Lessner (i)

Lessner was a journeyman tailor from North Germany who emigrated to London in the late 1840s and was an active associate of Marx both in the Communist League and in the First International. (For Lessner's reminiscences from the time of the latter, see below, no. 22.) In December 1847 Marx and Engels went from Brussels to London for an extended meeting of the Central Committee of the Communist League. The Committee entrusted them with the drafting of a policy document which was subsequently published as the *Communist Manifesto*. It was in the course of this visit that Lessner first met Marx.

About this time I saw Marx and Engels for the first time. I shall never forget the impression they made upon me.

Marx was then still a young man, about twenty-eight years old, but he greatly impressed us all. He was of medium height, broad-shouldered, powerful in build and energetic in his deportment. His brow was high and finely shaped, his hair thick and pitch-black, his gaze piercing. His mouth already had the sarcastic line that his opponents feared so much. Marx was a born leader of the people. His speech was brief, convincing and compelling in its logic. He never said a superfluous word; every sentence was a thought and every thought was a necessary link in the chain of his demonstration. Marx had nothing of the dreamer about him. The more I realised the difference between the communism of Weitling's time and that of the *Communist Manifesto*, the more clearly I saw that Marx represented the manhood of socialist thought.

SOURCE: *RME*, p. 153; from the German original in *Deutsche Worte* (1898) p. 151.

12 Carl Schurz

At the height of the revolutionary upheavals in 1848, Marx, then editor of the *Neue Rheinische Zeitung*, was instrumental in summoning a congress of Rhineland democrats to meet in Cologne to co-ordinate anti-government agitation.
   At the time of the Congress – August 1848 – Schurz was a student in Bonn. Soon afterwards he emigrated and made a distinguished career for himself as a United States Senator and Secretary of the Interior.

In the course of the summer Kinkel and I were invited to represent the club at a congress of democratic associations in Cologne. This assembly, in which I remained a shy and silent observer, became remarkable to me in bringing me into personal contact with some of the prominent men of that period, among others the leader of the communists, Karl Marx. He could not have been much more than thirty years old at that time, but he was already the recognised head of the advanced socialistic school. The somewhat thick-set man, with broad forehead, very black hair and beard and dark sparkling eyes, at once attracted general attention. He enjoyed the reputation of having acquired great learning, and as I knew very little of his discoveries and theories, I was all the more eager to gather words of wisdom from the lips of the famous man. This expectation was disappointed in a peculiar way. Marx's utterances were indeed full of meaning, logical and clear, but I have never seen a man whose bearing was so provoking and intolerable. To no opinion which differed from his own did he accord the honour of even condescending consideration. Everyone who contradicted him he treated with abject contempt; every argument that he did not like he answered either with biting scorn at the unfathomable ignorance that had prompted it, or with opprobrious aspersions upon the motives of him who had advanced it. I remember most distinctly the cutting disdain with which he pronounced the word 'bourgeois'; and as a 'bourgeois' – that is, as a detestable example of the deepest mental and moral degeneracy – he denounced everyone who dared to oppose his opinion. Of course, the propositions advanced or advocated by Marx in that meeting were voted down, because everyone whose feelings had been hurt by his conduct was inclined to support everything that Marx did not favour. It was very evident that not only had he not won any adherents, but had repelled many who otherwise might have become his followers.

SOURCE: *The Reminiscences of Carl Schurz* (London, 1909) vol. I, pp. 138 f.

13 Stephan Born

Born (whose real name was Simon Buttermilch) was a German typesetter who was briefly active as a revolutionary in 1848–9. The following extract is taken from his reminiscences, published fifty years later, and refers to a visit he paid to Marx as editor of the *Neue Rheinische Zeitung*, in January 1849.

Marx took me up in the most friendly manner, as did his wife. They would not let me move into a hotel, and treated me as their guest. And here there occurs to me a remark that Marx made at table and which, since it is characteristic of his manner and style, deserves to be preserved. While I was present the conversation turned for the first time on family relationships. The talk was of the political position of Herr von Westphalen in the year of the revolution, when he was an outspoken reactionary. 'Your brother', said Marx laughingly to his wife, 'is so stupid that he will become a Prussian Minister yet.' Mrs Marx blushed at this over-frank remark and turned the conversation to another subject. As we know, the prophecy of her husband was fulfilled. . . .

The most bitter complaints about Marx came from Engels. 'He is no journalist', he said, 'and will never become one. He pores for a whole day over a leading article that would take someone else a couple of hours as though it concerned the handling of a deep philosophical problem. He changes and polishes and changes the change and owing to his unremitting thoroughness can never be ready on time.' It was a real release for Engels to be able once in a while to sound off about what annoyed him. At bottom, however, he had a deep respect for Marx, whom he always recognised as having a mind superior to his own. And when Marx, who was much given to irasciblity, considered it necessary to put him in his place – once in my presence he called him an Elberfeld guttersnipe and then went out slamming the door – then Engels merely replied, 'I'll remember that!' For all that, he did not think about it for long.

SOURCE: trs. by the editor from S. Born, *Erinnerungen eines Achtundvierzigers* (Leipzig, 1898) pp. 196 ff.

14 Gustav Techow

This extract is from a long letter written in August 1850 by a former Prussian army officer active in the revolutionary cause in 1848 to a friend of his who was also an ex-army officer of radical political views. Techow had emigrated to London and here describes a meeting a few days previously at which Marx and Engels had tried to recruit him to the Central Committee of the Communist League. The tension in the League between the followers of Marx and those of Willich was to develop into an open split a month later.

Now at last we came to the main point: what I thought of their programme, whether I wished to join them on the basis of this programme; if so, I could immediately become a member of the Central Committee. Thereupon I adopted a tone of heartfelt gratitude, but explained to them that I must first get a more accurate knowledge of the persons and the organisation, then later I would be willing to come to a decision. At that, they broke in earnestly: organisation yes, but persons were not in question – they were constantly changing and also what I had previously said about leaders of the Party was totally inapplicable to theirs; it recognised no authorities and relied on its own strength, on the force of circumstances; no one in it thought about a provisional government, about dictatorship, about playing this or that role, seizing this or that title. As far as they themselves were concerned, they wanted nothing better than to remain for ever in opposition, otherwise the revolution would go to sleep and all the old class-shit, as Marx euphonically expressed himself, would be left in place. Any of those who prematurely undertook positions and roles must necessarily thereby revert to the reaction and thus betray their principles. I replied that, if it were not a question of positions and roles, all right then, but they had often and justifiably met with the reproach that during the times of unrest they had on several occasions merely twiddled their thumbs and prevented the workers from achieving their aims on the pretext that any effort in that direction was vain. That was what had happened in Cologne. To this Marx replied very animatedly that the reproach was unjustified. They had tried to stop the business in Cologne because it had become senseless, aimless and impracticable, otherwise they would certainly have proved on every occasion that every revolution was all right by them – even if it was a question of a bourgeois revolution; and, as for courage, Marx had given evidence of it here and there, in this way and that and in fact a quite different sort of courage from that which marches a little way towards bullets of which only one in a thousand hit the mark. Actually, it was the military people who had been present who had developed incredible stupidity: Anneke and also our good B. got their share of abuse. I listened to everything quietly and finally declared that I should give them a definite answer after a time; that I agreed with their programme; that, although I had always held them to be superior to the communist happiness stables of Cabet, yet that programme was the first indication to me of how practical their approach to the question was, and that therefore from this point of view I should be able unhesitatingly to join them.

Although I have here touched on the principal points of our discussion, it is nevertheless impossible for me to describe to you the animated exchanges, the growing warmth of the conversation, the way in which Marx dominated it.

First we drank port, then claret (which is red Bordeaux), then champagne. After the red wine he was completely drunk. That was exactly what I wanted, because he would be more openhearted than he probably would otherwise have been. I became certain of many things which would otherwise have remained mere suppositions. In spite of his condition Marx dominated the conversation up to the last moment.

He gave the impression not only of rare intellectual superiority but also of outstanding personality. If he had had as much heart as intellect and love as hate, I should have gone through fire for him, even if he had not just occasionally hinted at his complete contempt for me, which he finally expressed quite openly. He is the first and only one among us all whom I would trust to have the capacity for leadership and for never losing himself in small matters when dealing with great events.

In view of our aims, I regret that this man, with his fine intellect, is lacking in nobility of soul. I am convinced that the most dangerous personal ambition has eaten away all the good in him. He laughs at the fools who parrot his proletarian catechism, just as he laughs over the communists à la Willich and over the bourgeoisie. The only people he respects are the aristocrats, the genuine ones who are well aware of it. In order to drive them from government, he needs a source of strength, which he can find only in the proletariat. Accordingly, he has tailored his system to them. In spite of all his assurances to the contrary, and perhaps because of them, I took away with me the impression that the acquisition of personal power was the aim of all his endeavours.

Engels and all his old associates, in spite of their many fine talents, are all far inferior to him, and, if they should dare to forget it for a moment, he would put them in their place with an unashamedness worthy of a Napoleon.

SOURCE: trs. by the editor from Karl Vogt, *Mein Prozess wider die Allgemeine Zeitung* (Geneva, 1859) pp. 149 ff.

15 Jenny Marx (i)

A SHORT SKETCH OF AN EVENTFUL LIFE

These autobiographical notes were first written in 1865. Having remained in the Longuet archives until recently, they were first published in 1965.

19 June 1843, was my wedding-day.[1] We went from Kreuznach to Rhein-Pfalz via Ebernburg and returned via Baden-Baden. Then we stayed at Kreuznach till the end of September. My dear mother returned to Trier with my brother Edgar. Karl and I arrived in Paris in October and were met by Herwegh and his wife.

In Paris Karl and Ruge edited *Deutsch-französische Jahrbücher*, Julius Fröbel being the publisher. The enterprise came to grief after the very first issue. We lived in rue Vanneau, Faubourg St Germain and associated with Ruge, Heine, Herwegh, Mäurer, Tolstoi, Bakunin, Annenkov, Bernays and *tutti quanti*. There was a lot of gossip and quarrels over bagatelles. Our little Jenny was born on 1 May 1844. I went out for the first time after that to Laffitte's burial and six weeks later I took the mail coach to Trier with my mortally sick child. . . . In September I returned to Paris with a German nurse. By then little Jenny had four teeth.

During my absence Karl had had a visit from Frederick Engels.[2] During the autumn and winter Karl worked at his *Kritik der Kritischen Kritik*, which was published in Frankfurt.[3] Our circle comprised Hess and his wife, Ewerbeck and Ribbentrop and especially Heine and Herwegh. Suddenly, at the beginning of 1845, the police commissioner came to our house and showed us an expulsion order made out by Guizot on the request of the Prussian Government. 'Karl Marx must leave Paris within twenty-four hours', the order ran. I was given a longer delay, which I made use of to sell my furniture and some of my linen. I got ridiculously little for it, but I had to find money for our journey. The Herweghs gave me hospitality for two days. Ill and in bitter cold weather, I followed

Karl to Brussels at the beginning of February. There we put up at
Bois Sauvage Hotel and I met Heinzen and Freiligrath for the first
time. In May we moved into a small house that we rented from
Dr Breuer in rue de l'Alliance, outside Porte du Louvain.
Hardly had we settled down when we were followed by Engels.
Heinrich Bürgers, who had already visited us in Paris with his friend
Dr Roland Daniels, was also there. Shortly afterwards Hess arrived
with his wife, and a certain Sebastian Seiler joined the small German
circle. He set up a correspondence bureau and the small German
colony lived pleasantly together. Then we were joined by some
Belgians, among them Gigot, and several Poles. In one of the
attractive cafés that we went to in the evenings I made the
acquaintance of old Lelewel in his blue blouse.
During the summer Engels worked with Karl on the criticism of
German philosophy.[4] The external impulse for this work was the
publication of *Der Einzige und sein Eigenthum*.[5] The criticism was a
bulky work and was to be published in Westphalia.
In the spring Joseph Weydemeyer paid us his first visit, remaining
for some time as our guest. In April my dear mother sent her own
trusty maid[6] to Brussels to help me. I went with her once more to see
Mother, taking little Jenny who was then fourteen months old. I
stayed with her six weeks and returned to our small colony two weeks
before Laura was born, on 26 September. My brother Edgar spent
the winter with us in Brussels, hoping to find work there. He entered
Seiler's correspondence bureau. Later, in spring 1846, our dear
Wilhelm Wolff also joined the bureau. He was known as 'Kasemat-
tenwolff', having escaped from a fortress in Silesia where he had
been four years for a violation of the law on the press. His coming to
us was the beginning of the close friendship with our dear 'Lupus'
that was dissolved only by his death in May 1864. During the winter
we had visits from Georg Jung and Dr Schleicher....
In the meantime the storm-clouds of the revolution had been
piling higher and higher. The Belgian horizon too was dark. What
was feared above all was the workers, the social element of the
popular masses. The police, the military, the civil guard, all were
called out against them, all were kept ready for action. Then the
German workers decided that it was time to arm themselves too.
Daggers, revolvers, etc., were procured. Karl willingly provided
money, for he had just come into an inheritance. In all this the
government saw conspiracy and criminal plans: Marx receives
money and buys weapons, he must therefore be got rid of. Late at
night two men broke into our house. They asked for Karl: when he
appeared they said they were police sergeants and had a warrant to
arrest him and take him to be questioned. They took him away. I
hurried after him in terrible anxiety and went to influential men to

find out what the matter was. I rushed from house to house in the dark. Suddenly I was seized by a guard, arrested and thrown into a dark prison. It was where beggars without a home, vagabonds and wretched fallen women were detained. I was thrust into a dark cell. As I entered, sobbing, an unhappy companion in misery offered to share her place with me: it was a hard plank bed. I lay down on it. When morning broke I saw at the window opposite mine, behind iron bars, a cadaverous, mournful face. I went to the window and recognised our good old friend Gigot. When he saw me he beckoned to me, pointing downwards. I looked in that direction and saw Karl being led away under military escort. An hour later I was taken to the interrogating magistrate. After a two hours' questioning, during which they got little out of me, I was led to a carriage by gendarmes and towards evening I got back to my three poor little children. The affair caused a great sensation. All the papers reported on it. After a short while Karl too was released and ordered to leave Brussels immediately.

He had already intended to return to Paris and had applied to the Provisional Government in France for a repeal of the expulsion order issued against him under Louis Philippe. He at once received a paper signed by Flocon by which the Provisional Government cancelled the expulsion order in very flattering terms. So Paris was open to us again. Where could we feel more at ease than under the rising sun of the new revolution? We had to go there, we just had to! I hastily packed my belongings and sold what I could, but left my boxes with all my silver-plate and my best linen in Brussels in charge of the bookseller Vögler, who was particularly helpful and obliging during the preparations for my departure.

Thus we left Brussels after being there for three years. It was a cold, dull day and we had difficulty in keeping the children warm, the youngest of them was just a year old . . . .

At the end of May[7] Karl put out the last issue of *Neue Rheinische Zeitung*[8], printed in red – the famous 'red number' a real firebrand in form and content. Engels had immediately joined the Baden rising[9] in which he was adjutant to Willich. Karl made up his mind to go to Paris again for a while, as it was impossible for him to stay on in Germany.[10] Red Wolff followed him there. I went with the three children via Bingen . . . to see my old home town and my dear mother. I made a detour a little after Bingen in order to convert into ready money the silver-plate which I had just redeemed from the pawn broker's in Brussels. Weydemeyer and his wife again gave us hospitality and were very helpful to me in my dealings with the pawnbroker. Thus I managed again to get money for the journey. Karl went with Red Wolff to Baden-Pfalz and then on to Paris.

There the Ledru-Rollin affair of 13 June soon put an end to the short dream of revolution.[11] Reaction came on the scene in all its fury everywhere. The Hungarian revolution, the Baden insurrection, the Italian rising, all collapsed. Courts-martial were rife in Hungary and Baden. During the presidency of Louis Napoleon, who was elected with an enormous majority at the end of 1848, 50,000 Frenchmen entered the 'city of the seven hills' and occupied Italy.[12] *L'ordre règne à Varsovie*[13] and *Vae victis!*[14] were the mottos of the counter-revolution in the elation of victory. The bourgeoisie breathed relieved, the petty bourgeois went back to their business, the liberal petty philistines clenched their fists in their pockets, the workers were hounded and persecuted and the men who fought with sword and pen for the reign of the poor and oppressed were glad to be able to earn their bread abroad.

While in Paris Karl established contacts with many of the leaders of clubs and secret workers' societies. I followed him to Paris in July 1849 and we stayed there a month. But we were to get no rest there either. One fine day the familiar police sergeant came again and informed us that 'Karl Marx and his wife had to leave Paris within twenty-four hours.' By an act of clemency he was given permission to take up his residence in Vannes, in the Morbihan.[15]

Karl did not, of course, accept such an exile. I packed my goods and chattels again to look for a sure place of rest in London. Karl hastened there ahead of me and established close contact with Blind. Georg Weerth also came later on. It was he who met me when I arrived, sick and exhausted with my three poor persecuted small children. He found accommodation for me in a boarding-house in Leicester Square belonging to a master-tailor. We looked in haste for a larger lodging in Chelsea,[16] for the time was approaching when I would need a quiet roof over my head. On 5 November, while the people outside were shouting 'Guy Fawkes for ever!', small masked boys were riding the streets on cleverly made donkeys and all was in an uproar, my poor little Heinrich was born. We called him Little Fawkes, in honour of the great conspirator.

Shortly afterwards Engels also arrived in London via Genoa, fleeing from Baden. Willich had preceded him and immediately settled down among us like a communist *frère* and comrade. He made his appearance in our bedroom early in the morning like a Don Quixote, dressed in a grey woollen doublet with a red cloth round his waist instead of a belt, roaring with laughter in real Prussian style and ready to expatiate in a long theoretical discussion on so 'natural' communism. Karl hastily put an end to his attempts.... While we were in Chelsea we also had our first visit from W. Pieper, and W. Liebknecht. The Red Wolff had come to London with Karl.

Thousands of emigrants arrived daily. Few of them had any means of their own, all were in more or less dire straits, needing and looking for help. This was one of the most unpleasant periods of our life in emigration. Emigrant committees were founded to help them, meetings were arranged, appeals made, programmes drawn up and great demonstrations prepared. In all emigrant circles dissensions broke out. The various parties gradually split up completely. It came to an official separation between the German democrats on the one hand and the socialists on the other, and there was a clear rift even among the communist working men. The leaders of the groups attacked one another most viciously and a band of petty-bourgeois rabble eager for 'deeds' and 'action' pushed to the fore and were most hostile towards the section of the workers and their leaders who saw more clearly through the situation and knew that the era of the revolution could not dawn for a long time. Karl above all was persecuted beyond measure, calumniated and defamed. It was at this time that the duel between Conrad Schramm and August Willich took place.

Karl had started negotiations in the autumn of 1849 for a new journal to be edited in London and published in Hamburg. The first three or four issues appeared after countless difficulties under the title *Revue der Neuen Rheinischen Zeitung*. It was a great success, but the bookseller, bought over by the German Government, was so negligent and inefficient over the business side of it that it was soon obvious that it could not go on for long.

In the spring of 1850 we were forced to leave our Chelsea house. My poor little Fawkes was always ill and the anxieties about our daily life were also ruining my health. Harassed on all sides and pursued by creditors, we put up for a week in a German hotel in Leicester Square.[17] But we did not stay there long. One morning our worthy host refused to serve us our breakfast and we were forced to look for other lodgings. The small help I got from my Mother often saved us from the bitterest privations. We found two rooms in the house of a Jewish lace dealer[18] and spent a miserable summer there with the four children.

That autumn Karl and some of his closest friends broke completely off from the doings of the bulk of the emigrants and never took part in a single demonstration.[19] He and his friends left the Workers Educational Society . . . . Engels, after trying in vain to earn his living by writing in London, went to Manchester and worked as a clerk in his father's textile business on very hard terms. All our other friends tried to pay their way by giving lessons, etc. This and the next two years were for us a time of the greatest hardships, of continual acute anxiety, great privations of all kinds and actual need.

In August 1850, although I was not at all well, I made up my mind to leave my sick child and go to Holland to get consolation and help from Karl's uncle. I was desperate at the prospect of a fifth child and of the future. Karl's uncle was very ill-disposed by the unfavourable effect the revolution had had on his business and his sons'. He was embittered against the revolution and revolutionaries and in a very bad temper. He refused to give me any help. However, as I was going he pressed into my hand a present for my youngest child and I saw that it hurt him not to be able to give me more. The old man could not realise my feelings as I took leave of him. I returned home in despair. My poor little Edgar came leaping towards me with his friendly face and Little Fawkes stretched his tiny arms out to me. I was not to enjoy his caresses for long. In November the child died from convulsions caused by pneumonia. My sorrow was great. He was the first child I had lost. I had no idea then what other sufferings were in store for me which would make all others seem as nothing. Shortly after the child had been laid to rest we left the small flat for another one in the same street. . . .[20]

On 28 March 1851, our daughter Franzisca was born. We gave the poor little thing to a nurse, for we could not rear her with the others in three small rooms. That year there was a world exhibiton and visitors were streaming to London. Freiligrath came from Cologne in the spring to look for a situation in London. Later Lupus came from Switzerland and so did Dronke, Imandt and Schily. Seiler had returned earlier and Götz had joined the group of emigrants round Karl. 1851 and 1852 were the years of the greatest and at the same time the most paltry troubles, worries, disappointments and privations of all kinds.

In the early summer 1851 an event occurred which I do not wish to relate here in detail, although it greatly contributed to increase our worries, both personal and others.[21] During the spring the Prussian Government charged all Karl's friends in the Rhine province with the most dangerous revolutionary intrigues. They were all thrown into prison and treated in the most appalling way. The public trial did not start until the end of 1852. That was the famous Cologne Communist Trial. All the accused except Daniels and Jacoby were sentenced to from three to four years prison. . . .

At first W. Pieper was Karl's secretary, but soon I took over that post. The memory of the days I spent in his little study copying his scrawly articles is among the happiest of my life.

Louis Napoleon's *coup d'état* took place at the end of 1851 and the following year Karl wrote his *Eighteenth Brumaire*, which was published in New York. He wrote the book in our small lodgings in Dean Street amidst the noise of the children and the household bustle. By March I had copied the manuscript out and it was sent off, but it did not appear in print till much later and brought in next to nothing.

At Easter 1852 our little Franzisca had a severe bronchitis. For three days she was between life and death. She suffered terribly. When she died we left her lifeless little body in the back room, went into the front room and made our beds on the floor. Our three living children lay down by us and we all wept for the little angel whose livid, lifeless body was in the next room. Our beloved child's death occurred at the time of the hardest privations, our German friends being unable to help us just then. Ernest Jones, who paid us long and frequent visits about that time, promised to help us but he was unable to bring us anything . . . . Anguish in my heart, I hurried to a French emigrant who lived not far away and used to come to see us, and begged him to help us in our terrible necessity. He immediately gave me two pounds with the most friendly sympathy. That money was used to pay for the coffin in which my child now rests in peace. She had no cradle when she came into the world and for a long time was refused a last resting place. With what heavy hearts we saw her carried to her grave!

In August 1852 the trial of the communists, since become famous, came to an end. Karl wrote a pamphlet disclosing the infamy of the Prussian Government. It was printed in Switzerland by Schabelitz but was confiscated at the frontier by the Prussian Government and destroyed. Cluss had it printed again in America and many copies of the new edition were spread on the continent.

During the year 1853 Karl used to write two articles regularly for the New York *Daily Tribune*. They attracted great attention in America. This steady income enabled us to pay off our old debts to a certain extent and to live a less anxious life. The children grew up nicely, developing both physically and mentally, although we were still living in the poky Dean Street flat. Karl kept up contact with the Chartists all the time he was in London. He contributed to Ernest Jones's journal, the *People's Paper*, and in the summer of 1853 he passed on to that journal articles which had already appeared in the *Tribune* . . . . In answer to a vicious article against him published by Willich in America, Karl wrote a short pamphlet, *The Knight of the Noble Conscience*, which was also printed in America. It reduced that knight and his barking pack to silence.

Christmas that year was the first merry feast we celebrated in London. We were relieved from nagging daily worries by Karl's connection with the New York *Tribune*. The children had romped about more in the open air in the parks during the summer. There had been cherries, strawberries and even grapes that year, and our friends brought our three little ones all sorts of delightful presents:

dolls, guns, cooking utensils, drums and trumpets. Dronke came late in the evening to decorate the Christmas tree. It was a happy evening.

A week later our little Edgar showed the first symptoms of the incurable disease which was to lead to his death a year later. Had we been able to give up our small unhealthy flat then and take the child to the seaside, we might have saved him. But what is done cannot be undone. . . .

In September 1855 we returned to our old headquarters in Dean Street, firmly resolved to move out as soon as a small English inheritance[22] freed us from the chains and ties in which the baker, butcher, milkman, grocer and greengrocer and all the other 'hostile forces' held us. At last, in spring 1856 we received the small sum that was to release us. We paid all our debts, redeemed our silver, linen and clothes from the pawnbroker's and I went newly clothed with my little ones to my beloved old home for the last time. . . .

We spent that winter in great retirement. Nearly all our friends had left London and the few that remained lived a long way from us. Besides, our attractive little house,[23] though it was like a palace for us in comparison with the places we had lived in before, was not easy to get to. There was no smooth road leading to it, building was going on all around, one had to pick one's way over heaps of rubbish and in rainy weather the sticky red soil caked to one's boots so that it was after a tiring struggle and with heavy feet that one reached our house. And then it was dark in those wild districts, so that rather than have to tackle the dark, the rubbish, the clay and the heaps of stones one preferred to spend the evenings by a warm fire.

I was very unwell that winter and was always surrounded with stacks of medicine bottles and it was a long time before I could get used to the complete solitude. I often missed the long walks I had been in the habit of making in the crowded West End streets, the meetings, the clubs and our favourite public-house and homely conversations which had so often helped me to forget the worries of life for a time. Luckily I still had the article for the *Tribune* to copy out twice a week and that kept me in touch with world events.

In the middle of 1857 another great trade crisis faced the American workers. The *Tribune* again declined to pay for two articles a week and as a result there was another considerable ebb in our budget. Luckily Dana was then publishing an encyclopaedia and Karl was asked to write articles on military and economic questions. But as such articles were very irregular and the growing children and the larger house led to greater expenses, this was by no means a time of prosperity. It was not positive need, but we were permanently hard up and worried by petty fears and calculations. No matter how much we cut down expenses, we could never make ends meet and our debts mounted from day to day and year to year. . . .

On 6 July the seventh child was born to us, but it lived only long enough to breathe a while and then be carried to join its brothers and sisters.

In the summer of 1857 our good old Conrad Schramm came back from America too, but in such a poor state of health that we saw at the first glance that he was beyond saving. He spent six weeks in the German hospital and then went to Jersey. He there met Frederick Engels who had also been very ill for a year and had gone there to recuperate. Karl visited the two friends there in September of that year and came back loaded with fruit, nuts and grapes. In January 1858 our friend Julian Harney, who was editor of a paper in Jersey, informed us of the death of our dear friend Schramm.

1858 brought us neither good nor evil, one day was just like any other. . . . That winter Karl worked at his book *A Contribution to the Critique of Political Economy* for which he had been collecting material for years. Lassalle, with whom he had entertained friendship since 1848, found a publisher for the book in the person of Franz Duncker in Berlin. In spring Karl sent in the manuscript after I had copied it out and the proofs kept coming in to be read, which naturally delayed the printing considerably. But what delayed it still more was that Lassalle was in a hurry to have his 'inflammatory work', the drama *Franz von Sickingen*, published. Being a particular friend of his, Duncker published the drama before Karl's book.

In the summer of 1859 the *via sacra*, the Italian war between France and Austria, broke out. Engels published a pamphlet *Po and Rhine*, the success of which urged Lassalle to write a pamphlet *The War in Italy*.

In London Elard Biskamp published a weekly called *Das Volk*, to which Karl contributed and for which Engels also wrote several articles. A leaflet composed by K. Blind, reprinted in *Das Volk* and later passed on to *Augsburger Allgemeine Zeitung* by Liebknecht, was seized on by K. Vogt as a pretext for a defamatory attack on Karl. Vogt published a pamphlet in which he told the vilest lies about Karl. During 1860 Karl collected material to refute at a single blow the calumny which was being peddled *con amore* from town to town and village to village by the whole of the German press under the halo of the 'new era'. . . .

In spring 1860 Engels's father died. After that Engels's situation considerably improved, although he remained bound by the unfavourable contract signed with Ermen, which was valid until 1864, from which time Engels became a co-partner in the management of the firm.

In August 1860, I again spent a fortnight at Hastings with the children. On my return I began to copy the book Karl had written against Vogt and his associates. It was printed in London and did not appear till the end of December 1860 after much annoyance. At the time I was very ill with pox, having just recovered enough from the terrible disease to be able to devour *Herr Vogt* with half blinded eyes. That was a most dismal time. The three children had found a home and hospitality with the faithful Liebknecht.

Just then appeared the first forebodings of the great American Civil War that was to break out the next spring. Old Europe with its petty, old-fashioned pigmy-struggles ceased to interest America. The *Tribune* informed Karl that it was forced by financial circumstances to forgo all correspondence and that it would not need his collaboration for the time being. The blow was felt all the more as all other sources of income had completely dried up and all efforts to undertake something had proved to be failures. The hardest thing about it was that this complete helplessness came as our eldest daughters entered the beautiful golden age of maidenhood. So we had again to fight the same sorrows, troubles and privations as of old, the difference being that what the children had been unconscious of at the age of five and six, they had consciously to bear up with ten years later when they were fifteen and sixteen. Thus we learned in practice the German proverb 'Small children, small troubles, big children, big troubles.'

In the summer of 1860 we took in Eccarius for two months, for he was very poorly. In spring 1861 Karl went to Germany because it was absolutely necessary to get financial help. The King of Prussia, called the 'genial', had died at Christmas and left his throne to 'handsome Wilhelm'.[24] The corporal proclaimed an amnesty and Karl availed himself of it to make a trip to Germany and see the new lie of the land. In Berlin he lived at Lassalle's and saw a lot of Countess Hatzfeldt. Then he went to Holland to visit his uncle Lion Philips who had the real magnanimity to advance him a sum of money interest-free. Karl came home accompanied by Jacques Philips von Bommel just in time for Jennychen's seventeenth birthday. The loan put our finances afloat and we sailed on for a time happily, although always between rocks and sand-banks, drifting between Charybdis and Scylla.

Our eldest daughters left school in the summer of 1860 and attended only a few lessons held in the college for non-pupils too. They continued to learn French and Italian with M de Colme and Signor Maggioni and Jenny also took drawing lessons with Mr Oldfield until 1862. In autumn the girls began to take singing lessons with Mr Henry Banner.

In September 1861 Karl, with the help of A. Dana, managed to get an article a week accepted by the *Tribune* on the same conditions as before. At the same time he was introduced to the editor of *Wiener*

Presse by a cousin of Lassalle's and was invited to contribute to the 'liberal' paper. Unfortunately both these jobs only lasted the winter. In spring 1862 Karl gave up contributing to the *Tribune* and let all his work with the *Presse* die away slowly. . . .

Jenny's health was poor during the whole of spring 1863 and she was continually under the care of doctors. Karl was also extremely unwell. He was no better when he came back from a visit to Engels, one of his regular annual visits since 1850. We again spent three weeks at the seaside at Hastings, being with H. Banner twelve days. Karl came to fetch us but he looked very bad and continually felt unwell, until in November of that year it turned out that he had terrible illness called the 'carbuncle disease'. On 10 November a terrible abscess was opened and he was in danger for a fairly long time afterwards. The disease lasted a good four weeks and caused severe physical sufferings. These were accompanied by rankling moral tortures of all kinds. Just as we were on the edge of the abyss we suddenly got the news of my mother-in-law's death. The doctor decided that a change of air would be very beneficial for Karl, and on his advice Karl, although not yet quite recovered, left in the middle of the winter cold for Germany accompanied by our anxious and heartfelt wishes in order to see to his mother's legacy in Triers. He stayed there a short time with his brother-in-law Conradi and sister Emilie and then made a detour to Frankfurt to see his aunt, his father's sister. From there he went to Bommel to see his uncle.[25] He was very well looked after by his uncle and Nettchen. For unfortunately he required medical attention and careful nursing again, the illness, which had not been cured, breaking out very badly again as soon as he reached Bommel and forcing him to remain in Holland from Christmas until 19 February.

That lonely disconsolate winter was terrible! The small share in the legacy that Karl brought back in ready money enabled us to free ourselves from obligations, debts, pawnbroker, etc. We were lucky enough to find a very attractive and healthy dwelling[26] which we fitted out very comfortably and relatively smartly. At Easter 1864 we moved into the pleasant sunny house with the spacious airy rooms.

On 2 May 1864 we received a letter from Engels telling us that our good and faithful old friend Lupus was seriously ill. Karl hastened to go and see him and his faithful friend recognised him for a while. On 9 May Lupus breathed his last. In his will he made Karl, the children and myself his main legatees along with a few minor ones. It turned out that by his excessive industry and effort the homely, simply living man had saved up the appreciable sum of £1000. He did not have the consolation of enjoying the fruit of his life in a quiet, comfortable old age. He afforded us help and relief and a year free from worry. A stay at the seaside was absolutely necessary for Karl's

health, which was still precarious. He went to Ramsgate with Jenny, Laura and Tussy followed later. . . .
   During the year he managed to find a publisher for his big work on economics. Meissner in Hamburg promised to publish it on fairly favourable conditions. Karl is now working intensely to finish the book.

SOURCE: *RME*, pp. 221 ff.

LETTER TO WEYDEMEYER

This letter, written on 20 May 1850, gives a vivid picture of difficulties of the Marx household soon after moving to London.

Dear Herr Weydemeyer,
   It will soon be a year since I was given such friendly and cordial hospitality by you and your dear wife, since I felt so comfortably at home in your house.[27] All that time I have not given you a sign of life: I was silent when your wife wrote me such a friendly letter and did not even break that silence when we received the news of the birth of your child. My silence has often oppressed me, but most of the time I was unable to write and even today I find it hard, very hard.
   Circumstances, however, force me to take up my pen. I beg you *to send us as soon as possible any money that has been or will be received* from the *Revue. We need it very, very much.* Certainly nobody can reproach us with ever having made much case of the sacrifices we have been making and bearing for years, the public has never or almost never been informed of our circumstances; my husband is very sensitive in such matters and he would rather sacrifice his last than resort to democratic begging like officially recognised 'great men'. But he could have expected active and energetic support for his *Revue* from his friends, particularly those in Cologne. He could have expected such support first of all from where his sacrifices for *Rheinische Zeitung*[28] were known. But instead of that the business has been completely ruined by negligent and disorderly management, and one cannot say whether the delays of the bookseller or of the business managers or acquaintances in Cologne or the attitude of the democrats on the whole were the most ruinous.
   Here my husband is almost overwhelmed with the paltry worries of life in so revolting a form that it has taken all his energy, all his calm, clear, quiet sense of dignity to maintain him in that daily, hourly struggle. You know, dear Herr Weydemeyer, the sacrifices my husband has made for the paper. He put thousands in cash into

it, he took over proprietorship, talked into it by worthy democrats who would otherwise have had to answer for the debts themselves, at a time when there was little prospect of success. To save the paper's political honour and the civic honour of his Cologne acquaintances he took upon himself the whole responsibility; he sacrificed his printing-press, he sacrificed all income, and before he left he even borrowed 300 thalers to pay the rent of the newly hired premises and the outstanding salaries of the editors, etc. And he was to be turned out by force. You know that we kept nothing for ourselves. I went to Frankfurt to pawn my silver – the last that we had – and I had my furniture in Cologne sold because I was in peril of having my linen and everything sequestrated. At the beginning of the unhappy period of the counter-revolution my husband went to Paris and I followed him with my three children. Hardly had he settled down in Paris when he was expelled and even my children and I were refused permission to reside there any longer. I followed him again across the sea. A month later our fourth child was born. You have to know London and conditions here to understand what it means to have three children and give birth to a fourth. For rent alone we had to pay 42 thalers a month.[29] We were able to cope with this out of money which we received, but our meagre resources were exhausted when the *Revue* was published. Contrary to the agreement, we were not paid, and later only in small sums, so that our situation here was most alarming.

I shall describe to you just *one* day of that life, exactly as it was, and you will see that few emigrants, perhaps, have gone through anything like it. As wet-nurses here are too expensive I decided to feed my child myself in spite of continual terrible pains in the breast and back. But the poor little angel drank in so much worry and hushed-up anxiety that he was always poorly and suffered horribly day and night. Since he came into the world he has not slept a single night, two or three hours at the most and that rarely. Recently he has had violent convulsions, too, and has always been between life and death. In his pain he sucked so hard that my breast was chafed and the skin cracked and the blood often poured into his trembling little mouth. I was sitting with him like that one day when our land-lady came in. We had paid her 250 thalers during the winter and had an agreement to give the money in the future not to her but to her landlord, who had a bailiff's warrant against her. She denied the agreement and demanded £5 that we still owed her. As we did not have the money at the time (Naut's letter did not arrive until later) two bailiffs came and sequestrated all my few possessions – linen, beds, clothes – everything, even my poor child's cradle and the best toys of my daughters, who stood there weeping bitterly. They threatened to take everything away in two hours. I would then have had to lie on the bare floor with my freezing children and my bad breast. Our friend Schramm hurried to town to get help for us. He got into a cab, but the horses bolted and he jumped out and was brought bleeding back to the house, where I was wailing with my poor shivering children. We had to leave the house the next day. It was cold, rainy and dull. My husband looked for accommodation for us. When he mentioned the four children nobody would take us in. Finally a friend helped us, we paid our rent and I hastily sold all my beds to pay the chemist, the baker, the butcher and the milkmen who, alarmed at the sight of the sequestration, suddenly besieged me with their bills. The beds which we had sold were taken out and put on a cart. What was happening? It was well after sunset. We were contravening English law. The landlord rushed up to us with two constables, maintaining that there might be some of his belongings among the things, and that we wanted to make away abroad. In less than five minutes there were two or three hundred persons loitering around our door – the whole Chelsea mob. The beds were brought in again – they could not be delivered to the buyer until after sunrise next day. When we had sold all our possessions we were in a position to pay what we owed to the last farthing. I went with my little darlings to the two small rooms we are now occupying in the German Hotel, 1, Leicester St, Leicester Square. There for £5 a week we were given a human reception.

Forgive me, dear friend, for being so long and wordy in describing a single day of our life here. It is indiscreet, I know, but my heart is bursting this evening, and I must at least once unload it to my oldest, best and truest friend. Do not think that these paltry worries have bowed me down; I know only too well that our struggle is not an isolated one and that I, in particular, am one of the chosen, happy, favoured ones, for my dear husband, the prop of my life, is still at my side. What really tortures my very soul and makes my heart bleed is that he had to suffer so much from paltry things, that so little could be done to help him, and that he who willingly and gladly helped so many others was so helpless himself. But do not think, dear Herr Weydemeyer, that we make demands on anybody. The only thing that my husband could have asked of those to whom he gave his ideas, his encouragement and his support was to show more energy in business and more support for his *Revue*. I am proud and bold to make that assertion. That little was his due. I do not think that would have been unfair to anybody. That is what grieves me. But my husband is of a different opinion. Never, not even in the most frightful moments, did he lose his confidence in the future or even his cheery humour, and he was satisfied when he saw me cheerful and our loving children cuddling close to their dear mother. He does not know, dear Herr Weydemeyer, that I have written to you in such detail about our situation. That is why I ask you not to refer to these lines. All he knows is that I have asked you in his name to hasten as much as you can the collection and sending of our money. Farewell, dear friend. Give your wife my most affectionate remembrances and kiss your little angel for a mother who has shed many a tear over her baby. Our three eldest children are doing splendidly for all that, for all that. The girls are pretty, healthy, cheerful and good, and our chubby little boy is full of good humour and the most amusing notions. The little goblin sings the whole day long with astonishing feeling in a thunderous voice. The house shakes when he rings out in a fearful voice the words of Freiligrath's Marseillaise:

Come, June, and bring us noble feats!
To deeds of fame our heart aspires.

Perhaps it is the historic destiny of that month, as of its two predecessors,[30] to open the gigantic struggle in which we shall all join hands again. Farewell!

SOURCE: *RME*, pp. 236 ff.; from the German original in *MEW*, XXVII, pp. 607 ff.

NOTES

1. The marriage took place in Kreuznach, to which place Jenny's mother had temporarily moved.
2. This meeting was the beginning of their lifelong collaboration.
3. This work, written in collaboration with Engels, is usually known as *The Holy Family. Critique of Critical Criticism* was its subtitle.
4. This was *The German Ideology*, for which Marx and Engels did not manage to find a publisher.
5. *The Ego and His Own*, by the Young Hegelian Max Stirner, was published at the end of 1844.
6. Helene Demuth.
7. 1849.
8. Marx had been editor of the *Neue Rheinische Zeitung* since its foundation a year before.
9. This quickly suppressed revolt was the last desperate flicker of the revolutionary movement in Germany.
10. Marx had relinquished his Prussian citizenship in 1845.
11. On 13 June left-wing republican politicians in Paris, led by Ledru-Rollin, attempted a revolutionary uprising, which was easily suppressed.
12. In the summer of 1849 a French force under Oudinot overthrew the

Roman Republic and reinstated the authority of Pius IX.
13. 'Order reigns in Warsaw.'
14. 'Woe to the conquered.'
15. A maritime department in southern Brittany.
16. 4, Anderson Street, off the King's Road.
17. For an extended account of these circumstances, see the next extract, from a letter by Jenny Marx.
18. 64, Dean Street.
19. In September 1850, Marx and his followers withdrew from the Communist League and from the Workers Educational Society associated with it. For further details on this split, see K. Marx and F. Engels, *Collected Works* (London, 1975) vol. x, pp. 625 ff.
20. 28, Dean Street.
21. This alludes to the birth of Freddy Demuth, Marx's son by Helene Demuth. For further details, see Y. Kapp, *Eleanor Marx*, vol. I: *Family Life 1855–1883* (London, 1972) pp. 289 ff.
22. In May Jenny inherited about £150 from an uncle in Scotland and in July about £120 from her mother.
23. 9, Grafton Terrace.
24. In 1861 Friedrich Wilhelm IV of Prussia died and was succeeded by Wilhelm I.
25. Lion Philips.
26. 1, Modena Villas, Maitland Park.
27. Jenny and her children visited the Weydemeyers in Frankfurt immediately after the suppression of the *Neue Rheinische Zeitung*.
28. To be precise, the *Neue Rheinische Zeitung*, of which Marx had been editor from May 1848 to May 1849.
29. The exchange rate at the time was about 7 thalers to the pound.
30. The reference is to the revolt of the Paris proletariat in June 1848 and the Baden uprising in 1849.

16 Prussian Spy

This extract is the major part of a report from an anonymous German spy. It was probably written, at the bequest of the Prussian authorities in Berlin, in the autumn of 1852. At that time the Prussian Government was organising a show trial of communists – the onus for whose defence lay chiefly with Marx.

The leader of this party is Karl Marx; his lieutenants are Engels in Manchester, where there are thousands of German workmen; Freiligrath and Wolff (known as Lupus) in London; Heine in Paris; Weydemeyer and Cluss in America; Bürgers and Daniels were his lieutenants in Cologne, and Weerth in Hamburg. All the rest are merely Party members. The shaping and moving spirit, the real soul of the Party, is Marx; therefore I will go on to acquaint you with his personality.

Marx is of medium height, thirty-four years old. Although in the prime of life, his hair is already turning grey. He is powerfully built, and his features remind you very distinctly of Szemere, only his complexion is darker, and his hair and beard quite black. The latter he does not shave at all. His large piercing fiery eyes have something demonically sinister about them. The first impression one receives is of a man of genius and energy. His intellectual superiority exercises an irresistible power on his surroundings.

In private life he is an extremely disorderly, cynical human being, and a bad host. He leads the existence of a real bohemian intellectual. Washing, grooming and changing his linen are things he does rarely, and he likes to get drunk. Though he is often idle for days on end, he will work day and night with tireless endurance when he has a great deal of work to do. He has no fixed times for going to sleep and waking up. He often stays up all night, and then lies down fully clothed on the sofa at midday and sleeps till evening, untroubled by the comings and goings of the whole world.

His wife is the sister of the Prussian Minister von Westphalen, a cultured and charming woman, who out of love for her husband has accustomed herself to his bohemian existence, and now feels perfectly at home in this poverty. She has two daughters and one son, and all three children are truly handsome.

As husband and father, Marx, in spite of his wild and restless character, is the gentlest and mildest of men. Marx lives in one of the worst – therefore, one of the cheapest – quarters of London. He occupies two rooms. The one looking out on the street is the living room, and the bedroom is at the back. In the whole apartment there is not one clean and solid piece of furniture. Everything is broken down, tattered and torn, with a half inch of dust over everything and the greatest disorder everywhere. In the middle of the living room there is a large old-fashioned table covered with an oilcloth, and on it there lie his manuscripts, books and newspapers, as well as the children's toys, and rags and tatters of his wife's sewing basket, several cups with broken rims, knives, forks, lamps, an inkpot, tumblers, Dutch clay pipes, tobacco ash – in a word, everything topsy-turvy, and all on the same table. A seller of secondhand goods would be ashamed to give away such a remarkable collection of odds and ends.

When you enter Marx's room, smoke from the coal and fumes from the tobacco make your eyes water so much that for a moment you seem to be groping about in a cavern, but gradually, as you grow accustomed to the fog, you can make out certain objects which distinguish themselves from the surrounding haze. Everything is dirty and covered with dust, so that to sit down becomes a thoroughly dangerous business. Here is a chair with only three legs, on another chair the children are playing at cooking – this chair happens to have four legs. This is the one which is offered to the visitor, but the children's cooking has not been wiped away; and if you sit down, you risk a pair of trousers. But none of these things embarrass Marx or his wife. You are received in the most friendly way and cordially offered pipes and tobacco and whatever else there may happen to be; and eventually a spirited and agreeable conversation arises to make amends for the domestic deficiencies, thus making the discomfort tolerable. Finally you grow accustomed to the company, and find it interesting and original. This is a true picture of the family life of the communist chief Marx. Now I wish to discuss him as a politician and leader of a conspiracy.

As head and leader of a plot Marx is undoubtedly the most capable and well-suited man next to Mazzini, but when it comes to intrigues he is a worthy equal to the Small Roman. Marx is exceptionally cunning, crafty and reserved; he is difficult of access; on the other hand, he will support in every way and defend to the death anyone in whom he has once placed his trust. He will not admit that he could be mistaken in a man whom he had investigated. Marx is jealous of his authority as head of the Party; against his political rivals and opponents he is vengeful and implacable: he does not rest until he has destroyed them. His main quality is boundless ambition and lust for power. In spite of his programme of communist equality, he is the absolute ruler of his party. It is true that he does everything himself, but then only he commands and here he will brook no opposition. All this only concerns the secret workings and the secret sections; in open Party meetings, by contrast, he is the most liberal and popular of all.

SOURCE: trs. by the editor from G. Mayer, 'Neue Beiträge zur Biographie von Karl Marx', *Archiv für die Geschichte des Sozialismus und der Arbeiter bewegung*, X (1922) 56 ff.

17 Jenny Marx (ii)

This letter to Mrs Weydemeyer was written in March 1861.

Dear Mrs Weydemeyer,
    I received your kind letter this morning and to show you how glad I was I wish to sit down and write you a long letter at once, for I know

from your friendly letter that you like to hear from us sometimes and still have friendly memories of us, as we have of you. And how could such old Party comrades and friends for whom destiny has brought about the same sorrows and joys, the same sunny and gloomy days, ever feel estranged though time and the ocean separate them. So I stretch out my hand to you from afar as to a brave and faithful companion in sorrow, a fighter and a sufferer. Yes, dear Mrs Weydemeyer, our hearts have often been heavy and sad, and I can well imagine what you must have gone through recently. I can imagine all your struggles, worries and privations, for I have often suffered the same myself. But suffering steels us and love keeps us up!

We had a bitterly hard time in the first years of our stay here, but I do not wish to dwell today on all the melancholy memories and all the losses we have suffered, nor on the sweet departed loves whose images we still carry in silent grief in our hearts.

Let me tell you today about a new period in our lives, which has had more than one sunny spell as well as cloudy days.

In 1856 I went to Trier with the three girls. My dear mother's joy was too great for words when I arrived with her grandchildren. But unfortunately it did not last long. That truest and best of mothers fell ill and after eleven days' suffering bestowed her blessing on the children and me and closed her dear tired eyes. Your dear husband, who knew how affectionate my mother was, will best be able to fathom my bereavement. When we had laid her beloved head in its last resting-place I saw to my mother's modest legacy, dividing it between my brother Edgar and myself, and then we left Trier. So far we had lived in London, in miserable furnished rooms. With the few hundred thalers that Mother had left us after all her sacrifices for us, we rented a small house not far from beautiful Hampstead Heath (you who translated *The Woman in White* [1] certainly remember that name) and we still live there now.[2] It is a truly princely dwelling compared with the holes we used to live in, and although it did not cost us more than £40 to furnish it from top to bottom (second-hand junk helped a lot) I really felt magnificent at first in our snug parlour. All the linen and other small remains of past grandeur were redeemed from 'uncle's' and I again had the pleasure of counting the old Scottish damask napkins. Although the wonder did not last long – for one article after another soon had to go back to the pop-house – it was a real pleasure for us to be comfortable. Then came the first American crisis and our income was halved. We were again hard up and fell into debt. This could not be avoided because we had to carry on the education of the three girls as it had been begun.

Now I come to the bright aspect of our existence, the light side of our life – our dear children. I am sure that if your kind husband loved our daughters when they were children it would be a real joy for him to see them now that they have grown into budding maidens. I must now run the risk of your taking me for a doting mother by singing the praises of my darling daughters. They both have a very kind heart and good nature, really lovable modesty and maidenly virtue. Jenny will be seventeen on 1 May. She is particularly attractive, and even pretty, with thick, dark, glossy hair, equally dark, shining, gentle eyes and a dark, creole complexion which, however, has a typically English freshness. The pleasant, good-natured expression of her apple-round childish face makes one overlook the not so pretty turned-up nose and it is a pleasure when the smiling mouth opens and shows her beautiful teeth.

Laura, who was fifteen years old last September, is perhaps prettier and has more regular features than her sister and is a direct contrast to her. She is just as tall, as slim and as delicately built as Jenny, but she is in all respects fairer, lighter and more limpid. You could call the upper part of her face beautiful, so charming is her wavy chestnut hair, so sweet her lovely green-shimmering eyes, always sparkling with joy, so noble and well-shaped her brow. But the lower part of her face is not so regular and has not yet reached full development. Both sisters have a truly blooming complexion and they are so free from any vanity that I often admire them in silence, all the more as the same could not be said of their mother when she was younger and still in flowing frocks.

At school they always won the first prizes. They are quite at home in English and know a fair amount of French. They understand Dante in Italian and can read a little in Spanish. It is only with German that they have big difficulties, although I do all I can to give them a lesson now and then but they are not at all keen and I have no great authority with them or they much respect for me. Jenny is particularly good at drawing and her pencil drawings are the best ornaments in our rooms. Laura was so negligent as regards drawing that we discontinued her lessons to punish her. On the other hand, she applies herself to piano exercises and sings duets with her sister very charmingly in English and in German. Unfortunately it was not until late – about a year and a half ago – that they were able to begin taking music lessons. It was beyond our means to pay for them and, besides, we had no piano. The one we have now is only hired and is hardly worth calling a piano. Both the girls give us many a joy because of their lovable, modest disposition. But their younger sister[3] is petted and pampered by the whole house.

The child was born just as my poor dear Edgar was taken away from us and all the love for the little brother, all affection for him, was transferred to the baby sister. The elder girls fostered and fondled her with almost motherly care. It is true that there can hardly be a more lovable child, so pretty, simple and good-humoured. The most striking thing about her is her love for talking and telling stories. This she got from the Grimm Brothers, with whom she does not part night or day. We all read her those tales till we are weary, but woe betide us if we leave out a single syllable about the Noisy Goblin, King Brosselbart or Snow-White. It is through these tales that the child has learned German, besides English which she breathes here with the air, and that her speech is most correct and precise. She is Karl's real pet and her chatter dispels many of his worries.

As far as the household is concerned, Lenchen is still as steadfast and conscientious as ever. Ask your husband about her, he will tell you what a treasure she has been for me. She has sailed with us through fair and foul for sixteen years.

In the past year we were terribly annoyed by the infamous attacks about the 'rounded off nature', the base attitude of all the German, American, etc., press. You cannot imagine how many worries and sleepless nights the affair brought us.[4] The lawsuit against *National-zeitung* cost a lot of money, and when Karl had finished his book he could find no publisher for it. He was obliged to get it printed at his own expense (£25) and now that it has appeared it is passed over in silence by the base, cowardly, mercenary press. I am awfully glad to know that you liked it. Your opinion of it is the same, almost word for word, as that of all our friends. As a result of the deliberate silence of the press, the sale of the book is, of course, far from being as successful as we were entitled to expect. However, the appreciation of all people who matter must be enough for us at the present. Even opponents and enemies recognise it as being of great significance. Bucher calls it a compendium of contemporary history and Lassalle writes that such a work of art was an indescribable pleasure for him and his friends, who could not stop expressing their joy and delight at its wit. Engels considers it to be Karl's best book, so does Lupus. Congratulations pour in from all sides and even the old cur Ruge calls it a 'good piece of nonsense'. I am curious to know whether the same silence will be kept over it in America. It would be outrageous, all the more as all columns were open to worthless lies and calumnies. Perhaps your husband could help to spread it in some way?

Hardly had I finished copying the manuscript – it was still at the press – when I suddenly began to feel very poorly. A terrible fever came over me and a doctor had to be called in. He came on 20 November and examined me at length and with great care. After a long silence he said to me, 'My dear Mrs Marx, I am sorry to say you have got the smallpox – the children must leave the house immediately.' You can imagine the terror and the wailing that these words caused in the house. What could we do? The Liebknechts did not hesitate to take in our children and that very noon the girls, carrying their few belongings, went into exile. I got worse from hour to hour, pockmarks broke out fearfully. I was in great suffering. I had severe burning pains in my face and was completely unable to sleep. I was mortally anxious about Karl, who took the most tender care of me. In the end I lost all use of my outward senses although I was fully conscious all the time. I lay constantly by the open window so that the cold November air would blow over me, while there was a raging fire in the stove and ice on my burning lips, and I was given drops of claret from time to time. I could hardly swallow, my hearing was getting weaker, and finally my eyes closed, so that I did not know whether I would remain enveloped in eternal night.

My constitution, helped by the tenderest and truest care, took the upper hand, however, and so I am sitting here now in perfect health but with my face disfigured by pockmarks and of a red which is just the 'Magenta' that is now in fashion. The children were not allowed back to the paternal home that they had been so longing for until Christmas eve. Our reunion was indescribably moving. The girls were overwhelmed with emotion and could hardly keep back their tears when they saw me. Five weeks before I had looked quite respectable beside my healthy-looking girls. Surprisingly, I had no grey hair and my teeth and figure were good and therefore people used to class me among the well-preserved women. But that was all a thing of the past now and I seemed to myself a kind of cross between a rhinoceros and a hippopotamus whose place was in the zoo rather than among the members of the Caucasian race. But do not be too terrified. It is not so bad now, the marks are beginning to heal.

No sooner was I able to leave my bed than my dear Karl fell ill. The excessive anxiety, worries and torments of all sorts forced him to take to his bed. His chronic liver disease took an acute turn for the first time. But thank God he got better after four weeks' suffering. In the meantime the *Tribune* had again halved our income and instead of getting money for Karl's book we had to pay a bill of exchange. Added to that came all the enormous expenses of that terrible disease. In a word, you can imagine our situation that winter.

A a result of all this Karl decided to make a flying trip to Holland, the land of his fathers, tobacco and cheese. He wants to see whether he can get any money out of his uncle. So I am a grass widow for the time being, waiting for what success the trip to Holland will bring. On Saturday I got the first letter with some hope and 60 gulden. Such a matter cannot, of course, be hurried; tact, diplomacy and skill must be used. All the same, I hope that Karl will manage to rake something together there. As soon as he has any success in Holland` he wants to make a secret detour to Berlin to see the lie of the land and if possible to arrange a monthly or weekly journal. We have been only too well convinced by late experiences that no progress is possible unless we have our own paper. If Karl succeeds in founding a new Party paper he will certainly write to your husband to ask him for reports from America.

Almost immediately after Karl's departure our faithful Lenchen fell ill and she is still in bed, though on the way to recovery. So I have my hands full and have written off this letter in the greatest hurry. But I was unable and unwilling to remain silent, and it has done my heart good to have emptied it to my oldest and truest friends. That is why I do not beg your pardon for having written at such great length about everything. My pen ran away with me and I only hope and wish that these scribbled lines will bring you some of the pleasure I had in reading your letter.

I immediately settled the matter of the bill of exchange and put everything in order just as if my lord and master had been here.

My daughters send love and kisses to your children – one Laura to the other – and I send each of them a kiss. Friendliest remembrances to your dear self. Be brave and courageous in these hard times. The world belongs to the fearless. Be a faithful and firm support for your husband and keep agile in body and in mind and the true 'unrespectful' comrade of your dear children. And let us hear from you again when the occasion offers.

Yours,
Jenny Marx

SOURCE: *RME*, pp. 243 ff.; from the German original in *Die Neue Zeit*, XXV, pt 2 (1906/7) pp. 182 ff.

NOTES

1. A novel by Wilkie Collins.
2. 9, Grafton Terrace, where the Marx family lived from 1856 to 1864.
3. Eleanor.
4. In 1859, Karl Vogt, a professor of zoology in Geneva who had been active as a radical in Germany in 1848, published a book entitled *Mein Prozess wider die Allgemeine Zeitung* ('My Lawsuit against the *Allgemeine Zeitung*'). The book was a rebuttal of charges, emanating from Marx, that Vogt was in the pay of Louis Napoleon, but it also contained documents blackguarding Marx's role in refugee politics over the previous decade. (For an example, see above, no.14). Marx devoted much time and energy to a lawsuit against the *Nationalzeitung*, which had reprinted excerpts from Vogt's book, and to his own reply – a book entitled *Herr Vogt*.

18 Wilhelm Liebknecht

The lengthy excerpts below form the major part of a small book of his reminiscences of Marx published by Liebknecht in 1896. Born in 1826, Liebknecht took an active part in the 1848 revolutions in Germany and consequently spent the 1850s as a penniless exile in London. During this decade, he was an almost daily visitor to Marx's house and had closer contact with him than anyone outside Marx's immediate family. Following his return to Germany in 1862, Liebknecht became, with Bebel, one of the leaders of the German social democrats.

1   FIRST MEETING WITH MARX

My friendship with Marx's two eldest daughters – they were then six and seven years old respectively – began a few days after I arrived in London after being released from prison in 'Free Switzerland' and travelling via France on a compulsory passport. I met the Marx family at the summer fête of the Communist Workers Educational Society[1] somewhere near London. I do not remember whether it was at Greenwich or Hampton Court.

'Père Marx', whom I had never seen before, at once severely scrutinised me, looking searchingly into my eyes and attentively surveying my head. . . .

The scrutiny ended favourably and I endured the gaze of that lion-like head with the jet-black mane. Then came a lively, cheerful chat and we were soon in the middle of unconstrained rejoicing, Marx being the least constrained of all. I was immediately introduced to Mrs Marx, Lenchen, who had been their faithful housekeeper since she was a girl, and the children. From that day I was at home in Marx's house and not a day went by when I did not visit his family. They were living in Dean Street, off Oxford Street. I took up lodgings in Church Street, not far away.

2   FIRST CONVERSATION

I had my first long talk with Marx the day after I met him at the fête which I have just mentioned. We had naturally not been able to have a serious discussion there and Marx invited me for the next day to the premises of the Workers Educational Society, where Engels would probably be too.

I arrived somewhat before the appointed time. Marx had not yet arrived, but I met a number of old acquaintances and was in the middle of an animated conversation when Marx slapped me on the shoulder with a friendly greeting, telling me that Engels was downstairs in the private parlour and that we would be more to ourselves there.

I did not know what a private parlour was and I thought that the time for the big test had come, but I went trustingly with Marx. The impression he made on me was just as favourable as the day before – he had a gift for inspiring confidence. He slipped his arm through mine and took me to the private parlour where Engels, who was already sitting there with a pewter mug of dark stout, gave me a cheerful welcome.

Amy, the brisk barmaid, was immediately ordered to bring us something to drink – and to eat too, for food was one of the major questions for us emigrants – and we sat down, I on one side of the table, Marx and Engels on the other. The heavy mahogany table, the shining tankards, the frothing stout, the prospect of a real English beefsteak and all that goes with it, and the long clay pipes only asking to be smoked made one feel so comfortable that it reminded me of one of the English illustrations to *Boz*. But it was to be an examination after all! Well, I would manage it allright. The conversation got livelier. I soon found that my examiners had already gathered information concerning me. A lengthy composition on the June battle I had written for Hecker's *Volksfreund* in Muttenz in the summer of 1848 under the fresh impressions of the tragedy that marked a new historical era, had been read by Marx and Engels and had attracted their attention to me....

Both my examiners suspected me of pretty-bourgeois 'democracy' and 'South-German placidity', and some of the opinions I expressed on men and things met severe criticism. Nevertheless I succeeded in clearing myself of that suspicion.... On the whole the examination was not a failure and the conversation turned to broader questions.

Soon we were talking about natural sciences and Marx scoffed at the victorious reaction in Europe who imagined that they had stifled the revolution and had no idea that natural science was preparing a new one. King Steam, who had revolutionized the world the century before, had lost his throne and was being superseded by a still greater revolutionary – the electric spark. Then Marx told me with great enthusiasm about the model of an electric engine that had been on show for a few days in Regent Street and that could drive a railway train.

'The problem is now solved,' he said, 'and the consequences are unpredictable. The economic revolution must necessarily be followed by a political revolution, for the latter is but the expression of the former.'

The way Marx spoke of the progress of science and mechanics

showed so clearly his world outlook, especially what was later to be called the materialist conception of history, that certain doubts which I still entertained melted like snow in the spring sun. I did not return home that evening. We talked, laughed and drank until well into the morning and the sun was already up when I went to bed. But I did not stay there long; I could not get to sleep, for my mind was full of all I had heard and the tumult of my thoughts drove me out of bed and to Regent Street to see the model, the modern horse of Troy which bourgeois society in its suicidal blindness had brought into its Ilion amidst rejoicings like the Trojans of old and which was to be their inevitable ruin. *Essetai haemar* – the day will come when holy Ilion will fall.

A big crowd showed me where the engine was exhibited. I pushed my way through and there was the engine and the train racing round merrily.

That was in 1850, at the beginning of July....

Well, though Marx was a prophet looking into the future with sharp eyes and perceiving much more than ordinary human beings, he never was a prophesier, and when Messieurs Kinkel, Ledru-Rollin and other revolution-makers announced in every appeal to their folks *in partibus* the typical, 'Tomorrow it will start', none was so merciless with his satire as Marx.

Only on the subject of 'industrial crises' he fell a victim to the prophesying imp, and in consequence was subjected to our hearty derision which made him grimly mad. However, on the main point he was right none the less. The prophesied industrial crises did come – only not at the fixed time.

3   EDUCATIONAL AND OTHER NOTES: MARX AS TEACHER.

Marx endeavoured to make sure of his men and to secure them for himself. He was not such a zealous devotee of phrenology as Gustav Struve, but he believed in it to some extent, and when I first met him – I have already mentioned it – he not only examined me with questions, but also with his fingers, making them dance over my skull in a connoisseur's style. Later on he arranged for a regular investigation by the phrenologist of the party, the good old painter, Karl Pfaender, one of the 'oldest', who helped to found the Communist League, and was present in that memorable council to whom the *Communist Manifesto* was submitted, and by whom it was discussed and accepted in due form. On this occasion a comical incident happened.[2] One of the 'old ones' of the Communist Workers Educational Society was very enthusiastic over the manifesto that was read by Marx with passionate emotion – perhaps similarly as the *Robbers* once upon a time by Schiller – was quite beyond himself, like all others, applauded and shouted 'Bravo!' as loud as he could; but his pensive mien gave evidence that some dark point occupied his mind. On leaving he finally called Pfaender aside: 'That was magnificent, but one word I did not understand – what does Marx mean by *Achtblättler* [plant with eight leaves]? *Achtblättler*, *Achtblättler* – I have heard of plants, of clover, with four leaves, but *Achtblättler*?' Pfaender was puzzled. At last the riddle was solved. Marx had a little lisp in his youth and at that time still spoke the unadulterated Rhenish dialect; the mysterious *Achtblättler*, behind which the old Cabetist had scented a magic formula, were simple and honest – *Arbeiter* (working men). We laughed many a time over this misunderstanding which, however, was beneficial to Marx in that henceforth he strove to clip the wings of his Rhenish dialect.

Well, my skull was officially inspected by Karl Pfaender and nothing was found that would have prevented my admission into the Holiest of Holies of the Communist League. But the examinations did not cease.

'Moor', being five or six years older than us 'young fellows', was conscious of the advantage his maturity gave him over us and sounded us, particularly me, on every possible occasion. Well-read as he was and with his fabulous memory, he had no difficulty in making it hot for us. How he enjoyed it when he could give one of the 'student boys' a sticky question and prove at his expense *in corpore vile* the wretchedness of our universities and academic education.

But he educated us and there was a plan in his education. I can say that he was my teacher in both senses of the word, the stricter and the broader. We had to learn from him in all branches, not to mention political economy – you don't talk of the pope in his palace. I shall speak of his talks on that subject in the Communist League later. Marx was at his ease in ancient as well as modern languages. I was a philologist and it gave him childlike pleasure when he could show me some difficult passage from Aristotle or Aeschylus which I could not immediately construe correctly. How he scolded me one day because I did not know – Spanish! He snatched up *Don Quixote* out of a pile of books and began to give me a lesson. I already knew the principles of grammar and word-building from Diez's comparative grammer of the Romance languages and so I got on pretty well under his excellent direction and with his cautious help when I hesitated or got stuck. And what a patient teacher he was, he who was otherwise so fiery! The lesson was cut short only by the entrance of a visitor. Every day I was questioned and had to translate a passage from *Don Quixote* or some other Spanish book until he judged me capable enough.

Marx was a remarkable philologist, though more in modern than in ancient languages. He had a most exact knowledge of Grimm's German Grammar and he understood more about the part of the Grimm brother's dictionary that was published than I, a linguist. He could write English and French as well as an Englishman or Frenchman, though his pronunciation was faulty. His articles for the *New York Daily Tribune* were written in classical English, his *Poverty of Philosophy* against Proudhon's *Philosophy of Poverty* in classical French. The French friend to whom he showed the manuscript of the latter work before it was printed found but little to improve in it.

As Marx understood the essence of language and had studied its origin, its development and its structure, it was not difficult for him to learn languages. In London he learned Russian and during the Crimean War he even intended to study Turkish and Arabic, but he was not able to do so. As one who really wishes to master a language, he attached most importance to reading. A man with a good memory – and Marx's was of such extraordinary fidelity that it never forgot anything – quickly accumulates vocabulary and turns of phrase. Practical use is then easily learned.

In 1850 and 1851 Marx gave a course of lectures on political economy. He was reluctant to do so, but once he had given a few private lectures to some of his closest friends he let us persuade him to lecture to broader audiences. In this course, which was thoroughly enjoyed by all fortunate to attend, Marx fully developed the principles of his system as we see it expounded in *Capital*. In the overcrowded hall of the Workers Educational Society, which at the time was in Great Windmill Street – the very hall in which the *Communist Manifesto* had been adopted a year and a half before – Marx showed a great gift for popularising knowledge. Nobody was more against vulgarising science, i.e. falsifying, debasing and stultifying it, than he was. Nobody had a greater talent for expressing himself clearly. Clarity of speech is the fruit of clarity of thought: clear thought necessarily leads to clear expression.

Marx proceeded with method. He formulated a proposition – as briefly as possible – and then explained it at length, avoiding with the utmost care any expressions which the workers would not understand. Then he invited his listeners to ask questions. If none were asked he would begin examining, which he did with such pedagogical skill that no gap or misunderstanding escaped him.

Expressing my surprise at this skill one day, I was told that Marx had already given lectures in the Workers Society in Brussels.[3] In any case, he had all that makes an excellent teacher. In teaching he also made use of a blackboard on which he wrote formulas, including those that we all know from the beginning of *Capital*.

The pity was that the course only lasted about six months or less.

Elements which Marx did not like got into the Workers Educational Society. When the tide of emigration had ebbed, the Society shrivelled up and became somewhat sectarian, the old followers of Weitling and Cabet began to assert themselves again. Marx, who was not content with such a narrow scope of activity and could do more important things than sweep away old cobwebs, kept away from the Society. . . .

The Society was even the cause of a conflict with Marx. However high he stood to me and however much I loved him, infallibility was not recognised, and if I did not find in debate that I was wrong I did not admit of being overruled by another's opinion. Marx himself was, of course, within the confines of communistic conceptions, the most tolerant of men. He could stand opposition, although not infrequently he flew into a passion over it; and afterwards he even enjoyed having received a strong answer. But by men who were more 'Marxian' than Marx himself – who did not wish to be called a 'Marxist' and ridiculed the 'Marxists' to his heart's content – plots were woven against me, and one fine day I found myself charged with the crime of violating our principles by my actions in the London Communist League, of having made concessions to the Weitlingians and other sectarians that were inadmissible from a tactical and theoretical standpoint, of trying to gain an unorthodox counterbalance against the orthodoxy of the Communist League, and to have deviated from the straight road through the attempt of playing the role of a 'mediator' between the pure communistic doctrine and the practice, especially between Marx and the working men. The spirits met in a lively clash. Marx violently deprecated the 'mediator business'; if he had anything to say to the workers he could say it himself. This I did not deny, of course, but I maintained my right to serve the party in a way that seemed most appropriate to me, and declared it crazy tactics for a working men's party to seclude itself away up above the workers in a theoretic air-castle; without working men, no working men's party, and the workers we must take as we find them. You see, it was a conflict that has been repeated later on. By personal instigations this trifling incident was inflated to a conflict, and I remained in the minority. This embittered me; and for several months I eschewed the house of Marx. But one day the children met me on the street; they scolded me for staying away so long; their mamma, they said, was quite cross with me, and – I went along with them, was received as usual, and Marx himself, whose originally serious look melted when I stepped close to him, laughingly shook my hand. And that conflict was mentioned no more.

Disputations I have had by the score with Marx – a quarrel with him only twice. This was the first time. The second was some twenty years later, and, curiously enough, over the same subject. It was in

1874: the longing for unity between the Lassallians and the 'honest ones' made itself equally felt on both sides and the political conditions made union a necessity.[4] But there were still certain prejudices to respect, and in the programme for union outlined by ourselves we had to submit to certain concessions. Marx, who could not survey the conditions of things from abroad as well as we in Germany, would not hear of such concessions; and after a prolonged exchange of opinions with me that famous letter was written about which so much was said some years ago. Marx was highly incensed with me for a long time, but in the interest of the movement in Germany I had had no other choice. If it had been a question of sacrificing a principle, Marx certainly would have been right; but it was only a matter of yielding temporarily for the purpose of securing great tactical advantages for the Party. And it cannot be called a sacrifice of principle when the sacrifice is made in the interest of principle. That I did not make a wrong calculation in this respect has been brilliantly demonstrated by the consequences and the successes. The declaration of principles was accomplished within the united parties so speedily and so smoothly that, had not the 'law of exception' during the time of its validity forced the programme question into the background, we could have proceeded with the clarification of the programme as early as the close of the 1870s without any opposition worth mentioning. As it was, this had to be postponed to the beginning of the 1890s.

Marx has finally acknowledged this. He was charmed by the progress of the Party – movement in Germany, and shortly before his death he said to me, 'I am proud of the German workers: without a doubt they are leading the international labour movement.' Similarly Engels has expressed himself, although he retained his animosity on account of the programme for union for a longer time.

Marx was no orator – it was not his nature. In the Hague, at the last congress of the International Working Men's Association, he is said to have spoken very well, so I have been told. I was at that time with Bebel in the 'fortress' Hubertusburg. I have never heard him making a speech; neither was there any opportunity for him during the time of our association.

4   MARX'S STYLE

It is claimed that Marx had no 'style' – or at least a very bad style. This is claimed by those who have no idea of style – polishers of words and twisters of phrases who have not understood and were not capable of understanding Marx – not capable of following the flight of his genius to the highest peaks of science and passion and into the lowest depths of human misery and human baseness. If

Buffon's saying 'The style is the man' is true of anybody, it is of Marx – Marx's style is Marx. A man of such thorough truthfulness as Marx, who knew no other cult but that of the truth, who swept aside in a moment a proposition painfully arrived at, and therefore dear to him, as soon as he was convinced of its incorrectness, necessarily showed himself in his works as he was in reality. Incapable of hypocrisy, dissimulation or pretence, he was always himself, in his writings as in his life. Naturally, the style of such a many-sided, versatile and all-embracing nature as his could not have the uniformity, evenness or even monotony of a less complex, less comprehensive one. The Marx of *Capital*, the Marx of *The Eighteenth Brumaire* and the Marx of *Herr Vogt* are three different Marxes; yet in their variety they are *one* Marx, there is unity in their trinity, the unity of his great personality which manifests itself in different ways in different fields and yet is ever the selfsame. Marx's style is indeed Marx himself. He has been reproached with trying to squeeze as much content as possible into the minimum space, but that is precisely Marx.

Marx attached extreme importance to purity and correctness of expression. And he chose himself the highest masters in Goethe, Lessing, Shakespeare, Dante and Cervantes, from whom he made almost daily readings. He was most scrupulous as far as purity and correctness of language were concerned. I remember that he once gave me a lecture at the beginning of my stay in London for having used the expression *stattgehabte Versammlung* in an article. I pleaded usage as an excuse but Marx burst out, 'What wretched German gymnasiums where no German is taught! What wretched German universities!' and so on. I defended myself as best I could and quoted examples from the classics, but I never spoke of a *stattgehabte* or *stattgefundene* event again and tried to get others out of the habit. . . .

Marx was a strict purist, he often searched hard and long for the correct expression. He hated unnecessary foreign words and if he did frequently use foreign words where the subject did not call for them, the fact must be attributed to the long time he spent abroad, especially in England. . . . But the abundance of original, genuine German word constructions and uses which we find in Marx in spite of his having spent two-thirds of his life abroad make him highly deserving before the German language, of which he was one of the most prominent masters and creators. . . .

Marx was a purist in language to the extent of pedanticism. My Upper Hessian dialect, which clung to me like a skin – or perhaps I clung to it – let me in for countless lectures from him. If I speak of such trifles it is only because they show how much Marx felt himself to be the teacher of us 'young fellows'.

This was naturally manifested in another way. He was very exacting towards us. As soon as he discovered a deficiency in our knowledge he would insist most forcibly on our making it up and give us the right advice how to do so. Anybody who was alone with him would be put through a regular examination. Such examinations were no joke. You could not throw dust in his eyes. If he saw that his efforts were lost on anybody that was the end of his friendship. It was an honour for us to be 'school-mastered' by him. I was never with him but I learned something from him. And that I did not go to the bottom in the hard struggle for existence, for the naked physical life, or let us rather say for keeping from starving – because we had to hunger for years in London – that I did not perish in this desperate struggle for a piece of bread or a few potatoes, I owe to Marx and his family.

5 POPULARITY

For popularity Marx entertained a sovereign contempt. What he especially praised in Robert Owen was that whenever any of his ideas became popular he would come forth with a new demand making him unpopular. Free from all conceit, Marx could not attribute any value to the applause of the masses. The masses were to him a brainless crowd whose thoughts and feelings were furnished by the ruling class. And while socialism has not spiritually soaked through the masses, the applause of the crowd can, as a logical consequence, be bestowed only on men belonging to no party or to the adversaries of socialism. Today, when socialistic conceptions have begun to pervade the masses and to influence so-called 'public opinion', this is no longer true to the same extent as forty or fifty years ago.

In those days only a small minority in the working class itself had risen to the level of socialism, and among the socialists themselves only a minority were socialists in the scientific sense Marx gave the word – the sense of the *Communist Manifesto*. The bulk of the workers, if they were at all awakened to political life, were pinned down by the mist of sentimental democratic wishes and phrases, such as were characteristic of the 1848 movement and what preceded and followed it. The applause of the multitude, popularity, was for Marx a proof that one was on the wrong road, and his favourite motto was Dante's proud line '*Segui il tuo corso, e lascia dir le genti!*' – 'Go your own way and let tongues wag!'

How often he quoted that line, with which he also concluded his Preface to *Capital*. Nobody is insensitive to blows, jostling, or gnat or bug bites, and how often Marx, attacked from all sides and racked by the struggle for existence, misunderstood by the working people the weapons for whose emancipation he forged in the silence of the night, sometimes even disdained by them, whereas they followed vain prattlers, dissembling traitors or even avowed enemies – how often he must have repeated to himself in the solitude of his poor, genuinely proletarian study the words of the great Florentine to inspire himself with courage and fresh energy!

He would not be led astray. Unlike the prince in the *Thousand and One Nights* who surrendered victory and the prize of victory because, terrified by the noise and the fearful apparitions round him, he looked round and back, Marx went forward, always looking ahead at his bright goal. . . .

As great as his hatred for popularity was his anger at those who sought it. He loathed fine speakers and woe betide anyone who engaged in phrasemongering. With such people he was implacable. 'Phrasemonger' was the worst reproach he could make, and when he had once discovered that somebody was a phrasemonger it was all over with him. He kept impressing upon us 'young fellows' the necessity for logical thought and clarity in expression and forced us to study.

The magnificent reading-room of the British Museum with its inexhaustible treasure of books was completed about that time. Marx went there daily and urged us to go too. Study! Study! That was the categoric injunction that we heard often enough from him and that he gave us by his example and the continual work of his mighty brain.

While the other emigrants were daily planning a world revolution and day after day, night after night, intoxicating themselves with the opium-like motto 'Tomorrow it will begin!', we, the 'brimstone band', the 'bandits', the 'dregs of mankind', spent our time in the British Museum and tried to educate ourselves and prepare arms and ammunition for the future fight.

Sometimes we had not a bite to eat, but that did not keep us away from the Museum, for there we had comfortable chairs to sit on and in winter it was warm and cosy, which was far from being the case at home, for those who had a home.

Marx was a stern teacher: he not only urged us to study, he made sure that we did so.

For a long time I was studying the history of the English trade-unions. Every day he would ask me how far I had got and he left me no peace until I delivered a long speech to a large audience. He was present at it. He did not praise me, but neither did he inflict any devastating criticism, and as he was not in the habit of praising and did so only out of pity, I consoled myself for the absence of praise. Then, when he entered into a discussion with me over an assertion that I had made, I considered that as indirect praise.

As a teacher Marx had the rare quality of being severe without discouraging. And another of his remarkable qualities was that he compelled us to be critical of ourselves and would not allow us to be complacent over our achievements. He scourged bland contemplativeness cruelly with the lash of his irony. Marx could only become what he did become, as I said elsewhere, in England. In a country so undeveloped economically as Germany still was up to the middle of the present century it was just as impossible for Marx to arrive at his criticism of bourgeois economy and the knowledge of the capitalist process of production as for economically undeveloped Germany to have the political institutions of economically developed England. Marx depended just as much on his surroundings and the conditions in which he lived as any other man: without those conditions he would not have become what he is. Nobody proved that better than he did.

To observe such a mind letting conditions act upon it and penetrating deeper and deeper into the nature of society is in itself a profound mental enjoyment. I shall never be able to appreciate at its worth the good fortune that befell me, a young fellow without experience and craving for education, to have Marx as my guide and to profit by his influence and teaching.

Given the many-sidedness, I would go so far as to say the all-embracingness, of his universal mind, a mind that encompassed the universe, penetrated into every substantial detail and never scorned anything as secondary or insignificant, that teaching could not but be many-sided.

Marx was one of the first to grasp the significance of Darwin's research. Even before 1859, the year of the publication of *The Origin of Species* – and, by a remarkable coincidence, of Marx's *Contribution to the Critique of Political Economy* – Marx realised Darwin's epoch-making importance. For Darwin, in the peace of his country estate far from the hubbub of the city, was preparing a revolution similar to the one which Marx himself was working for in the seething centre of the world. Only the lever was brought to bear on a different point.

Marx kept up with every new appearance and noted every step forward, especially in the fields of natural sciences – including physics and chemistry – and history. The names of Moleschott, Liebig and Huxley, whose 'popular lectures' we attended scrupulously, were as often to be heard among us as those of Ricardo, Adam Smith, MacCulloch and the Scottish and Italian economists. When Darwin drew the conclusions from his research work and brought them to the knowledge of the public, we spoke of nothing else for months but Darwin and the enormous significance of his scientific discoveries. I emphasise this, because 'radical' enemies have spread the idea that Marx, from a certain jealousy, acknowledged the merit of Darwin very reluctantly and in a very limited degree.

No one could be kinder and fairer than Marx in giving others their due. He was too great to be envious, jealous or vain. But he had as deadly a hatred for the false greatness and pretended fame of swaggering incapacity and vulgarity as for any kind of deceit and pretence.

6 MASKS, MEN AND PHOTOGRAPHS

Of all the great, little or average men that I have known, Marx is one of the few who was free from vanity. He was too great and too strong to be vain, and too proud as well. He never struck an attitude, he was always himself. He was as incapable as a child of wearing a mask or pretending. As long as social or political grounds did not make it undesirable, he always spoke his mind completely and without any reserve and his face was the mirror of his heart. And when circumstances demanded restraint he showed a sort of childlike awkwardness that often amused his friends.

No man could be more truthful than Marx – he was truthfulness incarnate. Merely by looking at him you knew who it was you were dealing with. In our 'civilised' society with its perpetual state of war one cannot always tell the truth, that would be playing into the enemy's hands or risking being sent to Coventry. But even if it is often inadvisable to say the truth, it is not always necessary to say an untruth. I must not always say what I think or feel, but that does not mean that I must say what I do not feel or think. The former is wisdom, the latter hypocrisy. Marx was never a hypocrite. He was absolutely incapable of it, just like an unsophisticated child. His wife often called him 'my big baby', and nobody, not even Engels, knew or understood him better than she did. Indeed, when he was in what is generally termed society, where everything is judged by appearances and one must do violence to one's feelings, our 'Moor' was like a big boy and he could be embarrassed and blush like a child.

He detested men who acted a part. I still remember how he laughed when he told us of his first meeting with Louis Blanc. He was still living in Dean Street, in the small flat in which there were really only two rooms, the front one, the parlour, being used as study and reception-room, the back one for everything else. Louis Blanc gave Lenchen his card and she showed him into the front room while Marx quickly dressed in the back room. The door between the two rooms had been left ajar and Marx witnessed an amusing scene. The 'great' historian and politician was a very small man, hardly taller than an eight-year-old boy, but he was terribly vain. Looking round the proletarian reception-room, he discovered a very primitive mirror in a corner. He immediately stood in front of it, struck an attitude, stretching his dwarfish stature as much as he could – he had the highest heels I have ever seen – contemplated himself with delight and frisked like a March hare and tried to look imposing. Mrs Marx, who also witnessed the comic scene, had to bite her lips not to laugh. When he had finished dressing Marx coughed aloud to announce his arrival and give the foppish tribune time to step away from the mirror and welcome his host with a respectful bow. Acting and posing got one nowhere, of course, with Marx, and 'little Louis', as the Paris workers called Blanc in contrast to Louis Bonaparte, hastily adopted as natural an attitude as he was capable of. . . .

Of Marx I know no bad photographs. They are all good likenesses, because he has always given himself as he was. True, the photographs have not all the same value. The characteristic lines of a person's face do not always show equally well – bodily or mental uneasiness or disease, the domination of a certain thought or sensation may give a strange character to a face. But all photographs of Marx are good.

7   MARX AT WORK

'Genius is industry', somebody said and it is right to a point, if not completely.

There is no genius without extreme energy and extraordinary hard work. Anything which is called genius and in which neither the former nor the latter have any part is but a shimmering soap bubble or a bill backed by treasures on the moon. Genius is where energy and hard work exceed the average. I have often met people who were considered geniuses by themselves, and sometimes by others too, but had no capacity for work. In reality they were just loafers with a good gift of the gab and talent for publicity. All men of real importance whom I have known were hard workers. This could not be truer than it was of Marx. He was a colossal worker. As he was often prevented from working during the day – especially in the first emigration period – he resorted to night-work. When he came home late from some sitting or meeting it was a regular thing for him to sit down and work a few hours. And the few hours became longer and longer until in the end he worked almost the whole night through and went to sleep in the morning. His wife made earnest reproaches to him about it, but he answered with a laugh that it was in his nature. . . .

Notwithstanding his extraordinarily robust constitution, Marx began to complain of all sorts of troubles at the end of the 1850s. A doctor had to be consulted. The result was that Marx was expressly forbidden to work at night. And much exercise – walking and riding – was prescribed. Many were the walks I had with Marx at that time on the outskirts of London, mainly in the hilly north. He soon recovered, too, for his body was indeed made for great exertion and display of strength.

But he hardly felt better when he again gradually fell into his habit of night-work until a crisis came that forced him to adopt a more reasonable mode of life, though only as long as he felt the imperative necessity of it.

The attacks became more and more violent. A liver disease set in, malignant tumours developed. His iron constitution was gradually undermined. I am convinced – and the physicians who last treated him were of the same opinion – that had Marx made up his mind to a life in keeping with nature, that is, with the demands of his organism and of hygiene, he would still be alive today.

Only in his last years, when it was already too late, did he give up working at night. But he worked all the more during the day. He worked whenever it was at all possible to do so. He even had his notebook with him when he went for a walk and kept making entries in it. And his work was never superficial, for there are different ways of working. His was always intense, thorough. His daughter Eleanor gave me a little history table that he drew up for himself to get a general view for some secondary remark. Really nothing was secondary for Marx and the table that he made up for his own temporary use is compiled with as much industry and care as if it had been intended to be printed.

The endurance with which Marx worked often astonished me. He knew no fatigue. Even when he was on the point of breaking down he showed no signs of flagging strength.

If a man's worth is reckoned according to the work he does, as the value of things is reckoned by the amount of work embodied in them, even from that point of view Marx is a man of such value that only a few titanic minds can be compared with him.

What did bourgeois society give Marx in recompense for that enormous quantity of work?

Capital cost Marx forty years' work, and work such as Marx alone was capable of. I shall not be exaggerating if I say that the lowest paid day-labourer in Germany got more pay in forty years than Marx as honorarium or, to put it bluntly, as debt of honour for one of the two greatest scientific creations of the century. The other one is Darwin's work.

'Science' is not a marketable value. And bourgeois society cannot be expected to pay a reasonable price for the drawing up of its own death sentence.

8 MARX AND CHILDREN

Like every strong and healthy nature, Marx had an extraordinary love for children. He was not only a most loving father who could be a child for hours with his children, he felt drawn as by a magnet towards other children, especially helpless ones in distress whom he came across. Hundreds of times he left us as we were going through poor districts to go and pat the head of some child sitting in rags on the door-step and press a penny or a halfpenny into its hand. He distrusted beggars, for begging had become a regular trade in London, and one that paid too, even if only coppers at a time. Consequently Marx was not long taken in by men or women who went begging, though at first he never refused alms if he had any money. If any of them tried artfully to move him by feigning illness or need he was profoundly angry with them, for he considered the exploitation of human pity especially base and equivalent to stealing from the poor. But if a man or woman with a weeping child came to Marx begging, he could not resist the entreating eyes of the child, no matter how clearly roguery was written on the face of the man or woman.

Bodily weakness and helplessness always excited lively pity and sympathy in Marx. . . . He would have enjoyed having a man who beat his wife – which was common at the time in London – flogged to death. In such cases his impulsive nature often got him and us in trouble.

One evening he and I were going to Hampstead Road on the top of a bus. At a stop by a public-house there was a great hubbub and a woman could be heard screaming, 'Murder! Murder!' Marx was down in a trice and I followed him. I tried to keep him back but I might just as well have tried to stop a bullet with my hand. We immediately found ourselves in the middle of the tumult with people pressing behind us. 'What's the matter?' It was all too obvious what the matter was. A drunken woman had quarrelled with her husband, he wanted to take her home and she was resisting, shouting like one possessed. So far so good. As we saw, there was no reason for us to interfere. But the quarrelling couple saw it too and immediately made peace and went for us. The crowd around us grew and pressed closer and adopted a threatening attitude to the 'damned foreigners'. The woman, in particular, attacked Marx, making his fine black beard the object of her rage. I tried to calm the storm, but in vain. Only the arrival of two stalwart constables saved us from paying dearly for our philanthropic interference. We were glad when we were safe and sound on an omnibus again, on our way home. Later Marx was more cautious in his attempts to interfere in such cases. . . .

One had to see Marx with his children to have an idea of his profound affection and simplicity. When he had a minute to spare or during his walks he would run about with them and take part in their merriest, most boisterous games: he was like a child among children. Occasionally we would play 'cavalry' on Hampstead Heath. I would take one of the daughters on my shoulders and Marx the other, and then a jumping competition or races would start or the riders would fight a cavalry battle. The girls were as wild as boys and it took more than a bump to make them cry. Marx could not do without the society of children, which was his rest and refreshment. When his own children were grown up or had died his grandchildren took their place. Jennychen, who married Longuet, one of the Commune emigrants, at the beginning of the 1870s, brought Marx several turbulent grandsons. Jean or Johnny, the eldest – and the most turbulent – was his grandfather's favourite. He could do what he liked with him and he knew it.

One day when I was on a visit to London, Johnny, whose parents had sent him over from Paris as they did several times a year, got the idea of using his grandfather as an omnibus and riding on top, i.e. on Moor's shoulders, Engels and I being the horses. When we were properly harnessed there was a wild chase – I was going to say drive – round the little garden behind Marx's cottage in Maitland Park Road. Or perhaps it was at Engels's house in Regent Park Road, for London houses are all very much alike and it is easy to confuse them, and still more the gardens. A few square yards of gravel and grass covered with 'black snow' or London soot so that you cannot tell where the gravel ends and the grass begins – that is what a London 'garden' is like.

The ride started: Gee-ho! with international – English, German, and French – shouts: 'Go on! *Plus vite!* Hurrah!' And Moor had to trot until the sweat dripped from his brow. When Engels or I tried to slow down a little the merciless coachman's whip lashed down on us: 'You naughty horse! *En avant!*' And it went on until Marx was dropping and then we had to parley with Johnny and a truce was concluded.

It was pathetic and at the same time often comical how Marx, who in political and economical discussions did not eschew the strongest, yea most cynical expressions and phrases, would express himself in the presence of children and women with a gentleness that an English governess might have envied. When the conversation then took an ambiguous turn, he became nervously excited, shifted about on his chair, ill at ease and could colour like a girl six years old. We young fugitives were a wild set and we delighted among other things in singing worldy songs of a strong calibre; thus it happened one day that one of us who had quite a fine voice, a distinction I cannot claim for any of us others – politicians and especially communists and socialists seem to live in strained relations with the muse of music – began to sing the beautiful but not exactly chaste song of 'Jung, jung Zimmergesell' ('Young, young carpenter lad'). Mrs Marx was not at home – otherwise we should not have dared it – and nothing was to be seen of Lenchen and the children, therefore we believed we were 'by ourselves'. Suddenly Marx, who at first had also sung or rather shouted, became restless, and at the same time I heard in the adjoining room a noise indicating the presence of somebody; Marx, who evidently had also heard this noise, shifted about on his chair, the picture of highest embarrassment, until he suddenly jumped up and whispered or hissed with his face glowing red: 'Hush! hush! The girls!'

The girls were really so young then that the 'young, young carpenter lad' would not have been able to endanger their morality. We smiled a little – he stuttered that it would not be right to sing such songs in the hearing of children. And the 'young, young carpenter lad' like other similar songs was not sung any more by us in the house of Marx.

In such matters, by the way, Mrs Marx was even more sensitive than he. She had a look that made a word freeze to your tongue, if you showed a sign of boldness.

9   MARX AND CHESS

Marx was an excellent draughts player. He was so expert at the game that it was difficult to beat him at all. He enjoyed chess too, but he was not so skilful at it. He tried to make up for that by zeal and surprise attacks.

Chess was popular among us emigrants at the beginning of the 1850s. We had more time and, although 'time is money', less money than we could have wished for. We therefore engaged a lot in the 'game of the wise' under the Direction of Red Wolff who had frequented the best chess circles in Paris and learned something about it. Sometimes we had heated chess contests. The one who lost came in for plenty of banter and the games were merry and often very noisy.

When Marx was in a tight corner he got vexed, and when he lost a game he was furious. In the Model Lodging-House in Old Compton Street, where several of us lodged for a time for 3s. 6d. a week, we were always surrounded by Englishmen watching the game with keen interest – chess was popular in England, among the workers too – greatly amused by our boisterous good humour, for two Germans are noisier than a couple of dozen Englishmen.

One day Marx triumphantly informed us that he had discovered a new move that would lick all of us. His challenge was accepted. True enough, he beat us all one after the other. But we soon learned from our defeat and I succeeded in checkmating Marx. It was already quite late, so he insisted on a return game next day at his house.

At eleven sharp – quite early for London – I was at Marx's house. He was not in his room, but I was told he would soon be coming. Mrs Marx was not to be seen and Lenchen was not in a very good humour. Before I could ask what was the matter, Moor came in, shook hands with me and got the chess-board out. Then the fight began. Marx had improved on his move during the night, and before long I was in a hopeless position. I was checkmated and Marx was delighted. He ordered something to drink and some sandwiches. Then we had another game and I won. We played on with varying luck and a varying mood. . . . Mrs Marx kept out of sight and none of the children dared to come near. The contest raged, favouring now one, then the other. At last I beat Marx twice running. He insisted on continuing, but Lenchen said peremptorily, 'Enough of it!'.

Next morning, when I had just risen from my bed, somebody knocked at my door, and in came Lenchen.

'Library' – the children had dubbed me thus and Lenchen had accepted this title, for the title 'Mister' was not in use among us – 'Library, Mrs Marx begs that you play no more chess with Moor in the evening – when he loses the game, he is most disagreeable.' And she told me how his bad humour had vented itself so severely that Mrs Marx lost her patience.

Henceforth I did not accept any more invitations from Marx to play chess in the evening.

10 LENCHEN

Speaking of this diplomatic mission of Lenchen, let me mention in this place that she was often employed in family missions, especially also in missions to the enraged head of the family. Ever since the Marx family was founded Lenchen had been the life and soul of the house, as one of the daughters put it; she was the general maid in a high and noble sense. All the work she had to do! And she did it all gladly. I will only remind you of the many trips to that mysterious, deeply hated and still assiduously courted, all-benevolent relative: the 'uncle' with the three globes. . . . Always good-humoured, smiling, ready to help. And yet she could get angry, and she hated Moor's enemies bitterly.

When Mrs Marx was ill or out of sorts Lenchen replaced her as a mother, and in any case she was a second mother to the children. She had great strength and steadfastness of will: if she considered something necessary it just had to be done.

As has already been said, Lenchen was a kind of dictator in the house: to put it more exactly, Lenchen was the dictator but Mrs Marx was the mistress. And Marx submitted as meekly as a lamb to that dictatorship.

No man is great in the eyes of his servant, it is said. And Marx was certainly not in Lenchen's eyes. She would have sacrificed herself for him, she would have given her life a hundred times for him, Mrs Marx or any of the children had it been necessary and possible. She did, indeed, give her life for them. But Marx could not impose on her. She knew him with all his whims and weaknesses and she could twist him round her little finger. Even when he was irritated and stormed and thundered so that nobody else would go near him, Lenchen would go into the lion's den. If he growled at her, Lenchen would give him such a piece of her mind that the lion became as mild as a lamb.

.   11 WALKS WITH MARX

Those walks to Hampstead Heath! Were I to live to a thousand I would never forget them. . . . Forty years ago Hampstead Heath was much larger and less artificial than now and a Sunday there was our greatest treat.

The children used to speak about it the whole week and even the adults, young and old, looked forward to it. The journey there was a treat in itself. The girls were excellent walkers, as nimble and tireless as cats. From Dean Street, where the Marxes lived – quite near Church Street where I had settled down – it was a good hour and a half away and we generally set out at about eleven o'clock. Not always, however, for in London people do not get up early and by the time everything was in order, the children seen to and the hamper packed properly it was much later.

That hamper! It hovers before 'my mind's eye' as real and material, attractive and appetising as if it was only yesterday I had seen Lenchen carrying it.

When a healthy and vigorous person has not many coppers in his pocket (and it was no question of silver then) food is a thing of primary importance. Our good Lenchen knew that and her kind heart pitied her poor guests, who went short often enough and were therefore always hungry. A substantial joint of roast veal was the main course, consecrated by tradition for the Sunday outings to Hampstead Heath. A basket of a size quite unusual in London, brought by Lenchen from Trier, was the tabernacle in which the holy of holies was borne. Then there was tea and sugar and occasionally some fruit. Bread and cheese could be bought on the Heath, where crockery, hot water and milk were also to be had, just as in a Berlin *Kaffeegarten*. Besides you could get as much butter and, according to the local custom, shrimps, watercress and periwinkles, as you wanted and could afford.

Beer was available too, except during the short time when the hypocritical aristocracy who have liquor from all the world in plenty in their clubs and at home and for whom every day is a Sunday, wanted to teach the common people virtue and morals by forbidding the sale of beer on Sundays.

But the Londoners don't like jokes where their stomach is concerned. They paraded in hundreds of thousands in Hyde Park on the Sunday after the bill was introduced and shouted disdainfully at the devout ladies and lords riding and walking there, 'Go to church!' The mighty shouts inspired the virtuous ladies and lords with anxiety and terror. The next Sunday there were twice as many shouters and the 'Go to church!' was far more impressive. By the third Sunday the bill had been withdrawn.

We emigrants gave as much help as we could in the 'Go to church' revolution. Marx, who got particularly excited on such occasions, might have been grabbed by the scruff of the neck by a policeman and hauled before the judge had not a warm appeal to the thirst of the gallant guardian of law and order won the day.

So the victory of hypocrisy did not last long, and except for the brief interim we had the consoling thought of a well-justified and well-earned cool drink to bear us up as we were scorched by the sun on the way to Hampstead Heath.

The walk there took place as follows. I generally led the way with the two girls, entertaining them with stories or acrobatics or picking wild flowers, which were more abundant then than now. Behind us came a few friends and then the main body: Marx with his wife and one of the Sunday visitors who was deserving of special consideration. In the rear came Lenchen and the hungriest of our party, who helped her to carry the hamper. If there were more people in our company they were distributed among the different groups. Needless to say, the order of battle or march varied according to need or desire.

When we arrived at the Heath we first of all chose a place to pitch our tent, taking tea and beer facilities into consideration as much as possible.

Once food and drink had been partaken of, both sexes went in search of the most comfortable place to lie or sit. Then those who did not prefer a nap got out the Sunday papers bought on the way and spoke about politics. The children soon found playmates and played hide-and-seek among the gorse bushes.

But there had to be variety even in those pleasant occupations: races, wrestling, heaving stones and other forms of sport were organised. One Sunday we discovered a chestnut-tree with ripe nuts near by.

'Let's see who can bring the most down', somebody said, and we went at it with a cheer. Marx was as tireless as any of us. Not till the last nut was brought down did the bombardment stop. Marx was unable to move his right arm for a week and I was not much better off.

The best treat was when we all went for a donkey ride. How we laughed and joked! And what comical figures we cut! Marx had fun himself and gave us plenty, twice as much as himself; his horsemanship was so primitive and he exerted such fantasy to assure us of his skill! And his skill boiled down to having taken riding lessons once when he was a student – Engels maintained that he had never got further than the third lesson – and on his rare visits to Manchester he went riding a venerable Rosinante, probably a great-grandchild of the placid mare that the late old Fritz presented to the brave Gellert.

The walk home from Hampstead Heath was always a merry one, although the pleasure ahead gladdened us more than the one behind. We had grounds enough for melancholy, but we were charmed against it by our grim humour. Emigration misery did not exist for us; whoever started to complain was immediately most forcibly reminded of his duties to society.

The marching order for the return was not the same as going. The children were tired with the day's running and they brought up the rearguard with Lenchen, who, light-footed now that the hamper was empty, could take care of them. Generally someone struck up a song. We seldom sang political songs, ours were mostly folk songs, full of feeling and 'patriotism' – it is not a hunter's yarn I am telling – from *Vaterland* like 'O Strassburg, O Strassburg, du wunderschöne Stadt', which was especially popular. Or the children would sing us Negro songs and dance to them when their feet were not so weary. As little was said about politics while walking as about the misery of emigration. But literature and art were frequent topics, which gave Marx the opportunity of showing his astonishing memory. He used to recite long passages from *The Divine Comedy*, which he knew almost by heart, and scenes from Shakespeare. His wife, whose knowledge of Shakespeare was excellent, often recited instead of him. When in the highest of high spirits, he represented Seidelmann as Mephisto. He adored Seidelmann whom he had seen and heard in Berlin as a student, and *Faust* was his favourite German poem. I cannot say that Marx recited well – he exaggerated considerably – but he never missed the point and he always expressed the sense correctly – in short, he was effective, and the ludicrous impression caused by the first violent outburst of words soon passed when it became apparent that he had deeply penetrated into the spirit of the character, had fully grasped it and thoroughly mastered the role.

Jennychen, the elder of the two girls, was the very image of her father: she had the same black eyes, the same forehead. She sometimes had pythonic transports: 'the spirit came over her', as over Pythia. Her eyes would begin to shine and blaze and she would start declaiming, often the most astonishing fantasies. She had one of those fits one day on the way home from Hampstead Heath and spoke of life on the stars, her account taking the form of poetry. Mrs Marx, in her maternal anxiety, several of her children having died young, said, 'Children of her age do not say things like that, her precocity is a sign of bad health.' But Moor scolded her and I showed her Pythia, who had recovered from her prophetic trance, skipping about and laughing merrily, the very picture of health. . . .

Both Marx's sons died young, one, who was born in London, when still very young, the other, born in Brussels, after a long infirmity. The death of the latter was a terrible blow for Marx. I still remember the sad weeks of the hopeless disease. The boy, named Edgar after an uncle but called 'Mush', was very gifted but sickly from birth, a real child of sorrow. He had beautiful eyes and a promising head which seemed too heavy for his weak body. Poor Mush might have lived if he had had peace and constant care and had lived in the country or by the seaside. But in emigration, hunted from place to place and amid the hardships of London life, even the tenderest parental affection and motherly care could not give the frail plant the strength it needed to fight for its life. Mush died. . . .

I cannot forget the scene: the mother weeping in silence bending over her dead child, Lenchen standing by and sobbing, and Marx, in prey to a terrible agitation, answering violently and almost wrathfully any attempt to console him, the two girls weeping silently and pressing close to their mother who clung feverishly to them as if to defend them against death which had robbed her of her boys.

The burial took place two days later. Lessner, Pfänder, Lochner, Conrad Schramm, Red Wolff and I attended. I went in the coach with Marx. He sat there without a word, his head in his hands. . . .

Later Tussy was born, a merry little thing, as round as a ball and like cream and roses, first wheeled about in her perambulator, then sometimes carried and sometimes toddling along. She was six years old when I came back to Germany, just half the age of my eldest daughter, who in the previous two years had accompanied the Marx family on their Sunday walks to Hampstead Heath.

12 PATRIOTISM AND ITS CONSEQUENCES

One evening Edgar Bauer, acquainted with Marx from their Berlin time and then not yet his personal enemy in spite of *The Holy Family*, had come to town from his hermitage in Highgate for the purpose of 'making a beer trip'. The problem was to 'take something' in every saloon between Oxford Street and Hampstead Road – making the 'something' a very difficult task, even by confining yourself to a minimum, considering the enormous number of saloons in that part of the city. But we went to work undaunted and managed to reach the end of Tottenham Court Road without accident. There loud singing issued from a public house; we entered and learned that a club of Odd Fellows were celebrating a festival. We met some of the men belonging to the 'party', and they at once invited us 'foreigners' with truly English hospitality to go with them into one of the rooms. We followed them in the best of spirits, and the conversation naturally turned to politics – we had been easily recognised as German fugitives; and the Englishmen, good old-fashioned people, who wanted to amuse us a little, considered it their duty to revile thoroughly the German princes and the Russian nobles. By 'Russian' they meant Prussian nobles. Russia and Prussia are frequently confounded in England, and not alone on account of their similarity of name. For a while, everything went along smoothly. We had to drink many healths and to bring out and listen to many a toast. . . .

Edgar Bauer, hurt by some chance remark, turned the tables and ridiculed the English snobs. Marx launched an enthusiastic eulogy on German science and music – no other country, he said, would have been capable of producing such masters of music as Beethoven, Mozart, Handel and Haydn, and the Englishmen who had no music were in reality far below the Germans who had been prevented hitherto only by the miserable political and economical conditions from accomplishing any great practical work, but who would yet outclass all other nations. So fluently I have never heard him speaking English. For my part, I demonstrated in drastic words that the political conditions in England were not a bit better than in Germany (here Urquhart's pet phrases came in very handy), the only difference being that we Germans knew our public affairs were miserable, while the Englishmen did not know it, whence it was apparent that we surpassed the Englishmen in political intelligence.

The brows of our hosts began to cloud, similarly as formerly in the 'Häfelei'; and when Edgar Bauer brought up still heavier guns and began to allude to the English cant, then a low 'damned foreigners!' issued from the company, soon followed by louder repetitions. Threatening words were spoken, the brains began to be heated, fists were brandished in the air and – we were sensible enough to choose the better part of valour and managed to effect, not wholly without difficulty, a passably dignified retreat.

Now we had had enough of our 'beer trip' for the time being, and in order to cool our heated blood, we started on a double quick march, until Edgar Bauer stumbled over a heap of paving stones. 'Hurrah, an idea!' And in memory of mad student's pranks he picked up a stone, and Clash! Clatter! a gas lantern went flying into splinters. Nonsense is contagious – Marx and I did not stay behind, and we broke four or five street lamps – it was, perhaps, two o'clock in the morning and the streets were deserted in consequence. But the noise nevertheless attracted the attention of a policeman who with quick resolution gave the signal to his colleagues on the same beat. And immediately countersignals were given. The position became critical. Happily we took in the situation at a glance; and happily we knew the locality. We raced ahead, three or four policemen some distance behind us. Marx showed an activity that I should not have attributed to him. And after the wild chase had lasted some minutes, we succeeded in turning into a side street and there running through an alley – a back yard between two streets – whence we came behind the policemen who lost the trail. Now we were safe. They did not have our description and we arrived at our homes without further adventures. In Marburg, a similar adventure had not taken the same smooth course for my comrades, and had also had some disadvantage for myself who had not been caught right away. Here in London, where they have no sympathy for German students' pranks, the matter would have been much more serious than in Marburg, Berlin or Bonn; and I must confess that on the next morning – no, at noon of the same day – I was very glad to be in my room, instead of being locked up in a London prison cell together with the member of the 'Holy Family', Edgar Bauer, and the future creator of *Capital*, Karl Marx. But we laughed whenever we thought of this night's adventure.

13   TOBACCO

Marx was a passionate smoker. Like everything else, he carried on smoking with impetuousness. English tobacco being too strong for him, he provided for himself, whenever he had any chance of doing so, cigars which he half chewed in order to heighten the enjoyment or to have a double pleasure. As cigars are very dear in England, he was continually on the hunt for cheap brands. And what kind of stuff he secured in this way, may be imagined; 'cheap and nasty' is an English expression, and Marx's cigars were consequently dreaded by his friends. And with these abominable cigars he completely ruined his smoking taste and smell. He nevertheless believed and contended that he was an excellent connoisseur of cigars, until one evening we laid a trap for him, into which he unwarily fell. ·A visitor from Germany had brought some fine imported cigars with him during the year of the exposition of 1851, and we began to light and smoke them with ostentatious relish, when Marx entered. The unwonted aroma tickled his nose. 'Ah, that smells excellent!' 'Well, these are genuine Havanas brought over by X! Here, try one.' And the speaker offered to the guileless Marx, who delightedly accepted, a specimen of the most horrible brand of cigars we had been able to find in St Giles, the worst proletarian quarter of the West End, which brand resembled the genuine article in form and colour. The 'horrible example' in the way of a cigar was lighted, Marx blew the delicious smoke into the air with raptured mien. 'I was a little suspicious at first; generally they bring a miserable weed from Germany; but this one is really good!' – We assented with grave faces, although we were ready to burst. A few days later he learned the true state of things. He did not lose his temper, but maintained obstinately that the cigar had been a genuine Havana and that we were now trying to hoodwink him. And he could not be convinced of the contrary.

Marx's passion for cigars had also a stimulating effect on his talent for political economy – not in theory, but in practice. He had smoked for a long time a certain brand of cigars that was very cheap according to English ideas – and proportionately nasty – when he found on his way through Holborn a still cheaper brand – I believe for 1s. 6d. per pound and box. That brought forth his political-economic talent for saving: with every box he smoked he 'saved' 1s. 6d. Consequently, the more he smoked the more he 'saved'. If he managed to consume a box per day, then he could live at a pinch on his 'savings'. And to this system of saving which he had demonstrated to us one evening in a humorous speech he devoted himself with so much energy and self-sacrifice that after the lapse of some months the family physician had to interfere and to forbid Marx peremptorily to enrich himself by such a system of 'saving'.

We had many a laugh over this Marxian theory of saving. That equally practical theories of saving would be believed in and seriously considered as a solution of the social problem by the 'nation of thinkers' for many years – such a thing we did not suspect at that time. I learned this fact only after my return to Germany. In England, whenever similar allusions were made in English newspapers, I had always regarded them as inventions.

SOURCE: *RME*, pp. 96 ff; supplemented from W. Liebknecht, *Karl Marx Biographical Memoirs* (Chicago, 1901); from the German original, W. Liebknecht, *Karl Marx. Zum Gedächtnis* (Nuremberg, 1896).

NOTES

1. The German Workers Educational Society founded in 1840, was closely associated with the Communist League.
2. For another account of this incident, see below, no. 20.
3. Later published under the title *Wage-Labour and Capital*.
4. Unity between the followers of Lassalle, on the one hand, and

Liebknecht and Bebel on the other, was achieved at the Gotha Congress of 1875 – whose programme Marx criticised so strongly.

19 Paul Lafargue

The following reminiscences, written in 1890, are from Marx's son-in-law, who subsequently became one of the leading propagandists of Marxism in France. The son of successful planters of Franco-Caribbean origin, Lafargue married Laura Marx in 1868.

I met Karl Marx for the first time in February 1865. The First International had been founded on 28 September 1864 at a meeting in St Martin's Hall, London, and I went to London from Paris to give Marx news of the development of the young organisation there. M Tolain, now a senator in the bourgeois republic, gave me a letter of introduction.

I was then twenty-four years old. As long as I live I shall remember the impression that first visit made on me. Marx was not well at the time. He was working on the first book of *Capital*, which was not published until two years later, in 1867. He feared he would not be able to finish his work and was therefore glad of visits from young people. 'I must train men to continue communist propaganda after me', he used to say.

Karl Marx was one of the rare men who could be leaders in science and public life at the same time: these two aspects were so closely united in him that one can understand him only by taking into account both the scholar and the socialist fighter.

Marx held the view that science must be pursued for itself, irrespective of the eventual results of research, but at the same time that a scientist could only debase himself by giving up active participation in public life or shutting himself up in his study or laboratory like a maggot in cheese and holding aloof from the life and political struggle of his contemporaries.

'Science must not be a selfish pleasure', he used to say. 'Those who have the good fortune to be able to devote themselves to scientific pursuits must be the first to place their knowledge at the service of humanity.' One of his favourite sayings was 'Work for humanity.'

Although Marx sympathised profoundly with the sufferings of the working classes, it was not sentimental considerations but the study of history and political economy that led him to communist views. He maintained that any unbiased man, free from the influence of private interests and not blinded by class prejudices, must necessarily come to the same conclusions.

Yet while studying the economic and political development of human society without any preconceived opinion, Marx wrote with no other intention than to propagate the results of his research and with a determined will to provide a scientific basis for the socialist movement, which had so far been lost in the clouds of utopianism. He gave publicity to his views only to promote the triumph of the working class, whose historic mission is to establish communism as soon as it has achieved political and economic leadership of society. . . .

Marx did not confine his activity to the country he was born in. 'I am a citizen of the world', he used to say; 'I am active wherever I am.' And in fact, no matter what country events and political persecution drove him to – France, Belgium, England – he took a prominent part in the revolutionary movements which developed there.

However, it was not the untiring and incomparable socialist agitator but rather the scientist that I first saw in his study in Maitland Park Road. That study was the centre to which Party comrades came from all parts of the civilised world to find out the opinion of the master of socialist thought. One must know that historic room before one can penetrate into the intimacy of Marx's spiritual life.

It was on the first floor, flooded by light from a broad window that looked out on to the park. Opposite the window and on either side of the fireplace the walls were lined with bookcases filled with books and stacked up to the ceiling with newspapers and manuscripts. Opposite the fireplace on one side of the window were two tables piled up with papers, books and newspapers; in the middle of the room, well in the light, stood a small, plain desk (three foot by two) and a wooden armchair; between the armchair and the bookcase, opposite the window, was a leather sofa on which Marx used to lie down for a rest from time to time. On the mantelpiece were more books, cigars, matches, tobacco boxes, paperweights and photographs of Marx's daughters and wife, Wilhelm Wolff and Frederick Engels.

Marx was a heavy smoker. 'Capital', he said to me once, 'will not even pay for the cigars I smoked writing it.' But he was still heavier on matches. He so often forgot his pipe or cigar that he emptied an incredible number of boxes of matches in a short time to relight them.

He never allowed anybody to put his books or papers in order – or rather in disorder. The disorder in which they lay was only apparent, everything was really in its intended place so that it was easy for him to lay his hand on the book or notebook he needed. Even during conversations he often paused to show in the book a quotation or figure he had just mentioned. He and his study were one: the books and papers in it were as much under his control as his own limbs.

Marx had no use for formal symmetry in the arrangement of his books: volumes of different sizes and pamphlets stood next to one another. He arranged them according to their contents, not their size. Books were tools for his mind, not articles of luxury. 'They are my slaves and they must serve me as I will', he used to say. He paid no heed to size or binding, quality of paper or type; he would turn down the corners of the pages, make pencil marks in the margin and underline whole lines. He never wrote on books, but sometimes he could not refrain from an exclamation or question mark when the author went too far. His system of underlining made it easy for him to find any passage he needed in any book. He had the habit of going through his notebooks and reading the passages underlined in the books after intervals of many years in order to keep them fresh in his memory. He had an extraordinarily reliable memory which he had cultivated from his youth according to Hegel's advice by learning by heart verse in a foreign language he did not know.

He knew Heine and Goethe by heart and often quoted them in his conversations; he was an assiduous reader of poets in all European languages. Every year he read Aeschylus in the Greek original. He considered him and Shakespeare as the greatest dramatic geniuses humanity ever gave birth to. His respect for Shakespeare was boundless: he made a detailed study of his works and knew even the least important of his characters. His whole family had a real cult for the great English dramatist; his three daughters knew many of his works by heart. When after 1848 he wanted to perfect his knowledge of English, which he could already read, he sought out and classified all Shakespeare's original expressions. He did the same with part of the polemical works of William Cobbett, of whom he had a high opinion. Dante and Robert Burns ranked among his favourite poets and he would listen with great pleasure to his daughters reciting or singing the Scottish poet's sátires or ballads.

Cuvier, an untirable worker and past master in the sciences, had a suite of rooms, arranged for his personal use, in the Paris Museum, of which he was director. Each room was intended for a particular pursuit and contained the books, instruments, anatomic aids, etc. required for the purpose. When he felt tired of one kind of work he would go into the next room and engage in another; this simple change of mental occupation, it is said, was a rest for him.

Marx was just as tireless a worker as Cuvier, but he had not the means to fit out several studies. He would rest by pacing up and down the room. A strip was worn out from the door to the window, as sharply defined as a track across a meadow.

From time to time he would lie down on the sofa and read a novel;

he sometimes read two or three at a time, alternating one with another. Like Darwin, he was a great reader of novels, his preference being for those of the eighteenth century, particularly Fielding's *Tom Jones*. The more modern novelists whom he found most interesting were Paul de Kock, Charles Lever, Alexander Dumas senior and Walter Scott, whose *Old Mortality* he considered a masterpiece. He had a definite preference for stories of adventure and humour. He ranked Cervantes and Balzac above all other novelists. In *Don Quixote* he saw the epic of dying-out chivalry whose virtues were ridiculed and scoffed at in the emerging bourgeois world. He admired Balzac so much that he wished to write a review of his great work *La Comedie Humaine* as soon as he had finished his book on economics. He considered Balzac not only as the historian of his time, but as the prophetic creator of characters which were still in the embryo in the days of Louis Philippe and did not fully develop until after his death, under Napoleon III.

Marx could read all European languages and write in three: German, French and English, to the admiration of language experts. He liked to repeat the saying 'A foreign language is a weapon in the struggle of life.'

He had a great talent for language which his daughters inherited from him. He took up the study of Russian when he was already fifty years old, and although that language had no close affinity to any of the modern or ancient languages he knew, in six months he knew it well enough to derive pleasure from reading Russian poets and prose writers, his preference going to Pushkin, Gogol and Shchedrin. He studied Russian in order to be able to read the documents of official inquiries which were hushed over by the Russian Government because of the political revelations they made. Devoted friends got the documents for Marx and he was certainly the only political economist in Western Europe who had knowledge of them.

Besides the poets and novelists, Marx had another remarkable way of relaxing intellectually – mathematics, for which he had a special liking. Algebra even brought him moral consolation and he took refuge in it in the most distressing moments of his eventful life. During his wife's last illness he was unable to devote himself to his usual scientific work and the only way in which he could shake off the oppression caused by her sufferings was to plunge into mathematics. During that time of moral suffering he wrote a work on infinitesimal calculus which, according to the opinion of experts, is of great scientific value and will be published in his collected works. He saw in higher mathematics the most logical and at the same time the simplest form of dialectical movement. He held the view that a science is not really developed until it has learned to make use of mathematics. Although Marx's library contained over a thousand volumes carefully collected during his lifelong research work, it was not enough for him, and for years he regularly attended the British Museum, whose catalogue he appreciated very highly.

Even Marx's opponents were forced to acknowledge his extensive and profound erudition, not only in his own speciality – political economy – but in history, philosophy and the literature of all countries.

In spite of the late hour at which Marx went to bed he was always up between eight and nine in the morning, had some black coffee, read through his newspapers and then went to his study, where he worked till two or three in the morning. He interrupted his work only for meals and, when the weather allowed, for a walk on Hampstead Heath in the evening. During the day he sometimes slept for an hour or two on the sofa. In his youth he often worked the whole night through.

Marx had a passion for work. He was so absorbed in it that he often forgot his meals. He had often to be called several times before he came down to the dining-room and hardly had he eaten the last mouthful than he was back in his study.

He was a very light eater and even suffered from lack of appetite. This he tried to overcome by highly flavoured food – ham, smoked fish, caviare, pickles. His stomach had to suffer for the enormous activity of his brain. He sacrificed his whole body to his brain; thinking was his greatest enjoyment. I often heard him repeat the words of Hegel, the philosophy master of his youth: 'Even the criminal thought of a malefactor has more grandeur and nobility than the wonders of the heavens.'

His physical constitution had to be good to put up with this unusual way of life and exhausting mental work. He was, in fact, of powerful build, more than average height,[1] broad-shouldered, deep-chested, and had well-proportioned limbs, although the spinal column was rather long in comparison with the legs, as is often the case with Jews. Had he practised gymnastics in his youth he would have become a very strong man. The only physical exercise he ever pursued regularly was walking: he could ramble or climb hills for hours, chatting and smoking, and not feel at all tired. One can say that he even worked walking in his room, only sitting down for short periods to write what he thought out while walking. He liked to walk up and down while talking, stopping from time to time when the explanation became more animated or the conversation serious.

For many years I went with him on his evening walks on Hampstead Heath and it was while stroiling over the meadows with him that I got my education in economics. Without noticing it he expounded to me the whole contents of the first book of *Capital* as he wrote it.

On my return home I always noted as well as I could all I had heard. At first it was difficult for me fo follow Marx's profound and complicated reasoning. Unfortunately I have lost those precious notes, for after the Commune the police ransacked and burned my papers in Paris and Bordeaux.

What I regret most is the loss of the notes I took on the evening when Marx, with the abundance of proof and considerations which was typical of him, expounded his brilliant theory of the development of human society. It was as if scales fell from my eyes. For the first time I saw clearly the logic of world history and could trace the apparently so contradictory phenomena of the development of society and ideas to their material origins. I felt dazzled, and the impression remained for years.

The Madrid socialists[2] had the same impression when I developed to them as well as my feeble powers would allow that most magnificent of Marx's theories, which is beyond doubt one of the greatest ever elaborated by the human brain.

Marx's brain was armed with an unbelievable stock of facts from history and natural science and philosophical theories. He was remarkably skilled in making use of the knowledge and observations accumulated during years of intellectual work. You could question him at any time on any subject and get the most detailed answer you could wish for, always accompanied by philosophical reflections of general application. His brain was like a man-of-war in port under steam, ready to launch into any sphere of thought.

There is no doubt that *Capital* reveals to us a mind of astonishing vigour and superior knowledge. But for me, as for all those who knew Marx intimately, neither *Capital* nor any other of his works shows all the magnitude of his genius or the extent of his knowledge. He was highly superior to his own works.

I worked with Marx; I was only the scribe to whom he dictated, but that gave me the opportunity of observing his manner of thinking and writing. Work was easy for him, and at the same time difficult. Easy because his mind found no difficulty in embracing the relevant facts and considerations in their completeness. But that very completeness made the exposition of his ideas a matter of long and arduous work.

Vico said, 'The thing is a body only for God, who knows everything; for man, who knows only the exterior, it is only surface.' Marx grasped things after the fashion of Vico's God. He saw not only the surface, but what lay beneath it. He examined all the constituent parts in their mutual action and reaction; he isolated each of those parts and traced the history of its development. Then he went on from the thing to its surroundings and observed the reaction of one upon the other. He traced the origin of the object, the changes, evolutions and revolutions it went through, and proceeded finally to its remotest effects. He did not see a thing singly, in itself and for itself, separate from its surroundings: he saw a highly complicated world in continual motion.

His intention was to disclose the whole of that world in its manifold and continually varying action and reaction. Men of letters of Flaubert's and the Goncourts' school complain that it is so difficult to render exactly what one sees; yet all they wish to render is the surface, the impression that they get. Their literary work is child's play in comparison with Marx's: it required extraordinary vigour of thought to grasp reality and render what he saw and wanted to make others see. Marx was never satisfied with his work – he was always making some improvements and he always found his rendering inferior to the idea he wished to convey. *The Unknown Masterpiece*, a psychological study by Balzac deplorably plagiarised by Zola, made a deep impression on him because it partly described feelings that he had himself experienced. A painter of genius is so driven by the urge to represent things precisely according to their images in his mind that he constantly refines and retouches his picture until in the end all he has made is a formless mass of colour which nevertheless in his deluded eyes is the most complete representation of reality.

Marx had the two qualities of a genius: he had an incomparable talent for dissecting a thing into its constituent parts, and he was past master at reconstituting the dissected object out of its parts, with all its different forms of development, and discovering their mutual inner relations. His demonstrations were not abstractions – which was the reproach made to him by economists who were themselves incapable of thinking; his method was not that of the geometrician who takes his definitions from the world around him but completely disregards reality in drawing his conclusions. *Capital* does not give isolated definitions or isolated formulas; it gives a series of most searching analyses which bring out the most evasive shades and the most elusive gradations. . . .

Marx was always extremely conscientious about his work: he never gave a fact or figure that was not borne out by the best authorities. He was never satisfied with second-hand information, he always went to the source itself, no matter how tedious the process. To make sure of a minor fact he would go to the British Museum and consult books there. His critics were never able to prove that he was negligent or that he based his arguments on facts which did not bear strict checking.

His habit of always going to the very source made him read

authors who were very little known and whom he was the only one to quote. *Capital* contains so many quotations from little-known authors that one might think Marx wanted to show off how well-read he was. He had no intention of the sort. 'I administer historical justice', he said. 'I give each one his due.' He considered himself obliged to name the author who had first expressed an idea or formulated it most correctly, no matter how insignificant and little known he was.

Marx was just as conscientious from the literary as from the scientific point of view. Not only would he never base himself on a fact he was not absolutely sure of, he never allowed himself to talk of a thing before he had studied it thoroughly. He did not publish a single work without repeatedly revising it until he had found the most appropriate form. He could not bear to appear in public without thorough preparation. It would have been a torture for him to show his manuscripts before giving them the finishing touch. He felt so strongly about this that he told me one day that he would rather burn his manuscripts than leave them unfinished.

His method of working often imposed upon him tasks the magnitude of which the reader can hardly imagine. Thus, in order to write the twenty pages or so on English factory legislation in *Capital* he went through a whole library of Blue Books containing reports of commissions and factory inspectors in England and Scotland. He read them from cover to cover, as can be seen from the pencil marks in them. He considered those reports as the most important and weighty documents for the study of the capitalist mode of production. He had such a high opinion of those in charge of them that he doubted the possibility of finding in another country in Europe 'men as competent, as free from partisanship and respect of persons as are the English factory inspectors'. He paid them this brilliant tribute in the Preface to *Capital*.

From these Blue Books Marx drew a wealth of factual information. Many members of Parliament to whom they are distributed use them only as shooting targets, judging the striking power of the gun by the number of pages pierced. Others sell them by the pound, which is the most reasonable thing they can do, for this enabled Marx to buy them cheap from the old paper dealers in Long Acre whom he used to visit to look through their old books and papers. Professor Beesley said that Marx was the man who made the greatest use of English official inquiries and brought them to the knowledge of the world. He did not know that before 1845 Engels took numerous documents from the Blue Books in writing his book on the condition of the working class in England.

To get to know and love the heart that beat within the breast of Marx the scholar you had to see him when he had closed his books and notebooks and was surrounded by his family, or again on Sunday evenings in the society of his friends. He then proved the pleasantest of company, full of wit and humour, with a laugh that came straight from the heart. His black eyes under the arches of his bushy brows sparkled with pleasure and malice whenever he heard a witty saying or a pertinent repartee.

He was a loving, gentle and indulgent father. 'Children should educate their parents', he used to say. There was never even a trace of the bossy parent in his relations with his daughters, whose love for him was extraordinary. He never gave them an order, but asked them to do what he wished as a favour or made them feel that they should not do what he wanted to forbid them. And yet a father could seldom have had more docile children than he. His daughters considered him as their friend and treated him as a companion; they did not call him 'father,' but 'Moor' – a nickname that he owed to his dark complexion and jet-black hair and beard. The members of the Communist League, on the other hand, called him 'Father Marx' before 1848, when he was not even thirty years of age....

Marx used to spend hours playing with his children. These still remember the sea battles in a big basin of water and the burning of the fleets of paper ships that he made for them and set on fire to their great joy.

On Sundays his daughters would not allow him to work, he belonged to them for the whole day. If the weather was fine, the whole family would go for a walk in the country. On their way they would stop at a modest inn for bread and cheese and ginger beer. When his daughters were small he would make the long walk seem shorter to them by telling them endless fantastic tales which he made up as he went, developing and intensifying the complications according to the distance they had to go, so that the little ones forgot their weariness listening.

He had an incomparably fertile imagination: his first literary works were poems. Mrs Marx carefully preserved the poetry her husband wrote in his youth but never showed it to anybody. His family had dreamt of him being a man of letters or a professor and thought he was debasing himself by engaging in socialist agitation and political economy, which was then disdained in Germany.

Marx had promised his daughters to write a drama on the Gracchi for them. Unfortunately he was unable to keep his word. It would have been interesting to see how he, who was called 'the knight of the class struggle', would have dealt with that terrible and magnificent episode in the class struggle of the ancient world. Marx fostered a lot of plans which were never carried out. Among other works he intended to write a Logic and a History of Philosophy, the latter having been his favourite subject in his younger days. He would have needed to live to a hundred to carry out all his literary plans and present the world with a portion of the treasure hidden in his brain.

Marx's wife was his lifelong helpmate in the truest and fullest sense of the word. They had known each other as children and grown up together. Marx was only seventeen at the time of his engagement. Seven long years the young couple had to wait before they were married in 1843. After that they never parted.

Mrs Marx died shortly before her husband. Nobody ever had a greater sense of equality than she, although she was born and bred in a German aristocratic family. No social differences or classifications existed for her. She entertained working people in their working clothes in her house and at her table with the same politeness and consideration as if they had been dukes or princes. Many workers of all countries enjoyed her hospitality and I am convinced that not one of them ever dreamt that the woman who received them with such homely and sincere cordiality descended in the female line from the family of the Dukes of Argyll and that her brother was a minister of the King of Prussia.[3] That did not worry Mrs Marx; she had given up everything to follow her Karl and never, not even in times of dire need, was she sorry she had done so.

She had a clear and brilliant mind. Her letters to her friends, written without constraint or effort, are masterly achievements of vigorous and original thinking. It was a treat to get a letter from Mrs Marx. Johann Philipp Becker published several of her letters. Heine, a pitiless satirist as he was, feared Marx's irony, but he was full of admiration for the penetrating sensitive mind of his wife; when the Marxes were in Paris he was one of their regular visitors.

Marx had such respect for the intelligence and critical sense of his wife that he showed her all his manuscripts and set great store by her opinion, as he himself told me in 1866. Mrs Marx copied out her husband's manuscripts before they were sent to the print-shop.

Mrs Marx had a number of children. Three of them died at a tender age during the period of hardships that the family went through after the 1848 Revolution. At that time they lived as emigrants in London in two small rooms in Dean Street, Soho Square. I only knew the three daughters. When I was introduced to Marx in 1865 his youngest daughter, now Mrs Aveling, was a charming child with a sunny disposition. Marx used to say his wife had made a mistake as to sex when she brought her into the world. The other two daughters formed a most surprising and harmonious contrast. The eldest, Mrs Longuet, had her father's dark and vigorous complexion, dark eyes and jet-black hair. The second, Mrs Lafargue, was fair-haired and rosy-skinned, her rich curly hair had a golden shimmer as if it had caught the rays of the setting sun: she was like her mother. Another important member of the Marx household was Helene Demuth. Born of a peasant family, she entered the service of Mrs Marx long before the latter's wedding,[4] when hardly more than a child. When her mistress got married she remained with her and devoted herself with complete self-oblivion to the Marx family. She accompanied her mistress and her husband on all their journeys over Europe and shared their exile. She was the good genius of the house and could always find a way out of the most difficult situations. It was thanks to her sense of order, her economy and skill that the Marx family were at least never short of the bare essentials. There was nothing she could not do: she cooked, kept the house, dressed the children, cut clothes for them and sewed them with Mrs Marx. She was housekeeper and majordomo at the same time: she ran the whole house. The children loved her like a mother and her maternal feeling towards them gave her a mother's authority. Mrs Marx considered her as her bosom friend and Marx fostered a particular friendship towards her; he played chess with her and often enough lost to her.

Helene loved the Marx family blindly: anything they did was good in her eyes and could not be otherwise; whoever criticised Marx had to deal with her.She extended her motherly protection to everyone who was admitted to intimacy with the Marxes. It was as though she had adopted all of the Marx family. She outlived Marx and his wife and transferred her care to Engels's household. She had known him since she was a girl and extended to him the attachment she had for the Marx family.

Engels was, so to speak, a member of the Marx family. Marx's daughters called him their second father. He was Marx's *alter ego*. For a long time the two names were never separated in Germany and they will be for ever united in history.

Marx and Engels were the personification in our time of the ideal of friendship portrayed by the poets of antiquity. From their youth they developed together and parallel to each other, lived in intimate fellowship of ideas and feelings and shared the same revolutionary agitation; as long as they could live together they worked in common. Had events not parted them for about twenty years they would probably have worked together their whole life. But after the defeat of the 1848 Revolution Engels had to go to Manchester, while Marx was obliged to remain in London. Even so, they continued their common intellectual life by writing to each other almost daily, giving their views on political and scientific events and their work. As soon as Engels was able to free himself from his work he hurried from Manchester to London, where he set up his home only ten minutes away from his dear Marx. From 1870 to the death of his friend not a day went by but the two men saw each other, sometimes at one's house, sometimes at the other's.

It was a day of rejoicing for the Marxes when Engels informed them that he was coming from Manchester. His pending visit was spoken of long beforehand, and on the day of his arrival Marx was so impatient that he could not work. The two friends spent the whole night smoking and drinking together and talking over all that had happened since their last meeting.

Marx appreciated Engels's opinion more than anybody else's, for Engels was the man he considered capable of being his collaborator. For him Engels was a whole audience. No effort could have been too great for Marx to convince Engels and win him over to his ideas. For instance, I have seen him read whole volumes over and over to find the fact he needed to change Engels's opinion on some secondary point that I do not remember concerning the political and religious wars of the Albigenses. It was a triumph for Marx to bring Engels round to his opinion.

Marx was proud of Engels. He took pleasure in enumerating to me all his moral and intellectual qualities. He once specially made the journey to Manchester with me to introduce me to him. He admired the versatility of his knowledge and was alarmed at the slightest thing that could befall him. 'I always tremble,' he said to me, 'for fear he should meet with an accident at the chase. He is so impetuous; he goes galloping over the fields with slackened reins, not shying at any obstacle.'

Marx was as good a friend as he was a loving husband and father. In his wife and daughters, Helene and Engels, he found worthy objects of love for a man such as he was. . . .

The share Marx had to take in the international socialist movement took time from his scientific activity. The death of his wife and that of his eldest daughter, Mrs Longuet, also had an adverse effect upon it.

Marx's love for his wife was profound and intimate. Her beauty had been his pride and his joy, her gentleness and devotedness had lightened for him the hardships necessarily resulting from his eventful life as a revolutionary socialist. The disease which led to the death of Jenny Marx also shortened the life of her husband. During her long and painful illness Marx, exhausted by sleeplessness and lack of exercise and fresh air and morally weary, contracted the pneumonia which was to snatch him away.

On 2 December 1881, Mrs Marx died as she had lived, a communist and a materialist. Death had no terrors for her. When she felt her end approach she exclaimed, 'Karl, my strength is ebbing!' Those were her last intelligible words.

She was buried in Highgate Cemetery, in unconsecrated ground, on 5 December. Conforming to the habits of her life and Marx's, all care was taken to avoid her funeral being made a public one and only a few close friends accompanied her to her last resting-place. Marx's old friend Engels delivered the address over her grave. . . . After the death of his wife, Marx's life was a succession of physical and moral sufferings which he bore with great fortitude. They were aggravated by the sudden death of his eldest daughter, Mrs Longuet, a year later. He was broken, never to recover. He died at his desk[5] on 14 March 1883, at the age of sixty-four.

SOURCE: *RME*, pp. 71 ff. (with restoration of omission, trs. by the editor); from the German original in 'Karl Marx. Persönliche Erinnerungen', *Die Neue Zeit*, IX, pt 1 (1890–1) 10 ff. and 37 ff.

NOTES

1. Marx was, in fact, only 5ft 7 in. (171 cm) high.
2. After the Paris Commune, Lafargue briefly emigrated to Spain in order to counteract the influence of the Bakuninists there.
3. Ferdinand von Westphalen was Prussian Minister of the Interior.
4. Helene Demuth did not arrive in the Marx household until the spring of 1845.
5. Marx died in his armchair in his bedroom.

20 Franziska Kugelmann

Franziska was the daughter of Ludwig Kugelmann, a well-known gynaecologist in Hanover and an enthusiastic adherent of Marx's views. Marx paid extended visits to the Kugelmann family in 1867 and, accompanied by his daughter Jenny, in 1869. Franziska was born about 1858 and so most of the following reminiscences are second-hand, having been obtained from her parents. They were written in 1928 at the request of the Institute for Marxism-Leninism in Moscow.

When a young student, my father was an enthusiastic admirer of Karl Marx. He wrote to him, after getting his London address through Miquel, who was a member of the same students' club as he, the Normannia. To my father's immense pleasure Marx answered him, and gradually a regular correspondence was established between them. Letters were addressed to Marx under the name of A. Williams, for his correspondence was watched by the government, opened and often not forwarded. For the same reason my father was careful not to address Marx by his name in his letters but used the form of address 'My esteemed and dear Friend!'

Several years later, when Marx wrote that he intended to go to the continent, my father, who in the meantime had married, invited him to be his guest and Marx accepted the invitation for a few days.

My mother, a gay young Rhineland woman, was rather worried about the visit. She expected to see a great scholar, completely absorbed with political ideas and hostile to the contemporary system of society. My father was busy the whole of the morning and part of the afternoon with his work as a doctor, how could she entertain a man like Marx? My father assured her that she would remember those days with pleasure for the rest of her life. Never was a prophecy more exactly fulfilled.

When the men arrived from the station, instead of the morose revolutionary she had expected my mother was greeted by a smart, good-humoured gentleman whose warm Rhenish accent at once reminded her of home. Young dark eyes smiled at her from under a mane of grey hair, his movements and his conversation were full of youthly freshness. He would not let my father make the slightest allusion to politics. He silenced him with the remark, 'That is not for young ladies, we'll speak of that later.' On the very first evening his conversation was so entertaining, witty and merry that the hours seemed to fly.

It happened to be the beginning of Holy Week and my parents asked Marx to go and hear Bach's *Passion according to Saint Matthew* with them on Good Friday. Marx refused saying that, although he was a great lover of music and particularly of Bach's, he must leave on Maundy Thursday at the latest.

However, he stayed in Hanover for four weeks.[1] It was such a pleasure for my parents to recall those days in detail with all the conversations they had with him that they were like a sunny hilltop rising above their everyday life, never shrouded in the mist of oblivion, and also allowing those who did not experience them to share in them.

It was not only in our family circle that Marx was unpretentious and amiable. With my parents' acquaintances, too, he took an interest in everything and when he was particularly attracted by anybody or a witty remark was made he would adjust his monocle and survey the person in question with a friendly interest.

He was somewhat short-sighted but he wore spectacles only when he had to read or write for a long time.

My parents took particular pleasure in recalling the conversations they had with him in the early hours of the day, when they were least disturbed. My mother used even to get up earlier to finish her work about the house before breakfast. They would often sit for hours at the coffee table and my father was always sorry when he was called away by his work.

The subjects of conversation included not only the interior and exterior life of Marx, but all fields of art, science, poetry and philosophy. Marx, who was as noble and amiable as he was great, never showed the slightest trace of pedantry. My mother took a great interest in philosophy, although she had not made a deep study of it. Marx spoke to her about Kant, Fichte and Schopenhauer and also alluded to Hegel, whose enthusiastic follower he had been in his youth. He quoted Hegel himself as having said that Rosenkranz was the only one of his students who had understood him, and incorrectly at that. Schopenhauer, Hegel's so-determined opponent, was frequently very superficially condemned in an unacceptable manner by many who often had never read his writings. Many of his contemporaries, said Marx, objected to his peculiar personality and described him as a misanthrope; however, in the basic conception of his ethics, he formulates the injunction that, in view of the essential unity of everything organic, we should recognise it as our duty not to cause pain to man or beast. Not to harm any living thing is what Schopenhauer characterises, in view of the indigent state of all existence, as the simple command of justice which leads to compassion and to the advice to 'Help everyone, so far as you can'. No sentimental emotion had given a deeper ethical and social content to the injunction to love one's neighbour.

Marx had a deep hatred for sentimentality, which is but a caricature of real feeling. On occasion he would cite Goethe's words 'I have never had much of an opinion of sentimental people; if anything happens they are sure to prove bad comrades.' When anybody showed exaggerated feeling in his presence he liked to recall Heine's lines

> A girl stood by the seashore
> In such great pain and dread.
> What was all her grief for?
> Because the sun had set.

Marx had known Heine and visited the unfortunate poet during his last illness in Paris. Heine's bed was being changed as Marx entered. His sufferings were so great that he could not bear to be touched, and the nurses carried him to his bed in a sheet. But Heine's wit did not forsake him and he said to Marx in a feeble voice, 'See, my dear Marx, the ladies still carry me aloft.'

Marx was of the opinion that all Heine's wonderful songs about love were the fruit of his imagination, that he had never had any success with ladies and had been anything but happy in his married life. His lines

> At six he was executed,
> At seven laid in the grave
> And lo! as eight was striking
> She drank red wine in high glee.

Marx thought, applied perfectly to his death.

Marx's opinion of Heine's character was by no means a good one. He blamed him in particular for his ingratitude to friends who had helped him. For instance, the completely unjustified irony of the lines on Christiana: 'For a youth so amiable no praise is too great', etc.

For Marx friendship was sacred. Once a friend visiting him allowed himself the remark that Frederick Engels, being a well-to-do man, could have done more to save Marx his serious money troubles. Marx cut him short with the words 'Relations between Engels and me are so intimate and affectionate that nobody has the right to interfere.' When somebody said a thing that displeased him he generally answered with a joke. In general he never resorted to coarse means of defence but retaliated with sharp thrusts which never missed their mark.

There was probably no field of science into which he had not penetrated deeply, no art for which he was not an enthusiast, no beauty of nature which did not arouse his admiration. But he could not bear truthlessness, hollowness, boasting or pretence.

For about an hour and a half before lunch he would write letters, work or read newspapers in the room that he had at his disposal besides his bedroom. It was there too that he looked through the first volume of *Capital*.[2] There was a statue of Minerva Medica with her symbolical little owl. Marx, who had a great admiration for my mother, her kind-heartedness, ready wit and good humour and her knowledge, which was extensive for her age, particularly in the fields of poetry and literature, once said to her jokingly that she was a young goddess of wisdom herself. 'No, I am not,' my mother answered, 'I am only the little screech-owl that sits listening at her feet.' That was why he sometimes called her his dear little owl, a name which he later gave to a little girl whom he loved very much and who used to sit on his knee for hours playing and chatting with him.

He used to call my mother 'Madame la Comtesse' because of her self-assurance in society and because she attached great importance to good manners. Soon he never gave her any other name, no matter who happened to be present.

It was a habit in the Marx family to give nicknames to people. He himself was called Moor, by his daughters as well as by his friends. His second daughter Laura, Mrs Lafargue, was generally called 'das Laura' or Master Kakadou, after a fashionable tailor in an old novel, because of the exceptional taste and smartness with which she dressed. Marx called his eldest daughter Jenny 'Jennychen'. My mother also mentioned her nickname but I have forgotten what it was. Eleanor, the youngest daughter, was always called 'Tussy'. He gave my father the name Wenzel. The reason was that my father once said that a guide in Prague had bored him with details about two Bohemian rulers, the good Wenzel and the bad one. The bad one had St John Nepomuck thrown into the Moldau, the good one was very pious. My father was very outspoken in his sympathies and antipathies and Marx would call him the good or the bad Wenzel according to his attitude. Later he also sent him his photo dedicated to 'his Wenzel'.

He often gave my parents' friends and acquaintances other names in their absence and said they should be their real names, although he often chose names that were not very typical but common ones. As a result, every time Marx was introduced to any of our acquaintances my father would afterwards ask, 'Well, Marx, what should their name really be? . . .'

He was always merry, ready to joke and tease, and he was never more bored than when someone tactlessly asked him about his doctrine. He never answered such questions. In the family he called this curiosity about him 'travelling opinion'. But it was a rare occurrence.

Once a gentleman asked him who would clean shoes in the future state. He answered vexedly, 'You should.' The tactless questioner understood and was silent. That was perhaps the only time that Marx lost his temper. When the visit was over, my mother said frankly, 'Herr Doktor, I don't wish to defend the man's silly questions, but I did think after your answer that it was better that he kept silent than that he should perhaps have answered that he did not feel he had the vocation of a shoeblack.' When Marx agreed, she added, 'I cannot imagine you in an egalitarian age, since you have inclinations and habits that are so thoroughly aristocratic.' 'Neither can I', answered Marx. 'These times will come, but we must be away by then.'

Party comrades from everywhere, often from the most distant parts, came to visit Marx. He received them all in his room. Long conversations on politics often ensued and they were continued in my father's study. Once one of his followers appeared and was still with him by lunch-time. Naturally he was invited to stay for the meal. He was remarkable neither for pleasant conversation nor for good manners. Marx was glad when he finally took his leave, and my mother too made fun of some of his silly remarks. But my father said, 'You must not laugh at this man. People like him who consciously participate in the questions of their century, belong to the best of their time.' 'Ah,' replied my mother, sighing playfully, 'if that is how we regard the best of our time . . . .' Then Marx laughed merrily and called out, in an adaptation of Schiller, 'Whoever has seen the best of his own time has seen enough for all time!' This immediately became one of our stock sayings and was often jokingly quoted.

Marx's taste was most refined in poetry as well as in science and the imitative arts. He was extraordinarily well-read and had a remarkable memory. He shared my father's enthusiasm for the great poets of classical Greece, Shakespeare and Goethe; Chamisso and Rückert were also among his favourites. He would quote Chamisso's touching poem 'The Beggar and His Dog'. He admired Rückert's art in writing and especially his masterly translation of Hariri's *Maqāmas*, which are incomparable in their originality. Years later Marx presented it to my mother in remembrance of that time.

Marx was remarkably gifted for languages. Besides English, he knew French so well that he himself translated *Capital* into French,[3] and his knowledge of Greek, Latin, Spanish and Russian was so good that he could translate from them at sight. He learned Russian by himself 'as a diversion' when he was suffering from carbuncles.

He was of the opinion that Turgenev wonderfully renders the peculiarities of the Russian soul in its veiled Slavonic sensitivity. Lermontov's descriptions, he thought, were hardly to be excelled and seldom equalled.

His favourite among the Spaniards was Calderón. He had several of his works with him and often read us parts of them. . . .

In our flat there was a large room with five windows which we called the hall and where we used to play music. Friends of the house called it Olympus because of the busts of Greek gods around the walls. Throned above them all was Zeus Otricolus.

My father thought Marx greatly resembled the last mentioned and many people agreed with him. Both had a powerful head with abundant hair, a magnificent thoughtful brow, an authoritative and yet kind expression. Marx's calm yet warm and lively nature, knowing no absent-mindedness or excitement, my father thought, also made him resemble his Olympian favourites. He liked to quote Marx's pertinent answer to the reproach that 'the gods of the classics are eternal rest without any passions.' On the contrary, Marx said, they were eternal passion without any unrest. My father could get very irritated when expressing his opinion of those who tried to drag Marx into the agitation of their political party undertakings. He wanted Marx, like the Olympian father of the gods and of men, only to flash his lightning into the world and occasionally hurl his thunder against it but not to waste his precious time in everyday agitation. The days thus flowed quickly by, filled with serious or merry conversation. Marx himself often called that period an oasis in the desert of his life.

Two years later my parents again had the pleasure of entertaining Marx for a few weeks, this time with his eldest daughter Jenny. The latter, an attractive slender girl with dark curly hair, greatly resembled her father in nature and appearance. She was merry, lively and amiable and most refined and tactful in her manners; she hated anything noisy and showy.

My mother quickly made friends with her and maintained her affection for her as long as she lived. She often said how well-read Jenny was, how broadminded and how enthusiastic for all that was noble and beautiful. She was a great admirer of Shakespeare and must have possessed dramatic talent, for she once played Lady Macbeth in a London theatre. Once at our house, but only in the presence of my parents and her father, she played that role in the diabolical scene of the letter. With the money that she earned on the occasion mentioned in London she bought a velvet coat for the faithful maid who had left Trier with the family for England and in joys, sorrows and privations remained firm in her love and attachment to them.

None of the Marx family had the gift of being economical or practical in money affairs. Jenny related that when, shortly after her marriage, her mother inherited a small sum, the young couple had it paid out to them entirely, and put it in a little chest with two handles. They had it in the coach with them and during their wedding journey they took it to the different hotels at which they stayed. When they had visits from friends or fellow-thinkers in need they put the chest open on the table in their room and any one could take as much as he pleased. Needless to say it was soon empty. They later suffered frequent and bitter want in London. Marx related how they were obliged to pawn or sell everything valuable that they had. The von Westphalen family were distant relations to the family of the Dukes of Argyll. When Jenny von Westphalen married Marx, her dowry included silver bearing the arms of the Argylls which had been in the family for a long time. Marx himself took a few heavy silver spoons to the pawnshop and was immediately asked to explain how those objects with the well-known crest came into his possession. This of course he easily did. When his only son died, their need was so great that they were unable to pay the burial expenses and buried him themselves in the yard of their house. Marx's hair went grey that night.[4]

For someone who does not have the gift of handling money, it is very difficult to learn it – even in so hard a school. Thus, Liebknecht related that he and his family too once lived in extreme poverty. The Marx ladies wanted to provide a Christmas treat for his children and sent them very large dolls which they had furnished with many beautiful dresses made of high quality material. The children were overjoyed, but Mrs Liebknecht would have preferred to use the material for the children themselves, who were in dire need of it.

During her stay in Hanover, Jenny made my mother a present of what was called a 'Confession Book'. They were then the fashion in England and later they appeared in Germany under the name *Erkenne dich selbst*.[5] Marx was to be the first to write in it, and Jenny wrote the prescribed questions for him on the first page. But they are still unanswered.[6] . . .

When we had company, Joseph Rissé, an excellent concert singer, used sometimes to sing. He had a baritone voice of remarkable power and scale and was very talented. Among other things he published a collection of Irish folk songs by Thomas Moore in his own translation and musical adaptation under the title *Erin's Harp*. One book was dedicated to my father. Marx, like the whole of his family, had great sympathy for unfortunate oppressed Ireland and loved to listen to these moving songs. Tussy manifested her sympathy for Ireland by making green her favourite colour and dressing mostly in green.

O'Donovan Rossa, an Irish freedom fighter, was put in prison and odiously treated by the English. Jenny, who had never seen him, wrote to him under her pen-name, J. Williams, full of admiration for his steadfastness. Mrs Rossa, hearing that the writer of the letters was a girl, is said to have been extremely jealous. This greatly amused Marx. If I am not mistaken, O'Donovan later went to America but did not particularly distinguish himself there. . . .

It was quite out of character for Marx to condemn anyone's point of view: he knew how to value each in his own way. For example, he enjoyed talking to Giniol, a lieutenant of dragoons from Bruchsal, who was then at a riding school in Hanover. . . .

Marx gave proof of his psychological insight in connection with Maybach, who later became a Minister and whom Marx saw, I think, on only one occasion. He was then president of the railway company in Hanover, an earnest man of wide cultural interests and very pleasant manner. The two gentlemen got on very well with each other. Later Marx said of him, 'That is the wood from which Ministers are hewn.' . . .

When, after a small midday gathering, Marx, Jenny and my parents sat chatting together, my mother said that it was a pity that she knew nothing whatsoever of Marx's writings and asked my father whether she should not at least make an effort to gain some understanding of them. Marx replied that in his opinion she had instinctive fellow feeling – but at this moment there was a loud crash with an accompanying scream from the adjoining dining room. My mother hurried out and, since only the door-curtains were closed, those who remained behind heard my mother ask in alarm, 'Have you hurt yourself?' There followed a muffled sobbing reply. Then more comforting words and the advice 'Calm yourself down now – you look as though you were about to faint. Sit down and I'll give you a glass of wine.' Then the doors were closed. After some time my mother came back in and said, 'Louise stumbled on the doorstep and fell with large tray full of crystal, which shivered into a thousand splinters. She could really have hurt herself. But, God be thanked, her only pain is the thought of having caused us loss.' Jenny embraced my mother with the words 'And don't you think of this loss?' 'Well, certainly,' she answered, 'there were beautiful and irreplacable things there, but I value human beings more than things.' 'If everyone thought likewise in matters both small and large,' said Marx, 'then our aims would be realised. This is in a very real sense a striking proof of what I have just said. Madame la Comtesse can occupy her time more practically and cheerfully than in the study of political economy.'

Party friends often came to see Marx during this period. One of them was Herr Dietzgen, a calm, distinguished man whom Marx and Jenny held in high esteem. It was his quiet way accompanied by a great capacity for work and action that inspired their sympathy. They jokingly called him 'das Dietzchen', -chen and -lein being neuter suffixes in German.

One day a visitor behaved in a rather obstinate and autocratic way. 'To hear him,' Marx said, 'You wonder why nobles are not worse than they are, considering their education and surroundings.'

We once came to talk about the wretched Emperor Maximilian of Mexico who had been so shamelessly abandoned by Napoleon III. 'He should have had the sense to go as soon as he saw that a large proportion of his people did not want him, as Gottlieb did in Spain', Marx observed. He meant Prince Amadeo of Savoy, and translated his name from Italian into German.[7] Meeting revolutionary opposition, Amadeo gave up the Spanish throne and is said to have stated that the people need not get exited, as he had no intention of forcing himself upon them. It seems that Marx did not have a high opinion of that considerate, reasonable prince; otherwise he would not have called him Gottlieb.

It was rather ironically that he called people by their Christian names. Kinkel, for instance, he always called Gottfried. He had a poor opinion of him and considered that his capture after his adventurous share in the Baden insurrection which cut short his insignificant teaching career, and then his romantic rescue by the faithful and courageous Karl Schurz, had so well set off his pleasant but by no means outstanding talent as a poet that he should have been thankful to fate for it.

Sometimes, though seldom, he also called Liebknecht by his Christian name. He held him in high esteem and thought that his talent as a reformer was a direct legacy from Luther. But he sometimes disagreed with him. He would then say with a smile, as a slight reproach, 'Yes, yes, Wilhelm.'

He said that Edgar and Bruno Bauer had founded a mutual admiration society. He never violently or insultingly manifested his displeasure during a conversation. He would unhorse his opponent, as in a tournament, but he never knocked him down. . . .

When people spoke of the enthusiasm of the workers for him, his attitude was very sceptical. 'These people have, understandably, only one wish – to escape from their poverty; they have very little understanding of how this might be possible.'

Once, after a talk he gave in the Rhineland, a worker came up and said, 'Very nice talk, Herr Doktor.' 'I'm glad that you enjoyed it.' 'Yer wouldn't have a copper to spare, would yer?' Once, too, a deputation came to Marx with the request to solve the social question quickly, for they were in great need.

On the whole, he continued, Bonaparte had known how to evaluate the enthusiasm of the masses correctly when he replied to a follower who pointed out how the people were thronging to him, 'If I were being executed, they would throng even more.' There was an amusing little event after a large meeting in which Marx had spoken of the need for the workers to unite. His well-known call, which he issued from London, whence he had fled after the reaction to the 1848 revolutions, ran, 'workers of the world, unite!' After the speech, which was received with great enthusiasm, one of the workers asked whether the association of *Achtblattler* (eight-leaved) was a secret society. Marx's Rhineland accent had caused him to understand *Arbeiter* (workers) as *Achtblattler*. There was a similar misunderstanding when Marx announced that a party of democrats, misheard as 'timocrats', was to be founded.

In connection with the first small episode, my mother had the beautiful idea of making Marx an embroidered wallet, in which there was a notebook on whose silk cover she embroidered the trunk of an oak surrounded by eight ivy leaves. The oak tree was naturally the symbol of Marx, the evergreen leaves that of the *Achblattler*. Beside it was a stone with the inscription 'Unite'. Marx was very pleased with it.

Contrary to his habit of sparing people in his judgements, he spoke very disapprovingly of Bakunin. He said his motto was 'Everything must be ruined' and that it was absolute nonsense to destroy values, to pull down one's own and other people's houses and then run away without knowing where and how to build another one. He acknowledged Lassalle's talents but he definitely had no sympathy with him. Even his eloquence amused Marx because of his lisp. He used to relate how Lassalle once recited a passage from Sophocles's *Antigone* with great fire as follows:

She shows herself fierth child of a fierth thire,
And before troubleth knowth not how to bend.

Marx thought Lassalle's attitude to Helene von Doenniges ridiculous in all respects and the duel which he provoked because of a person whom he professed to despise, senseless. He wanted to show off as an aristocrat in the whole affair and thus proved that he had chosen a wrong way of imitating the aristocracy. If he had taken his mission seriously he would not have exposed his life for a farce of the kind.

Considering Lassalle's extraordinary vanity, one could not conjecture how he would have behaved had he lived longer. It was typical of him to dream of marching into Berlin with the red-haired Helene at the head of battalions of workers. . . .

Marx, the true apostle of love of humanity, was an example of the Pentecostal miracle – like the apostles who, by the right of the all-embracing love of the Holy Spirit, were enabled to speak to everyone in their own language.

My father's mother lived with us and naturally everyone who came to see my parent also visited her. So did Engels when he once stopped in Hanover on a journey. But it did not come easily to him to converse with the old lady and she did not like him. With Marx, on the other hand, she was delighted, and she liked Jenny very much too. During Marx's first visit, she was away on her travels, so he only made her acquaintance the second time. He liked to chat with her and sought her out daily, particularly in her own rooms. Both he and Jenny often brought her flowers, which she liked very much. Without any preceding illness my grandmother died quite suddenly in her sleep.

The aforementioned small girl, who was the darling of Marx and on whom he had bestowed the nickname 'little owl', previously my mother's, sat anxiously and intimidated in a corner of the room that was to be arranged for the funeral. Although she had no accurate conception of death, the funereal atmosphere of the house lay heavily on her tiny heart. Marx took the child in his arms and brought her into his room, where he gave her *eau de Cologne* (which she liked very much) and read her a fairy story from a Spanish book, translating it simultaneously, as was his wont. She was completely captivated and was so inspired that after several days she recounted it all to my parents and declared it the most beautiful fairy-tale she had ever heard. My parents liked it very much too, and she often had to repeat it to friends. . . .

Marx and Jenny's long stay with us naturally led to lively correspondence when they returned to London.

. . . Jenny preferred to use French for letter-writing and English for brief notes. Eleanor always wrote in English, Marx and his wife in German. Mrs Marx wrote perfectly charming letters giving not only a vivid description of her life but even mentioning details about the life of my parents, which showed how well she had got to know them from what her husband and Jenny told her and what cordial interest she took in all that concerned us. My mother could read and speak both French and English, but her mother tongue came more naturally and fluently in correspondence.

Marx once told us about a silly Rhineland boy who always said, 'If only I had learned French instead of Latin.' 'Why, young man,' Marx rejoined, 'you can probably hardly decline *mensa*.' 'What's *mensa* got to do with it?' the boy answered. 'I learned *tabula*.'

Thanking Jenny for a letter my mother once wrote, '*Vivat sequens*',[8] and then in brackets, 'If only I had learned French instead of Latin!' At the bottom of Jenny's next letter Marx added in French, 'I beg Madame la Comtesse not to regret having preferred Latin to French. It not only shows a classical and highly developed taste, it explains why Madame is never *au bout de son latin*.'[9]

For Christmas the whole of the Marx family sent us fondly chosen keepsakes and pretty pieces of needlework. One was a silk theatre hat of their own making decorated with flowers. It could not be worn in Germany but my mother kept it for a long time as a souvenir. Several times they sent us a huge home-made plum-pudding. . . .

In order to see Marx again and make acquaintance with Mrs Marx and the Lafargues my father overcame his dislike for occasions and meetings of the sort and went to the Hague to the Congress of the Social Democrats.

My father described Mrs Lafargue as a beautiful, elegant and amiable woman. Mrs Marx, slim and young-looking, he said, took a passionate interest in Party life and seemed to have given herself up to it entirely. . . . My parents suspected that it was she particularly who drew Marx into these activities. This was confirmed by Jenny, who once, without naming any names, declared, 'Unfortunately, someone is always driving the Moor into political agitation – one could hate them for that.'

The following event showed how right Jenny was here – as was also my father, who was ever energetic in trying to restrain Marx. Some excited people were slinging mud at Marx. My father was beside himself with rage. Not because of the riff-raff, which always shouts 'Hurrah' one day and 'Boo' the next, but because Marx made himself so vulnerable and gave in to pressure from injudicious Party comrades.

A few years later my parents met Marx and Eleanor in Karlsbad, thus making personal acquaintance with the latter, with whom they had often chatted by letter. Jenny was already Mrs Longuet and could not leave her husband and child.

Eleanor – 'Tussy' as they called her – was very much unlike her elder sister both in character and figure. Her features were not so fine, but she too had her father's intelligent brown eyes. Although she was not beautiful she was certainly attractive. She had beautiful dark blonde hair with a golden shimmer; one day she undid it and wore it long and flowing, which was indeed very fetching but also rather flashy. But she did not care about that. She also dressed elegantly and with great taste but with the same flashiness. Her father let her have her way and said, 'Young women must smarten themselves up.'

My mother had the impression that as the youngest of the family she would be particularly indulged by all and sundry and like a spoilt child she followed her own whims. She was like Jenny in her reverence and adoration of her father. She was very intelligent, warm-hearted, and unlimitedly frank, in that she would say straight out to anyone what she thought, even when it was something she disliked about the person. She sat in the restaurants smoking cigarettes and buried in newspapers, which raised even more eyebrows then than it would today.

I think she was then nineteen years old and considered herself engaged to Lissagaray, with whom she kept up a lively correspondence. Once she showed my mother a letter from him which began with 'Ma petite femme'.

My father saw Lissagaray in the Hague and was not very favourably impressed. He was insignificant in his appearance and considerably older than Tussy. He was a count, but had given up his title and had been cast out by his whole family because of his socialist opinions. Marx did not seem to recognise the engagement and never spoke about it.

Marx was the same as before – unchanged even in his appearance. He watched with interest the international life of the health-resort and conferred the usual witty nicknames on a few of the more conspicuous passers-by.

He was delighted at the various beautiful walks in the wooded mountains, especially the romantic Egertal. Legend has personified some curiously shaped rocks there and given them the name of Hans Heiling's Rocks.

Hans Heiling is related to have been a young shepherd who won the heart of the beautiful nymph Eger. She demanded eternal faithfulness under pain of terrible vengeance. Hans Heiling swore never to abandon her, but after a few years he violated his vow and married a girl from the village. The wrathful nymph suddenly appeared out of the river at the wedding and turned the whole company into stone.

Marx took pleasure in looking for the figures of the musicians walking at the head of the wedding cortège with their horns and trumpets, the bride's coach and a festively attired old woman gathering her skirts together to step into the coach. At the same time he would listen to the quick-flowing seething river whose gurgling in the magic valley was supposed to represent an immortal being ever weeping over the fickleness of man.

In Dallwitz we visited the Oaks of Körner, under which the famous poet often spent his time while recovering from serious wounds and composed the beautiful poem 'The Oaks'.

Marx greatly enjoyed a visit to the Aich porcelain works, where he watched porcelain being made. First a soft grey mass is cut through with threads; then it is pressed into various moulds. One worker was tending a peculiar turning machine like a spinning-wheel on which most delicate cups were made.

'Is this always your job?' Marx asked him, 'or have you some other?' 'No,' the man answered, 'I have not done anything else for years. It is only by practice that one learns to work the machine so as to get the difficult shape smooth and faultless.' 'Thus division of labour makes man an appendage of the machine', Marx said to my father as we went on. 'His power of thinking is changed into muscular memory.'

The baking and certain details and then the painting and gilding of the finished objects in a large well-lit room, a further baking and lastly the careful sorting into defect-free and less perfect products, even the packing room – everything was excellently organised. We bought various articles as souvenirs.

Marx took pleasure in listening to the excellent resort orchestra which was conducted by Master Labitsky. As for serious talks on politics or discussion of Party affairs, he confined them to an absolute minimum during the short morning walk he had with my father or other men of his acquaintance. Among the latter was a

Polish revolutionary, Count Plater, who was so taken up with his ideas that he obviously found it difficult to take part in a light conversation, which was what Marx insisted upon in broader society or in the pleasant company of ladies. The Count was under average height, black-haired and somewhat clumsy. The historical artist Otto Knille, a friend of my father's, was of the opinion that if anybody was asked which of the two was the count, Marx or Plater, the answer would certainly be the former. Marx liked frequent conversations on art with Knille. Thus the days went by in a variety of pleasant occupations.

Suddenly, during a long walk Marx and my father had together towards the end of our stay, a difference occurred between them which was never smoothed down. My father only made vague allusions to it. It seems that he tried to persuade Marx to refrain from all political propaganda and complete the third book of *Capital* before anything else. My father was of the opinion that not only would precious time be uselessly wasted, but also that Marx had no talent for organisation. . . . 'Marx was a hundred years ahead of his time,' he often said later, 'but they are more likely to have immediate success who are in step with their time: those who look too far ahead miss things near at hand which shorter-sighted people see more clearly.'

Perhaps my father was over-zealous at the time, rather like the 'bad Wenzel'. This Marx could not countenance in a man so much younger than he and took for an encroachment upon his freedom. As a result their correspondence broke off. Tussy indeed wrote now and again but I do not know whether Jenny did. Tussy always gave wishes from her father, who also sent my mother books in memory of earlier talks together: Rückert's translation of Hariri's *Maqāmas*, Chamisso's works, and E. T. A. Hoffmann's *Klein Zaches*. This satire in the form of a legend particularly amused Marx. He himself never wrote any more. He probably did not intend to hurt my father by ignoring him and yet he could not forget the past.

My father never got over the pain that the break with a friend whom he still respected to the same degree caused him. However, he never made any attempt at a reconciliation, for he could not go back on his conviction. After Marx's death my mother seldom received letters from Tussy. She sent her back the much-used eight-leaved wallet as a souvenir of the pleasure that it had given to her father. Also a carved box for letters on whose inlaid lid my mother had placed a beautiful embroidery: on a background of revolutionary red there was inset a photograph of Marx surrounded by a laurel wreath woven into his initials.

The association between my parents and Marx, whom they held so dear that they always lovingly remembered every detail of it, can be described in the words of Schiller: 'Time hurries without tarrying, seeking what is permanent. Be faithful, and you will enchain her for ever.'

SOURCE: *RME*, pp. 273 ff. (with restoration of substantial omissions, trs. by the editor); from the German original in F. Kugelmann, 'Kleine Züge zu dem grossen Charakterbild von Karl Marx', *Mohr und General* (Berlin, 1970) pp. 280 ff.

NOTES

1. Marx's visit to Hanover lasted from 17 April to the middle of May 1867.
2. These were the proof sheets of volume I sent down from the publisher, Meissner, in Hamburg.
3. Marx did not translate volume I of *Capital* into French; but he did make many amendments to the translation by Roy.
4. Marx's eight-year-old son Edgar died in April 1855. He was buried in an ordinary cemetery. See above, no. 18, section 11.
5. 'Know yourself.'
6. But see Marx's answers to another Confession Book, no. 43 below.
7. In Italian 'Amadeo' means 'love God', in German 'Gottlieb' means 'God-love'.
8. 'Here's to the next!'
9. Literally, 'at the end of her Latin' – a colloquial expression meaning 'at a loss for words'.

21 Jenny Marx (iii)

This letter was written on Christmas Eve 1867 to thank Lugwig Kugelmann for the gift of a bust of Zeus. This statue had previously been on display in Kugelmann's house and he had observed a striking similarity between it and Marx when the latter had visited the house a few months previously. The reference at the end of the letter is to volume I of *Capital*, published in October 1867.

You cannot imagine what a great joy and surprise you provided for us yesterday and I really do not know how I am to thank you for all your friendship and sympathy – and now, for latest visible sign of your interest, the divine Father Zeus who now occupies the place of the 'Christchild' in our house. Our Christmas this year is again a very gloomy one, as my poor husband is once again laid low with his old illness. Two new outbreaks have appeared, of which one is important and in a painful position, so that Karl is compelled to lie on his side. I hope that we shall soon master this illness and that in the next letter you will no longer see the interim private secretary.

Yesterday, we were all sitting together in the rooms at the bottom of the house – the cooking region in English house designs, from which all creature comforts for the higher regions emerge – busy preparing the Christmas pudding with conscientious thoroughness. Raisins must have their pips removed (a very loathsome, sticky job), almonds and the peel of oranges and lemons be very finely chopped, kidney fat hacked into atoms, and, with eggs and flour, the whole mishmash kneaded into a peculiar potpourri. Then all of a sudden there is a ring, a wagon stops before the door, mysterious steps go up and down, a rustling whisper sweeps through the house; at last, a voice rings out from above, 'A big statue has arrived.' If someone had shouted, 'Fire, fire, the house is burning', or that the Fenians had come, we should not have rushed up any more confused and perplexed. And there he stood, in his colossal magnificence, his ideal purity, the old Jupiter Tonans quite undamaged (a little corner of the pedestal is broken off) before our staring, captivated eyes!! Afterwards, when the confusion had somewhat abated, we read your friendly accompanying letter that Borkheim had forwarded. After thinking of you in the most heartfelt and friendly terms there immediately began the debates as to where we could find the most worthy niche for our new 'God which art in heaven and on earth'. We have not come to any conclusion about this large question and we shall make many experiments before the proud head finds its position of honour.

I also thank you warmly for your great interest in Karl's book and your continuous efforts on its behalf. It appears that the Germans prefer to mask its arrival with silence and complete dumbness.

You can believe me, dear Herr Kugelmann, that seldom has a book been written under more difficult circumstances. I could write a secret history that would uncover an infinite amount of worry, trouble and anxiety. If the workers had an inkling of the sacrifice that was necessary to complete this work that is written only for them and in their interest, then perhaps they would show a little more interest.

SOURCE: trs. by the editor from *MEW*, vol. XXXI, pp. 595 f.

22 Friedrich Lessner (ii)

These reminiscences, first published in 1892, describe Marx mainly in the
mid 1860s, when Lessner worked closely with Marx in the International.
(On Lessner, see also the introductory note to no. 11.)

Marx always attached particular importance to meetings and talks
with workers. He considered it highly important to hear their
opinion of the movement and sought the company of those who
spoke frankly to him and spared him flattery. He was always ready to
discuss the most important political and economic problems with
them. He was quick in ascertaining whether they understood those
questions well enough, and the more they did, the greater was his
joy.

During the time of the International he never missed a sitting of
the General Council. After the sittings Marx and most of us
members of the Council generally went to a decent public-house for
a glass of beer and a chat. On the way home Marx often spoke of
the normal working-day in general and of the eight hour day
in particular. He often said, 'We are fighting for the eight-
hour working-day, but we frequently work more than twice as
long. . . .'

In fact, Marx unfortunately worked far too much. It is beyond the
conception of outsiders how much labour power and time the
International alone cost him. And yet he had to work hard for his
living and to study for hours in the British Museum to collect
material for his works on history and economics. On his way home to
Maitland Park Road, Haverstock Hill, in the north of London, he
often dropped in to see me, for I lived not far from the Museum, to
discuss some question concerning the International. When he got
home he would have his meal, after which he rested for a while and
then resumed his work. Often, too often, he worked late into the
night or even the early hours of the morning, especially as his short
evening rest was frequently cut short by visits from Party comrades.
Marx's house was open to every reliable comrade. I shall never
forget the pleasant hours which, like many others, I spent among
Marx's family. Mrs Marx produced a particularly vivid impression.
She was a tall, very beautiful woman, very distinguished and yet so
good-natured, lovable, witty and so free from pride and stiffness
that one felt as much at ease and at home in her presence as with
one's own mother or sister. Her whole being recalled the world of

the Scottish popular poet, Robert Burns[1]: 'Woman, lovely woman, heaven destined you to temper man.' She was full of enthusiasm for the labour movement and every smallest success in the struggle against the bourgeoisie afforded her the greatest satisfaction and joy.

From their early youth Marx's three daughters also took a most heartfelt interest in the Labour movement of the time, which was always the main topic in Marx's family. Relations between Marx and his daughters were the most intimate and unconstrained that one can imagine. The girls treated their father more as a brother or friend, for Marx scorned the exterior attributes of paternal authority. In serious matters he was his children's adviser, otherwise, according as his time allowed, their playmate.

Marx had an extreme liking for children generally. He often said that what he liked most in the Christ of the Bible was his great love for children. Often, when he had nothing to do in town and went for a walk to Hampstead Heath, the author of *Capital* could be seen bustling about with a lot of children.

Like all really great men, Marx was not at all conceited. He appreciated every honest striving and every opinion based on self-reliant thinking. As I have already said, he was always keen to hear the opinion of the most ordinary workers on the labour movement. Thus he often came to me in the afternoon, took me with him on his walk, and spoke to me about all sorts of things. I naturally let him do as much of the talking as possible, for it was a real pleasure to hear him talk and develop his arguments. I was always fascinated by his conversation and found it hard to leave him. In general he was splendid company and exerted a powerful attraction and even fascination on all who came into contact with him. His wit was inexhaustible and his laughter came right from the heart. When our Party comrades managed to achieve a victory in any country he would express his joy in the most unconstrained way and rejoice noisily, his joy infecting all those around him.

How he rejoiced over every electoral success of our comrades in Germany, over every strike won, and how he would have rejoiced if he had lived to see the giant demonstrations of May. As for the attacks of his opponents, he would merely make fun of them, and the irony and sarcasm with which he spoke of them was delicious. The lack of concern that he showed for his own works from the day when they had served their purpose was most noticeable. Whenever the conversation turned to his writings of earlier times, he used to say to me, 'If you want to have a complete set of my works, then you must go to Lassalle, who has collected them all. I myself have not got a single copy of most of them.' How much this reflected the true situation was shown by the fact that he often asked me to lend him for a time one or another of his writings of which he did not have a copy.

The death in 1883 of his eldest daughter, who had all the qualities of her mother – and she had only good ones – was a new blow to Marx at a time which was most difficult and fateful for him. Hardly twelve months earlier, on 2 December 1881, he had lost the faithful companion of his life. These were blows from which he never recovered.

Marx already had a nasty cough. When you heard it you thought his broad powerful figure would burst. This cough troubled him all the more as his constitution had been undermined by years of continuous overworking. In the middle of the 1870s the doctors forbade him to smoke and as Marx was a heavy smoker, this was a terrible sacrifice. On my first visit to him after the doctors' order he was quite pleased and proud to be able to tell me that he had not smoked for so and so many days, and that he would not do so until the doctors allowed him to. On every subsequent visit he would tell me how long it was since he had given up smoking and that he had not smoked all that time. He did not seem able to believe himself that he would manage it. His pleasure was all the greater when some time later the doctor allowed him a cigar a day.

SOURCE: *RME*, pp. 163 ff. and 169 (with restoration of omissions, trs. by the editor); from F. Lessner, 'Erinnerungen eines Arbeiters an Karl Marx', *Die Neue Zeit*, XI, pt 1 (1892–3) 748 ff.; and 'Von 1848 und nachher', *Deutsche Worte*, 1898, pp. 154 ff.

NOTE

1. Not Burns, but Thomas Otway in *Venice Preserved*.

23   Eleanor Marx (iii)

These reminiscences were written for an Austrian socialist journal in 1895.

My Austrian friends ask me to send them some recollections of my father. They could not well have asked me for anything more difficult. But Austrian men and women are making so splendid a fight for the cause for which Karl Marx lived and worked, that one cannot say nay to them. And so I will even try to send them a few stray, disjointed notes about my father.

Many strange stories have been told about Karl Marx, from that of his 'millions' (in pounds sterling, of course, no smaller coin would do), to that of his having been subventioned by Bismarck, whom he is supposed to have constantly visited in Berlin during the time of the International (!). But after all, to those who knew Karl Marx no legend is funnier than the common one which pictures him a morose, bitter, unbending, unapproachable man, a sort of Jupiter Tonans, ever hurling thunder, never known to smile, sitting aloof and alone in Olympus. This picture of the cheeriest, gayest soul that ever breathed, of a man brimming over with humour and goodhumour, whose hearty laugh was infectious and irresistible, of the kindliest, gentlest, most sympathetic of companions, is a standing wonder – and amusement – to those who knew him.

In his home life, as in his intercourse with friends, and even with mere acquaintances, I think one might say that Karl Marx's main characteristics were his unbounded good-humour and his unlimited sympathy. His kindness and patience were really sublime. A less sweet-tempered man would have often been driven frantic by the constant interruptions, the continual demands made upon him by all sorts of people. That a refugee of the Commune – a most unmitigated old bore, by the way – who had kept Marx three mortal hours, when at last told that time was pressing, and much work still had to be done, should reply 'Mon cher Marx, je vous excuse' is characteristic of Marx's courtesy and kindness.

As to this old bore, so to any man or woman whom he believed honest (and he gave of his precious time to not a few who sadly abused his generosity), Marx was always the most friendly and kindly of men. His power of 'drawing out' people, of making them feel that he was interested in what interested them was marvellous. I have heard men of the most diverse callings and positions speak of his peculiar capacity for understanding them and their affairs. When he thought anyone really in earnest his patience was unlimited. No question was too trivial for him to answer, no argument too childish for serious discussion. His time and his vast learning were always at the service of any man or woman who seemed anxious to learn.

But it was in his intercourse with children that Marx was perhaps most charming. Surely never did children have a more delightful playfellow. My earliest recollection of him is when I was about three years old, and 'Moor' (the old home name will slip out) was carrying me on his shoulder round our small garden in Grafton Terrace, and putting convolvulus flowers in my brown curls. Moor was admittedly a splendid horse. In earlier days – I cannot remember them, but have heard tell of them – my sisters and little brother – whose death just after my own birth was a lifelong grief to my parents – would 'harness' Moor to chairs which they 'mounted', and that he had to pull. In Dean Street, Soho, several chapters of the *Eighteenth Brumaire* were actually written in his capacity as steeplechaser of his three small children, who sat behind him on stools and whipped him up. Personally – perhaps because I had no sisters of my own age – I preferred Moor as a riding-horse. Seated on his shoulder, holding tight by his great mane of hair, then black, with but a hint of grey, I have had magnificent rides round our little garden, and over the fields – now built over – that surrounded our house in Grafton Terrace.

One word as to the name 'Moor'. At home we all had nicknames. (Readers of *Capital* will know what a hand at giving them Marx was.) 'Moor' was the regular, almost official, name by which Marx was called, not only by us, but by all the more intimate friends. But he was also our 'Challey' (Originally I presume a corruption of Charley!) and 'Old Nick'. My mother was always our 'Mohme'. Our dear old friend Helene Demuth – the lifelong friend of my parents, became after passing through a series of names our 'Nym'. Engels, after 1870, became our 'General'. A very intimate friend – Lina Schöler – our 'Old Mole'. My sister Jenny was 'Qui Qui, Emperor of China' and 'Di'. My sister Laura (Madame Lafargue) 'the Hottentot' and 'Kakadou'. I was 'Tussy' – a name that has remained – and 'Quo Quo, Successor to the Emperor of China', and for a long time the 'Getwerg Alberich' (from the *Niebelungen Lied*).

But if Moor was an excellent horse, he had a still higher qualification. He was a unique, an unrivalled story-teller. I have heard my aunts say that as a little boy he was a terrible tyrant to his sisters, whom he would 'drive' down the Markusberg at Trier full speed, as his horses, and worse, would insist on their eating the 'cakes' he made with dirty dough and dirtier hands. But they stood the 'driving' and ate the 'cakes' without a murmur, for the sake of the stories Karl would tell them as a reward for their virtue. And so many and many a year later Marx told stories to his children. To my sisters – I was then too small – he told tales as they went for walks, and these tales were measured by miles ' not chapters. 'Tell us another mile', was the cry of the two girls. For my own part, of the many wonderful tales Moor told me, the most wonderful, the most delightful one, was 'Hans Röckle'. It went on for months and months; it was a whole series of stories. The pity no one was there to write down these tales so full of poetry, of wit, of humour! Hans Röckle himself was a Hoffmann-like magician, who kept a toyshop, and who was always 'hard up'. His shop was full of the most wonderful things – of wooden men and women, giants and dwarfs, kings and queens, workmen and masters, animals and birds as numerous as Noah got into the Ark, tables and chairs, carriages, boxes of all sorts and sizes. And though he was a magician, Hans could never meet his obligations either to the devil or the butcher, and was therefore – much against the grain – constantly obliged to sell his toys to the devil. These then went through wonderful adventures – always ending in a return to Hans Röckle's shop. Some of these adventures were as grim, as terrible, as any of Hoffmann's; some were comic; all were told with inexhaustible verve, wit and humour.

And Moor would also read to his children. Thus to me, as to my sisters before me, he read the whole of Homer, the whole *Niebelungen Lied*, *Gudrun*, *Don Quixote*, the *Arabian Nights*, etc. As to Shakespeare, he was the Bible of our house, seldom out of our hands or mouths. By the time I was six I knew scene upon scene of Shakespeare by heart.

On my sixth birthday Moor presented me with my first novel – the immortal *Peter Simple*. This was followed by a whole course of Marryat and Cooper. And my father actually read every one of the tales as I read them, and gravely discussed them with his little girl. And when that little girl, fired by Marryat's tales of the sea, declared she would become a 'post-captain' (whatever that may be) and consulted her father as to whether it would not be possible for her 'to dress up as a boy' and 'run away to join a man-of-war' he assured her he thought it might very well be done, only they must say nothing about it to anyone until all plans were well matured. Before these plans could be matured, however, the Scott mania had set in, and the little girl heard to her horror that she herself partly belonged to the detested clan of Campbell. Then came plots for rousing the Highlands, and for reviving 'the '45'. I should add that Scott was an author to whom Marx again and again returned, whom he admired and knew as well as he did Balzac and Fielding. And while he talked about these and many other books he would, all unconscious though she was of it, show his little girl where to look for all that was finest and best in the works, teach her – though she never thought she was being taught, to that she would have objected – to try and think, to try and understand for herself.

And in the same way this 'bitter' and 'embittered' man would talk 'politics' and 'religion' with the little girl. How well I remember, when I was perhaps some five or six years old, feeling certain religious qualms and (we had been to a Roman Catholic Church to hear the beautiful music) confiding them, of course, to Moor, and how he quietly made everything clear and straight, so that from that hour to this no doubt could ever cross my mind again. And how I remember his telling me the story – I do not think it could ever have been so told before or since – of the carpenter whom the rich men killed, and many and many a time saying, 'After all we can forgive

Christianity much, because it taught us the worship of the child.' And Marx could himself have said 'suffer little children to come unto me', for wherever he went there children somehow would turn up also. If he sat on the Heath at Hampstead – a large open space in the north of London, near our old home – if he rested on a seat in one of the parks, a flock of children would soon be gathered round him on the most friendly and intimate terms with the big man with the long hair and beard, and the good brown eyes. Perfectly strange children would thus come about him, would stop him in the street, and animals were just as trusting towards him. Once I remember a small schoolboy of about ten quite unceremoniously stopping the dreaded 'chief of the International' in Maitland Park and asking him to 'swop knives'. After a little necessary explanation that 'swop' was schoolboy for 'exchange', the two knives were produced and compared. The boy's had only one blade; the man's had two, but these were undeniably blunt. After much discussion a bargain was struck, and the knives exchanged, the terrible 'chief of the International' adding a penny in consideration of the bluntness of his blades.

How I remember, too, the infinite patience and sweetness with which, the American war and Blue Books having for the time ousted Marryat and Scott, he would answer every question, and never complain of an interruption. Yet it must have been no small nuisance to have a small child chattering while he was working at his great book. But the child was never allowed to think she was in the way. At this time too, I remember, I felt absolutely convinced that Abraham Lincoln badly needed my advice as to the war, and long letters would I indite to him, all of which Moor, of course, had to read and post. Long long years after he showed me those childish letters that he had kept because they had amused him.

And so through the years of childhood and girlhood Moor was an ideal friend. At home we were all good comrades, and he always the kindest and best humoured. Even through the years of suffering when he was in constant pain, suffering from carbuncles, even to the end.

I was speaking of Marx and how he communicated with children. His relationships with animals were just as friendly, and, if there were space and time, I could tell many stories of our menagerie in Maitland Park, the cats, dogs, birds and tortoises. . . .

I sometimes think that almost as strong a bond between my parents as their devotion to the cause of the workers was their immense sense of humour. Assuredly two people never enjoyed a joke more than these two. Again and again – especially if the occasion were one demanding decorum and sedateness, have I seen them laugh till tears ran down their cheeks, and even those inclined to be shocked at such awful levity could not choose but laugh with them. And how often have I seen them not daring to look at one another, each knowing that once a glance was exchanged uncontrollable laughter would result. To see these two with eyes fixed on anything but one another, for all the world like two schoolchildren, suffocating with suppressed laughter that at last despite all efforts would well forth, is a memory I would not barter for all the millions I am sometimes credited with having inherited. Yes, in spite of all the suffering, the struggles, the disappointments, they were a merry pair,-and the embittered Jupiter Tonans is a figment of bourgeois imagination. And if in the years of struggle there were many disillusions, if they met with strange ingratitude they had what is given to few – true friends. . . .

To those who are students of human nature it will not seem strange that this man, who was such a fighter, should at the same time be the kindliest and gentlest of men. They will understand that he could hate so fiercely only because he could love so profoundly; that if his trenchant pen could as surely imprison a soul in hell as Dante himself it was because he was so true and tender; that if his sarcastic humour could bite like a corrosive acid, that same humour could be as balm to those in trouble and afflicted.

My mother died in the December of 1881. Fifteen months later he who had never been divided from her in life had joined her in death. After life's fitful fever they sleep well. If she was an ideal woman, he – well, he 'was a man, take him for all in all, we shall not look upon his like again'.

SOURCE: *RME*, pp. 249 ff. (with restoration of omissions, trs. by the editor).

24 Anselmo Lorenzo

A printer by trade, Lorenzo attended the London Conference of the International in September 1871. These reminiscences were written thirty years later.

In a short time we stopped before a house. Framed in the doorway appeared an old man with a venerable patriarchal appearance.

I approached him with shy respect and introduced myself as a delegate of the Spanish Federation of the International. He took me in his arms, kissed me on the forehead and showed me into the house with words of affection in Spanish. He was Karl Marx.

The family had already retired and he himself served me an

appetising refreshment with exquisite amiability. Then we had tea and spoke for a long time of revolutionary ideas, propaganda and organisation. Marx showed great satisfaction with what we had achieved in Spain, which he judged on the basis of my summary of the report that I was to convey and present to the Conference. Whether we had exhausted the subject or whether my honourable host desired to expand on some subject of his preference I do not know, but he spoke about Spanish literature, of which he had a detailed and profound knowledge. I was surprised at all he said about our ancient theatre, the history, vicissitudes and progress of which he was perfectly familiar with. Calderón, Lope de Vega, Tirso and other great masters, not only of the Spanish theatre, he said, but of European drama, were given a concise analysis and what seemed to me a very correct appraisal.

In the presence of that great man I could not help feeling very, very small, and, were it not for the great joy that I experienced, I should have preferred to be quietly in my own home, where I should certainly not have been assailed by such varied impressions, but then neither could I have been reproached with finding myself out of harmony with the situation and the personalities. However, I made a tremendous effort not to give a deplorable impression of my ignorance and made the usual comparisons between Calderón and Shakespeare and also recalled Cervantes. Marx spoke of all that with great brilliance and expressed his admiration for the Ingenious Hidalgo de la Mancha. It must be noted that the conversation was in Spanish, which Marx spoke correctly although with pronunciation defects, due mainly to the difficulty of our *cc*, *gg*, *jj* and *rr*.

In the early hours of the morning he took me to the room reserved for me. . . .

Next day I was introduced to Marx's daughters and then to various delegates and other people. His eldest daughter, a girl of ideal beauty, differed from all the types of feminine beauty I had so far met. She knew Spanish but pronounced it badly like her father. She asked me to read something for her so that she could hear the correct pronunciation. I went to the bookcase and took out *Don Quixote* and a collection of Calderón's dramatic works. From the former I read Don Quixote's speech to the shepherds and from the latter a few noble and sonorous passages from *Life Is a Dream* which are acknowledged to be gems of Spanish and sublime conceptions of human thought. The explanations that I tried to give about content and form proved superflous, for my young and beautiful inter-locutor had abundant knowledge of and feeling for the work, as she showed by the many pertinent remarks which she added to my explanation and which would never have occurred to me.

When I expressed my desire to send a telegram to Valencia to report my safe arrival in London, Marx's youngest daughter was sent with me to show me the way. I was most surprised and touched by the alacrity with which the young lady helped a foreigner whom she did not know, this being contrary to the customs of the Spanish bourgeoisie.

This young lady, or rather girl, as beautiful, merry and smiling as the very personification of youth and happiness, did not know Spanish. She could speak English and German well but was not very proficient in French, in which language I could make myself understood. Every time one of us made a blunder we both laughed as heartily as if we had been friends all our life.

SOURCE: *RME*, pp. 288 ff. (with restoration of omissions, trs. by the editor); from the Spanish original in A. Lorenzo, *EL proletariado militante* (Barcelona, n.d.) pp. 313 ff.

25 Interview with the New York *World*

The following interview with their correspondent R. Landor was published in the New York *World* on 18 July 1871. Marx was already known to American readers through his articles as one of the foreign correspondents of the New York *Tribune* from 1851 to 1862. In addition, the International had supported the Union in the Civil War and by 1871 had three sections in America. But what particularly prompted interest in Marx was his supposed direction of the Paris Commune, which had been bloodily suppressed two months prior to this interview.

London, 3 July. – You have asked me to find out something about the International Association, and I have tried to do so. The enterprise is a difficult one just now. London is indisputably the headquarters of the Association, but the English people have got a scare, and smell International in everything as King James smelt gunpowder after the famous plot. The consciousness of the Association has naturally increased with the suspiciousness of the public; and if those who guide it have a secret to keep, they are of the stamp of men who keep a secret well. I have called on two of their leading members, have talked with one freely, and I here give you the substance of my conversation. I have satisfied myself of one thing, that it is a society of genuine working men, but that these workmen are directed by social and political theorists of another class. One man whom I saw, a leading member of the Council, was sitting at his workman's bench during our interview, and left off talking to me from time to time to receive a complaint, delivered in no courteous tone, from one of the many little masters in the neighbourhood who employed him. I have heard this same man make eloquent speeches in public inspired in every passage with the energy of hate towards the classes that call themselves his rulers. I understood the speeches after this glimpse at the domestic life of the orator. He must have felt that he had brains enough to have organised a working government, and yet here he was obliged to devote his life to the most revolting task work of a mechanical profession. He was proud and sensitive, and yet at every turn he had to return a bow for a grunt and a smile for a command that stood on about the same level in the scale of civility with a huntsman's call to his dog. This man helped me to a glimpse of one side of the nature of the International, the revolt of labour against capital, of the workman who produces against the middleman who enjoys. Here was the hand that would smite hard when the time came, and as to the head that plans, I think I saw that, too, in my interview with Dr Karl Marx.

Dr Karl Marx is a German doctor of philosophy[1] with a German breadth of knowledge derived both from observation of the living world and from books. I should conclude that he has never been a worker in the ordinary sense of the term. His surroundings and appearance are those of a well-to-do man of the middle class. The drawing-room into which I was ushered on the night of my interview would have formed very comfortable quarters for a thriving stockbroker who had made his competence and was now beginning to make his fortune. It was comfort personified, the apartment of a man of taste and of easy means, but with nothing in it peculiarly characteristic of its owner. A fine album of Rhine views on the table, however, gave a clue to his nationality. I peered cautiously into the vase on the side-table for a bomb. I sniffed for petroleum, but the smell was the smell of roses. I crept back stealthily to my seat, and moodily awaited the worst.

He has entered and greeted me cordially, and we are sitting face to face. Yes, I am *tête à tête* with the revolution incarnate, with the real founder and guiding spirit of the International Association, with the author of the address in which capital was told that if it warred on labour it must expect to have its house burned down about its ears – in a word, with the apologist for the Commune of Paris. Do you remember the bust of Socrates, the man who died rather than profess his belief in the gods of the time – the man with the fine sweep of profile for the forehead running meanly at the end into a little snub, curled-up feature like a bisected pothook that formed the nose? Take this bust in your mind's eye, colour the beard black, dashing it here and there with puffs of grey; clap the head thus made on a portly body of the middle height, and the Doctor is before you. Throw a veil over the upper part of the face and you might be in the company of a born vestryman. Reveal the essential feature, the immense brow, and you know at once that you have to deal with that most formidable of all composite forces – a dreamer who thinks, a thinker who dreams.

Another gentleman accompanied Dr Marx, a German too, I believe, though from his great familiarity with our language I cannot be sure of it.[2] Was he a witness on the doctor's side? I think so. The 'Council',[3] hearing of the interview, might hereafter call on the Doctor for his account of it, for the *Revolution* is above all things suspicious of its agents. Here, then, was his evidence in corroboration.

I went straight to my business. The world, I said, seemed to be in the dark about the International, hating it very much, but not able to say clearly what thing it hated. Some, who professed to have peered further into the gloom than their neighbours, declared that they had made out a sort of Janus figure with a fair, honest workman's smile on one of its faces, and on the other a murderous, conspirator's scowl. Would he light up the case of mystery in which the theory dwelt?

The professor laughed, chuckled a little I fancied, at the thought that we were so frightened of him. 'There is no mystery to clear up, dear sir,' he began, in a very polished form of the Hans Breitmann dialect, 'except perhaps the mystery of human stupidity in those who perpetually ignore the fact that our Association is a public one and that the fullest reports of its proceedings are published for all who care to read them. You may buy our rules for a penny, and a shilling laid out in pamphlets will teach you almost as much about us as we know ourselves.

R. – Almost – yes, perhaps so; but will not the something I shall not know constitute the all-important reservation? To be quite frank with you, and to put the case as it strikes an outside observer, this general claim of depreciation of you must mean something more than the ignorant ill-will of the multitude. And it is still pertinent to ask, even after what you have told me, what is the International Association?

Dr M. – You have only to look at the individuals of which it is composed – workmen.

R. – Yes, but the soldier need be no exponent of the statecraft that sets him in motion. I know some of your members, and I can believe that they are not of the stuff of which conspirators are made. Besides, a secret shared by a million men would be no secret at all. But what if these were only the instruments in the hands of a bold, and I hope you will forgive me for adding, not over-scrupulous conclave.

Dr M. – There is nothing to prove it.

R. – The last Paris insurrection[4]?

Dr M. – I demand firstly the proof that there was any plot at all – that anything happened that was not the legitimate effect of the circumstances of the moment; or, the plot granted, I demand the proofs of the participation in it of the International Association.

R. – The presence in the communal body of so many members of the Association.

Dr M. – Then it was a plot of the Freemasons, too, for their share in the work as individuals was by no means a slight one. I should not be surprised, indeed, to find the Pope setting down the whole insurrection to their account. But try another explanation. The insurrection in Paris was made by the workmen of Paris. The ablest of the workmen must necessarily have been its leaders and administrators; but the ablest of the workmen happen also to be members of the International Association. Yet the Association as such may in no way be responsible for their action.

R. – It will still seem otherwise to the world. People talk of secret instructions from London, and even grants of money. Can it be affirmed that the alleged openness of the Association's proceedings precludes all secrecy of communication?

Dr M. – What association ever formed carried on its work without private as well as public agencies? But to talk of secret instruction from London, as of decrees in the matter of faith and morals from some centre of Papal domination and intrigue, is wholly to misconceive the nature of the International. This would imply a centralised form of government of the International, whereas the real form is designedly that which gives the greatest play to local energy and independence. In fact the International is not properly a government for the working class at all. It is a bond of union rather than a controlling force.

R. – And of union to what end?

Dr M. – The economical emancipation of the working class by the conquest of political power. The use of that political power to the attainment of social ends. It is necessary that our aims should be thus comprehensive to include every form of working-class activity. To have made them of a special character would have been to adapt them to the needs of one section – one nation of workmen alone. But how could all men be asked to unite to further the objects of a few? To have done that the Association must have forfeited its title of International. The Association does not dictate the form of political movements; it only requires a pledge as to their end. It is a network of affiliated societies spreading all over the world of labour. In each part of the world some special aspect of the problem presents itself, and the workmen there address themselves to its consideration in their own way. Combinations among workmen cannot be absolutely identical in detail in Newcastle and in Barcelona, in London and in Berlin. In England, for instance, the way to show political power lies open to the working class. Insurrection would be madness where peaceful agitation would more swiftly and surely do the work. In France a hundred laws of repression and a moral antagonism between classes seem to necessitate the violent solution of social war. The choice of that solution is the affair of the working classes of that country. The International does not presume to dictate in the matter and hardly to advise. But to every movement it accords its sympathy and its aid within the limits assigned by its own laws.

R. – And what is the nature of that aid?

Dr M. – To give an example, one of the commonest forms of the movement for emancipation is that of strikes. Formerly, when a strike took place in one country it was defeated by the importation of workmen from another. The International has nearly stopped all that. It receives information of the intended strike, it spreads that information among its members, who at once see that for them the seat of the struggle must be forbidden ground. The masters are thus left alone to reckon with their men. In most cases the men require no other aid than that. Their own subscriptions or those of the societies to which they are more immediately affiliated supply them with funds, but should the pressure upon them become too heavy and the strike be one of which the Association approves, their necessities are supplied out of the common purse. By these means a strike of the cigar-makers of Barcelona was brought to a victorious issue the other day. But the society has no interest in strikes, though it supports them under certain conditions. It cannot possibly gain by them in a pecuniary point of view, but it may easily lose. Let us sum it all up in a word. The working classes remain poor amid the increase of wealth, wretched among the increase of luxury. Their material privation dwarfs their moral as well as their physical stature. They cannot rely on others for a remedy. It has become then with them an imperative necessity to take their own case in hand. They must revise the relations between themselves and the capitalists and landlords, and that means they must transform society. This is the general end of every known workmen's organisation; land and labour leagues, trade and friendly societies, co-operative stores and co-operative production are but means towards it. To establish a perfect solidarity between these organisations is the business of the International Association. Its influence is beginning to be felt everywhere. Two papers spread its views in Spain, three in Germany, the same number in Austria and in Holland, six in Belgium, and six in

Switzerland. And now that I have told you what the International is you may, perhaps, be in a position to form your own opinion as to its pretended plots.

R. – I do not quite understand you.

Dr M. – Do you not see that the old society, wanting strength to meet it with its own weapons of discussion and combination, is obliged to resort to the fraud of fixing upon it the imputation of conspiracy?

R. – But the French police declare that they are in a position to prove its complicity in the late affair, to say nothing of preceding attempts.

Dr M. – But we will say something of those attempts, if you please, because they best serve to test the gravity of all the charges of conspiracy brought against the International. You remember the last 'plot' but one. A plebiscite had been announced.[5] Many of the electors were known to be wavering. They had no longer a keen sense of the value of the imperial rule, having come to disbelieve in those threatened dangers of society from which it was supposed to have saved them. A new bugbear was wanted. The police undertook to find one. All combinations of workmen being hateful to them, they naturally owed the International an ill turn. A happy thought inspired them. What if they should select the International for their bugbear, and thus at once discredit that society and curry favour for the imperial cause? Out of that happy thought came the ridiculous 'plot' against the Emperor's life – as if we wanted to kill the wretched old fellow. They seized the leading members of the International. They manufactured evidence. They prepared their case for trial, and in the meantime they had their plebiscite. But the intended comedy was too obviously but a broad, coarse farce. Intelligent Europe, which witnessed the spectacle, was not deceived for a moment as to its character, and only the French peasant elector was befooled. Your English papers reported the beginning of the miserable affair; they forget to notice the end. The French judges, admitting the existence of the plot by official courtesy, were obliged to declare that there was nothing to show the complicity of the International. Believe me, the second plot is like the first. The French functionary is again in business. He is called in to account for the biggest civil movement the world has ever seen. A hundred signs of the times ought to suggest the right explanation – the growth of intelligence among the workmen, of luxury and incompetence among their rulers, the historical process now going on of that final transfer of power from a class to the people, the apparent fitness of time, place and circumstance for the great movement of emancipation. But to have seen these the functionary must have been a philosopher, and he is only a *mouchard*.[6] By the law of his being, therefore, he has fallen back upon the *mouchard*'s explanation – a 'conspiracy'. His old portfolio of forged documents will supply him with the proofs, and this time Europe in its scare will believe the tale.

R. – Europe can scarcely help itself, seeing that every French newspaper spreads the report.

Dr M. – Every French newspaper! See, here is one of them [taking up *La Situation*], and judge for yourself of the value of its evidence as to a matter of fact. [Reads] 'Dr Karl Marx, of the International, has been arrested in Belgium, trying to make his way to France. The police of London have long had their eye on the society with which he is connected, and are now taking active measures for its suppression.' Two sentences and two lies. You can test the evidence of your own senses. You see that instead of being in prison in Belgium I am at home in England. You must also know that the police in England are as powerless to interfere with the International Association as the Association with them. Yet what is most regular in all this is that the report will go the round of the continental press without a contradiction, and could continue to do so if I were to circularise every journal in Europe from this place.

R. – Have you attempted to contradict many of these false reports?

Dr M. – I have done so till I have grown weary of the labour. To show the gross carelessness with which they are concocted I may mention that in one of them I saw Félix Pyat set down as a member of the International.

R. – And he is not so?

Dr M. – The association could hardly have found room for such a wild man. He was once presumptuous enough to issue a rash proclamation in our name, but it was instantly disavowed, though, to do them justice, the press of course ignored the disavowal.

R. – And Mazzini, is he a member of your body?

Dr Marx [laughing]. – Ah, no. We should have made but little progress if we had not got beyond the range of his ideas.

R. – You surpise me. I should certainly have thought that he represented the most advanced views.

Dr M. – He represents nothing better than the old idea of a middle-class republic. We seek no part with the middle class. He has fallen far to the rear of the modern movement as the German professors, who, nevertheless, are still considered in Europe as the apostles of the cultured democratism of the future. They were so at one time – before '48, perhaps, when the German middle class, in the English sense, had scarcely attained its proper development. But now they have gone over bodily to the reaction, and the proletariat knows them no more.

R. – Some people have thought they saw signs of a positivist element in your organisation.[7]

Dr M. – No such thing. We have positivists among us, and others not of our body who work as well. But this is not by virtue of their philosophy, which will have nothing to do with popular government, as we understand it, and which seeks only to put a new hierarchy in place of the old one.

R. – It seems to me, then, that the leaders of the new international movement have had to form a philosophy as well as an association for themselves.

Dr M. – Precisely. It is hardly likely, for instance, that we could hope to prosper in our war against capital if we derive our tactics, say, from the political economy of Mill. He has traced one kind of relationship between labour and capital. We hope to show that it is possible to establish another.

R. – And as to religion?

Dr M. – On that point I cannot speak in the name of the society. I myself am an atheist. It is startling, no doubt, to hear such an avowal in England, but there is some comfort in the thought that it need not be made in a whisper in either Germany or France.

R. – And yet you make your headquarters in this country?

Dr M. – For obvious reasons; the right of association is here an established thing. It exists, indeed, in Germany, but it is beset with innumerable difficulties; in France for many years it has not existed at all.

R. – And the United States?

Dr M. – The chief centres of our activity are for the present among the old societies of Europe. Many circumstances have hitherto tended to prevent the labour problem from assuming an all-absorbing importance in the United States. But they are rapidly disappearing, and it is rapidly coming to the front there with the growth as in Europe of a labouring class distinct from the rest of the community and divorced from capital.

R. – It would seem that in this country the hoped-for solution, whatever it may be, will be attained without the violent means of revolution. The English system of agitating by platform and press until minorities become converted into majorities is a hopeful sign.

Dr M. – I am not so sanguine on that point as you. The English middle class has always shown itself willing enough to accept the verdict of the majority so long as it enjoyed the monopoly of the voting power. But mark me, as soon as it finds itself outvoted on what it considers vital questions we shall see here a new slave owners' war.

I have here given you as well as I can remember them the heads of my conversation with this remarkable man. I shall leave you to form your own conclusions. Whatever may be said for or against the probability of its complicity with the movement of the Commune we may be assured that in the International Associaton the civilised world has a new power in its midst with which it must soon come to a reckoning for good or ill.

NOTES

1. Marx obtained a doctorate of philosophy *in absentia* from the University of Jena in 1841.
2. Probably Engels, who had moved to London the previous year and spoke excellent English.
3. That is, the General Council of the International, which met weekly in London.
4. This refers to the Paris Commune, which was established on 18 March 1871 and fell exactly two months later.
5. This plebiscite – to approve constitutional changes and generally provide evidence of popular support for the Empire – was held on 7 May 1870. The International had recommended abstention; many of its members were arrested and sentenced to imprisonment.
6. That is, 'informer'.
7. The followers of Auguste Comte were known as positivists. Comte had advocated a positive science of society for which he coined the term 'sociology'. His disciples displayed a favourable attitude to the Commune.

26 Theodor Cuno

Cuno was an Austrian engineer, very active in the cause of the International. The following passage concerns the 1872 Congress, to which Cuno was sent as a delegate from Hamburg. He emigrated to America soon afterwards and became a journalist in New York. These reminiscences were written in 1932 at the request of the Institute for Marxism–Leninism, Moscow.

Marx was sitting behind Engels. I recognised him immediately with his big, woolly head. His complexion was dark, his hair and beard were grey. He wore a black broadcloth suit, and when he wanted to look at anybody or anything intently he pressed a monocle into his right eye. Engels took me to him; and he received me affably, requesting me to give him an account of different occurrences in Spain and Italy when the session was adjourned. . . . Then the report of the General Council was read, Marx, Engels and other members of the Council alternating in the reading. The report was written in

English, French and German. As the delegates from Italy and Spain did not speak any other language but their own, I was appointed to be interpreter for Italian and Spanish and it was a big job for me to translate the contents of the report as well as any remarks made regarding it from the floor, Marx and Engels replying extensively. When speaking, Marx was not very fluent; in fact he was not a practical orator, while Engels spoke in a conversational tone, often sarcastic and humorous, *'burschicosically'*, as we Germans are in the habit of describing the conversation among college students. When Marx was speaking he from time to time dropped his monocle and then slowly reinserted it in its place at his right eye. Being fifty-five years at that time, Marx was still in a vigorous physical condition, his bushy hair and beard being only in part streaked with grey or white. His complexion was a pale yellow.... His fellow-students had conferred upon him the nickname 'Der Mohr', American boys would probably call him 'Nigger'. His wife and children always called him 'Der Mohr', considering him to be more of a jolly comrade than a stern and bossy parent.

SOURCE: *RME*, pp. 209 f.

27 S. M. N. Calisch

The following comes from a contemporary report on the 1872 Hague Congress of the International written by a Dutch journalist of liberal sympathies.

Karl Marx was the pope of the International, the infallible lord, the autocratic chief to whom Bakunin had to leave the field, before whom Jung trembled.

Marx is a man of distinguished appearance. His beautiful grey hair falls in regular locks over his strongly developed head, a grey beard frames his chin and his upper lip is adorned by a moustache whose original black is not completely grey but has already arrived at the pepper and salt stage.

His gait is measured, he speaks strongly, pithily, hotly, but not rhetorically. He does not deny his German character. His eyes do not have the expression that one would have expected from the sort of full-blooded internationalist described in the *Dagblad*.

It is said that he is of Dutch origin and has relations who live in Amsterdam. If that is correct, then his family will have no worries about introducing him to society or drinking tea with him in the Zoo

Café. The impression he makes in his grey suit is exactly *comme il faut*. Anyone who did not know him and had no connexion with the nightmare of the feared International would take him for a tourist making a sortie on foot.

He has not spoken at Congress meetings – at least, those that were public; but he seems to have influenced the direction of the resolutions. He took a seat diagonally behind Ranvier and was often to be seen involved in lively conversation with him.

Marx has something magisterial about him. And the delegates treated him with a certain distinction. One of them, extremely pleased with himself, showed me the autographed portrait that Marx had presented him with.

SOURCE: trs. by the editor from S. Calisch, *Een Zesdaagsch Internationaal Debat* (Dordrecht, 1872) pp. 69 ff.

28 Franz Mehring

Mehring became one of the major intellectual leaders of the German Social Democratic Party and author of the classic biography of Marx. The following sketch was written about 1896.

Marx was squat and stocky, with glittering eyes and a lion's mane of ebony black hair which accorded with his semitic origins; nonchalant in his external manner; a harassed paterfamilias who lived at a distance from the social bustle of the outside world; given to exhausting mental labour which scarcely allowed him to take a quick midday meal and then consumed his bodily strength until deep into the night; a restless thinker to whom thinking was the highest pleasure; therein a true successor to Kant, Fichte and particularly Hegel, whose saying he liked to repeat: 'Even the criminal thought of a malefactor has more grandeur and nobility than the wonders of the heavens' – except that his own thinking tended incessantly towards action: impractical in small things, but practical in large ones: much too clumsy to organise a small household, but unequalled in the ability to recruit and lead an army to change the world.

SOURCE: trs. by the editor from F. Mehring, 'Friedrich Engels und Karl Marx', *Gesammelte Schriften*, vol. III (Berlin, 1960) pp. 238 f.

29 Mikhail Bakunin (ii)

These impressions were written in 1871 at the height of the struggle in the International between Marxists and Bakuninists. They precede a detailed account of the meetings between Marx and Bakunin – one of which is recalled in item no. 9.

Marx is a man of great intelligence and also a scholar in the broadest and deepest sense of the word. He is a profound student of economics in comparison with whom Mazzini, whose knowledge of economics is superficial in the extreme, can scarcely be called a disciple. Marx is, moreover, passionately devoted to the cause of the proletariat. Nobody has the right to doubt this, for he has served this cause for nearly thirty years with undeniable constancy and fidelity. He has dedicated his whole life to it. Mazzini, whose present impotence seeks a sad consolation in the poison of unjust invective and in arbitrarily invented fables and calumnies, asserts that Marx is inspired only by hate and not by love. Let us be clear: deep, earnest and passionate human love is always accompanied by hate. You cannot love justice without detesting injustice, nor freedom without detesting authority, nor humanity without detesting the spiritual and moral sources of all despotism, the immoral fiction of the heavenly despot, the Lord God. You cannot love the oppressed without detesting the oppressors and therefore cannot love the proletariat without hating the bourgeoisie. Marx loves the proletariat, therefore he hates the bourgeoisie. You cannot serve a cause for thirty years with passionate devotion without loving it, and only the hateful prejudice of calumny can dare to deny the love of Marx for the cause of the proletariat.

In addition to these great and incontestable services, Marx was the initiator and chief inspirer of the founding of the International. These are the services that he has rendered. But every medal has its obverse, every light its shade, and every man his faults. Therefore one should never trust to a single man the power over society as a whole, even when he is a genius crowned with virtue, nor to a minority, be it ever so intelligent and well-meaning: for all power by an inherent law involves its own misuse and every government, even one nominated by universal suffrage, inevitably leads to despotism.

So Marx too has his faults. They are as follows.

First, he has the fault of all professional scholars: he is *doctrinaire*. He has an absolute faith in his theories and from the summit of these theories he disdains the whole world. As a learned and clever man he naturally has his party, a core of blindly devoted friends, who swear by him alone, think through him alone, have only his will at heart – in short, who deify and worship him, and through this worship, corrupt him – a process which has already gone quite far. Thus he regards himself in all seriousness as the pope of socialism or rather of communism, for his whole theory leads him to be an authoritarian communist. Like Mazzini – though with other ideas and in a much more realistic and earthy manner – he aims to free the proletariat through the centralised power of the state.

Secondly, this self-adoration in his absolute and absolutist theories has a natural corollary in the hate that Marx nurtures not only against the bourgeoisie but against all – even revolutionary socialists – who contradict him and dare to follow a line of ideas different from his theories.

Marx is extremely vain, a vanity which causes him to descend to filth and madness. This is strange in so intelligent and honestly devoted a man and can only be explained by his education as a German scholar and man of letters and particularly by his nervous Jewish character. Anyone who is unlucky enough to wound, albeit unintentionally, this pathological, ever sensitive and ever irritable vanity becomes his mortal enemy, and then he considers any means justified – and in fact uses the most abusive and impermissible means – to destroy his enemy's reputation. Thus, in this respect Mazzini was right when he spoke of Marx's detestable character, but I ask you, dear friends, to note well that, in spite of his natural magnanimity and driven by his increasing powerlessness, he treated his opponents in his latest polemics in nearly the same manner.

However different they may be in every other respect (and this comparison is not always to Marx's advantage), Mazzini and Marx are driven by the same passion, by a political ambition – religious with Mazzini, scientific and doctrinaire with Marx – to regulate, educate and organise the masses in accordance with their own conceptions. Mazzini, whose high personal unselfishness, whose pure and elevated soul are well-known, feels a need to see his ideas, his party, his apostles conquer. Marx, whose instincts are much less unselfish than those of Mazzini, passionately wills the victory of his ideas, the proletariat and thereby his own person. The ambition of the one is thus loftier and above all less selfish, that of the other more personal, but both lead to the same manner of proceeding.

The evil lies in the seeking of power, the love of domination, the thirst for authority – and Marx is deeply imbued with this evil.

Thirdly, his theory gives great support for this. Although not the organisational leader of the German Communist Party – in general he does little organisation and has more talent for splitting through intrigues than for organising – he is the Party's inspirational head and as such is an authoritarian communist who believes that the proletariat should be reorganised and liberated through the state. This process would be from the top to the bottom, through the intelligence and knowledge of an enlightened minority which naturally professes socialism and exercises a legitimate authority over the ignorant and stupid masses for their own good. This political system is almost the same as Mazzini's, only with the programme changed. This partly explains their great mutual hatred and the inability of either of them to do justice to the other. In addition to the division over ideas and programme, they are contenders for the same power. For both of them – one through his ideas and his disciples, the other through his ideas and himself – comfort themselves with the hope that one day they will rule their own land. They dream of universal power and a universal state: Mazzini, that Italy will achieve organisation through his ideas and then become queen of the world; Marx through Germany and the German race, who, he believes, are called upon to regenerate the world. Mazzini is an Italian nationalist, and Marx a Pan-Germanist, to his very marrow.

The following difference between them is entirely in Mazzini's favour. Mazzini loves his faithful friends, his disciples more than himself; he is very lenient with them, sometimes too much so, and is noble enough to forgive from the bottom of his heart the injustices, offences and wrongs that he has suffered at their hands. But he never forgives infidelity to his religion, to his divine ideas. . . .

Marx loves his own person more than his friends and disciples and no friendship can withstand the wounding of his vanity, be it ever so slight. He will more readily forgive infidelity to his philosophical and socialist system; he will treat it as proof of the stupidity, or at least of the intellectual inferiority, of his friend and that will amuse him. If he no longer perceives him as a rival who could attain to his own eminence, then he will perhaps like him all the more. But he will never forgive anyone an offence against his own person: to be loved by him you must worship and deify him, to be tolerated by him you must at least fear him. He loves to surround himself with the smallest, with lackeys and flatterers. Nevertheless, there are some outstanding men in his intimate circle.

But in general it can be said that in Marx's intimate circle there is very little fraternal frankness; on the contrary, there is a lot of ulterior motives and diplomacy. A sort of silent struggle exists, a compromise between the self-interests of the individuals; and where vanity is at stake there is no longer room for fraternity. Everyone is on his guard and is afraid of being sacrificed and destroyed. It is mainly Marx who disposes of the honours, but he also constantly instigates – perfidiously and spitefully, never freely and openly – the persecution of people whom he suspects or who had the misfortune not to show him respect in the degree that was expected.

Once he has ordered a persecution, then it does not shrink from any baseness or infamy. Himself a Jew, he has surrounded himself, in London and France but above all in Germany, with crowds of minor, more or less clever, scheming, glib, speculating Jews. Like Jews everywhere else, they are banking or commercial agents, literary people, political people, correspondents for newspapers of all shades – in a word, brokers both of literature and of finance, with one foot in the bank, the other in the socialist movement and their behinds firmly planted in the German daily press – they have got control of all the newspapers – and you can imagine what nauseating literature that produces!

Now, this whole Jewish world, which constitutes an exploiting sect, a leech-like people, a single voracious parasite that remains close-knit and intimate not only beyond national boundaries but also beyond differences of political opinion – this Jewish world is for the most part today at the disposal of Marx on the one hand and Rothschild on the other. I am sure that the Rothschilds, on the one side, set great store by the merits of Marx, and that, on the other side, Marx feels an instinctive attraction to, and great respect for, the Rothschilds.

This may seem strange: what can there be in common between communism and high finance? Well! Marx's communism aims at powerful state centralisation, and, if that happens, then these days there must inevitably be a central state bank, and, when such a bank exists, then the parasitical Jewish nation, which speculates in the labour of the people, will always find a means to exist.

However that may be, the fact remains that the greater part of this Jewish world, above all in Germany, is at Marx's disposition. It is sufficient that he mark down a person for persecution by this world, and a flood of insults, filthy invective and ridiculous, shameless slanders breaks over him in all newspapers, socialist and non-socialist, republican and monarchist. In Italy, where reciprocal tact and human respect are closely observed at least in form, it is impossible to imagine the dirty tone and truly infamous style of day-to-day polemic in the German press. Jewish men of letters are peculiarly outstanding in the art of cowardly, hateful and perfidious insinuation. They rarely accuse openly, but they insinuate 'they have heard it said – it is claimed – it may not be true, but still . . .' and then they sling the most absurd calumnies in your face.

I know something of this from personal experience. Marx and I have known each other a long time.

SOURCE: trs. by the editor from M. Bakunin, 'Persönliche Beziehungen zu Marx', *Gesammelte Werke*, vol. III (Berlin, 1924) pp. 205 ff.

.

30 Edward Aveling

In the following reminiscence, written in 1897, Aveling, the future common-law husband of Marx's daughter Eleanor, describes his only meeting with her father.

A good many years ago now, when I was quite a young man, I gave a lecture on 'Insects and Flowers' at the Orphan Working School, Haverstock Hill, London. It was a fête-day at the school, and besides the children and their teachers a number of those interested in the school were present. As I was a young man of only one or two and twenty, I do not doubt that the lecture was a very bumptious, self-sufficient performance. After it was over a number of the visitors were introduced to me. I only remember three of them. One of the three was a not very tall, but very powerfully built, man, with a tremendous leonine head, and the strongest and yet gentlest eyes I think I ever saw. The second was a lady of singular refinement and high-breeding. The third was a young girl. The man was Karl Marx. The woman was his wife, Jenny von Westphalen. The young girl is now my wife. I remember with what kindness and generosity Marx spoke to me. He spoke in very high terms, terms far too high, of the lecture, and prophesied all sorts of good things in the way of future work. It was really as if I were the teacher and he the learner. I fear that at that time I did not nearly properly estimate the inestimable value of such a criticism from such a man.

SOURCE: E. Aveling, 'Charles Darwin and Karl Marx. A Comparison, Part 3', *New Century Review*, Apr 1897, p. 321.

31 Wilhelm Blos (ii)

Blos was a social-democratic journalist who suffered imprisonment for his political views. The incident he refers to occurred in September 1874. Blos wrote his reminiscences some forty years later.

Liebknecht had told me on the day before my release that he would be waiting for me at the prison door. 'You will find a surprise', he said mysteriously, 'a big surprise'.

The next morning came the surprise. Joyful and excited I strode through the prison door. Outside stood Liebknecht with one of his small sons. Near him, with a beautiful young lady on his arm, stood a tall slim man in his fifties with a long white beard, only his moustache remaining deep black. His complexion was rosy and he could have been taken for a jovial old Englishman. But I recognised him immediately from his picture: it was Karl Marx. The young lady was his daughter Eleanor, who was also known as Tussy.

This man, who was so mysterious in the eyes of the bourgeois philistines and whom the police regarded as the incarnation of international revolution, approached me with engaging friendliness. There was by then a well-developed Marx legend and the alarmists among the upper ten thousand saw in him a man who undermined every social order and crept into its innermost recesses. They knew nothing of his true greatness. . . .

Marx has been described by many contemporaries as a grim, arrogant man whose manner was spiteful and bilious. It is possible that, having to endure so many unbelievable insults, he dealt bluntly with many a stupid individual who believed he could treat him with disrespect. But we were charmed by his extraordinary kindness.

SOURCE: trs. by the editor from W. Blos, *Denkwürdigkeiten eines Sozial demokraten* (Munich, 1914) vol. I, pp. 159 ff.

32 Friedrich Sorge

Sorge emigrated to the United States from Germany, where he had taken part in the 1848–9 Revolution. He became active in the International, was a delegate to the Hague Congress in 1872 and General Secretary of the International when it moved to New York. These reminiscences were published in 1902.

Marx has been accused of ambition and reproached with heartless, inhumane conduct. What injustice!

He never showed ambition or sought to dominate, and it was only thanks to his superior knowledge, his vast erudition, his all-round learning and his imposing character that he won the influence that he had, especially in the old General Council of the International in London, about four-fifths of which were Englishmen or Frenchmen, only two or three members being Germans in the most important period. . . .

In personal associations Marx was a friendly, pleasant, likable man, as all will agree who had the happiness of any close relations with this extraordinary man.

But he was relentless towards hypocrites, and ignorant or pretentious people, and it was these who blackened Marx's character and invested and spread the legend of his ambition, etc.

Anybody with Marx's experience of the hardships of life was always ready to help and did help when he could. Countless cases could be quoted. Let one suffice. When the Congress of the North-American Federation of the International Working Men's Association closed its session in July 1872 and elected delegates to the Hague Congress, a worker went up to one of those delegates and gave him a sum of money for Marx. He was a Rhineland worker, a strict follower of Lassalle, who had been obliged to leave his family and home in 1864 or 1865, had arrived in London penniless and asked Marx for help to continue his journey to America. Marx had helped him, although he was in by no means a good situation at the time.

When the emigrants of the Commune arrived in London Marx and his family made extraordinary efforts to help and support them. And besides the emigrants who came and went, one could often meet in his house workers from the provinces, from Manchester and Liverpool, from the continent, from America and other distant parts.

SOURCE: *RME*, pp. 199 f.; from the German original in F. Sorge, 'Zum 14. März', *Die Neue Zeit*, XXI, pt 1 (1902–3) 719 ff.

33 Dimitri Richter

Richter was a Russian émigré journalist who worked in the mid 1870s for the newspaper *Vpered!* ('Forward!') in Leipzig. He recounts below a visit he paid Marx in 1875 seeking a letter of introduction to contacts in Stockholm.

Marx lived in the north of London, not far from the editorial offices of *Vpered!* The door was opened by Eleanor, a remarkably pretty girl. She greeted Peter Lavrovitch in a very friendly manner and said that Papa was at home and would certainly be pleased to see us.

Marx was indeed at home and sitting, as usual, in his study. This was a large room with three or four windows looking onto the street. The arrangement was the simplest imaginable: bookshelves along the length of the walls; almost in the middle of the room a plain writing table that was not exactly large. Then there were a few armchairs and seats; I do not remember whether there was any sort of a divan or paintings or portraits around. Only one thing struck me: on the mantelpiece there stood a photo of Chernychevsky, in a simple frame, a copy of the well-known picture taken during his exile. Marx later told me that it was a present from a Russian friend, probably Lopatin.

Even Marx's external appearance was impressive. He was fairly stout and stocky, an elderly man (then fifty-seven years old) with light grey in the dark hair that covered his head like a hood.

He gave us a very welcoming reception and was evidently pleased to comply with the request of his Russian comrade. Although he knew no one in Stockholm and could not even say whether there was anything approaching a socialist organisation there, he gave me a letter for the leader of the Danish social democrats, a member of Parliament and a lawyer by profession who would do everything in his power.

Marx served us red wine. That seemed to be his custom, for the next time I visited him he again presented me with red wine. With Lavrov he discussed some scientific work, with me the 'young' Leipzig comrades Liebknecht (then fifty years old) and Bebel (around forty).

For my second visit I came alone. Both Marx and later Engels, who joined us during my visit was introduced to me, had highly differentiated comments on their Russian acquaintances. Towards some they were extremely tender – Lopatin, for example, and Nikolai Frantsevitch Danielson (this latter they both only knew by letter). By contrast they spoke – particularly Marx – rather condescendingly of Lavrov. They clearly admired the breadth of his knowledge but had no high opinion of his understanding. They called him an eclectic.

SOURCE: trs. by the editor from 'Zitejskie vstreĉi', *Russkie sovremmeniki o K. Markse i F. Engelse* (Moscow, 1969) pp. 57 f.

34 Julius Walther

The following is from a report in the gossip columns of a Viennese newspaper. Julius Walther is probably the pseudonym of Ferdinand Fleckles, a doctor whose acquaintance Marx made while in Karlsbad.

Right now, just before the close of the season, another very interesting guest has come to the spa – Karl Marx is staying in Karlsbad for a cure. . . .

Marx is now sixty-three years old. But his slim form of above average height has a youthful strength and elasticity about it. On the firm neck sits a head formed of prominent features – a finely rising forehead, white locks which flow in thick and often overflowing waves down onto his sturdy shoulders, his snowy beard surges far down and under his thick black bushy eyebrows a pair of highly glowing eyes sparkle out. Marx himself is as interesting and arresting as his appearance. He is a man of exceptional learning, which is as deep as it is broad, and he is well versed in all branches of knowledge. You feel immediately that he is one of those who has something to say and says it with well measured breath and only has recourse to heavy blows when opposing opinions that he thinks are wrong; in his sarcastic dismissal of personalities he uses a soft voice to cover the sharp point of his caustic wit, with an effect that is all the harsher. But when he is expounding his own views and giving an account of his teaching, he does not act the professor and scorns both a lecturing tone and an appeal to pathos. It speaks lightly and agreeably and yet always with a cultivated refinement: he always has to hand the *mot juste*, the striking simile, the suddenly illuminating joke. If you share his society accompanied by a woman of evident wit – women and children are the best *agents provocateurs* in conversation and, because they appreciate the general only in relationship to the personal, constantly summon one into the cosy arbour of personal encounters – then Marx will bestow on you with full hands the rich and well-ordered treasure of his memories. He then prefers to direct his steps back into past days when romanticism was singing its last free woodland song, when he sat, a black-locked enthusiastic young fellow, at the feet of A. W. Schlegel, when he was in contact with the child Bettina – who was of course already a grandmother then – and Heine brought poems into his study with the ink still wet. Marx is a riveting *raconteur*, he has mastered the art of story-telling like few others, he is a brilliant conversationalist, a dazzling dialectician, who is also capable of adopting a warm and feeling tone. He can excite, teach and captivate, but his meditative nature, his speculative, critical mind, his delight in artistic matters, his essential neatness do not seem conducive to converting the heavy bullion of his knowledge into the common currency of the crowd, to stirring up the masses and inspiring them to action and fanning the secretly glimmering fire of the crowd into a full and lofty blaze. He is indubitably more a philosopher than a man of action and has in him more of the historian or perhaps strategist of a movement than of the experienced fighter.

SOURCE: trs. by the editor from J. Walther, 'Carl Marx', *Sprudel*, 19 Sep 1875; repr. in E. Kisch, *Karl Marx in Karlsbad* (Berlin, 1968) pp. 63 ff.

35 Maxim Kovalevsky

Kovalevsky was a well-to-do Russian intellectual of liberal reformist opinions. As a historian and sociologist he subsequently produced works of note on primitive systems of land tenure. In his late twenties he got to know Marx in London and Karlsbad from 1875 to 1878. The two sets of reminiscences below were written in 1895 and 1909 respectively.

1

The first impression that I got from my acquaintance with Marx was extremely uncomfortable. He received me in his famous drawing-room, which was adorned by a bust of Zeus. His closely knit brows and – as it seemed to me on my first visit – his harsh glare led me, despite myself, to compare him with the bust, above all in view of his projecting forehead and the curly exuberance of already greying hair that fell behind. On this occasion Marx explained to me that, with few exceptions, all Russians living abroad were agents of Pan-Slavism, and that Herzen too was one of them; that was why he avoided contact with him. Bakunin, whom he (it could well be said) had first introduced to socialist agitation, had paid him back with the blackest ingratitude in that he had founded his so-called Alliance in order to bring down the International. I left feeling scalded – with the firm resolve never to see Marx again. But I soon met him again in Karlsbad. No doubt through lack of other society he attached himself to me. We went for our morning and evening walks together and sabotaged the diet with many bottles of Rüdesheimer, to which he was particularly partial. Far from his usual entourage, this great man became a simple merry interlocutor, inexhaustible in story-telling, full of humour and always ready to laugh at himself.

On my return to England, I got to know another side of Marx which surprised me: namely, as an affectionate father who joked with his daughters and grandchildren, and as a loyal friend – a loyalty that showed itself in his truly brotherly attachment to Engels. . . .

Never during his life was Marx blessed with an abundance of worldly possessions, and not infrequently he was short of money, but Jenny treated these adversities of fortune with a cheerful philosophic imperturbability and was only concerned that her 'dear Karl' should not waste too much time in worrying about their living.

During my acquaintance with Marx he and his family lived a completely retired life. It was rare to find a real Englishman in his house, with the exception of Hyndman, the leader of the English socialists. The orthodox economists did not then think it necessary even to take note of Marx's existence. He told me of the following occurrence. Lewis, author of a book on the history of commerce, gave a public lecture on the harmony of economic interests. After the lecture the audience could enter into the discussion. Hyndman stood up and declared that among the economists who had taken up one position or another on the harmony and non-harmony of interests, the lecturer had not mentioned Marx. 'I don't know him', came the reply.

I was all the more surprised at this attitude of the English economists, since Wagner and Engel in Berlin did at least often mention Marx, sometimes agreeing with and sometimes attacking him.

When Spencer had the first volume of *Capital* sent to him by its author, he thought it necessary to tell his acquaintances that ignorance of the German language prevented him from reading the book. Darwin's attitude was different. He wrote a detailed letter which Marx preserved in his papers as a precious document.[1]

2

I owed my acquaintance with Marx to a man who saved the life of his son-in-law Longuet, a member of the Paris Commune. I got a recommendation from one of the two authors of a diary kept all through the insurrection and entitled *The Revolution of 18 March*.[2] In spite of such an introduction, Marx at first displayed great mistrust towards me, so strongly prejudiced against Russians was he since the time of the treachery (as he expressed it) of Bakunin. Our first talks were mainly about Bakunin, whom Marx himself had introduced into international emigrant circles in London and who intended to translate the first book of *Capital* into Russian. We know that it was later Nikolai-on[3] who did this work with the help of Hermann Lopatin.

I was at Marx's only a few times in the first winter. He lived not far from Regent's Park – to be more exact, the continuation of it called Maitland Park – in a crescent. I can still remember the number of his house – 41. Marx occupied the whole of the house. On the ground-floor was his library and drawing-room where he usually received his guests. His two eldest daughters were already married, one to a member of the Paris Commune, Longuet, the other to Paul Lafargue, now a well-known writer. Eleanor, the youngest, known in the family as Tussy, was then very keen on the theatre, especially on Irving's acting of Shakespeare and at one time she even considered going on the stage.

It was especially at the waters at Karlsbad that I got to know Marx closely. We went for walks in the mountains together almost every day and we became so intimate that in his letters at that time, which have recently been published in the journal *Byloye* ('The Past'), Marx counted me among his 'scientific friends'.

Marx was then working on the second book of his work, a large portion of which he intended to devote to the accumulation of capital in two relatively new countries, America and Russia. For this purpose he was receiving numerous books from New York and Moscow. Marx could be considered a polyglot. He not only fluently spoke German, English and French but could also read Russian, Italian, Spanish and Rumanian. He read an extraordinary lot and often borrowed books from me, including a two-volume treatise on the history of land-ownership in Spain and Morgan's well-known work *Ancient Society*, which I brought back from my first journey to America. It provided material for Engels's sensational work *The Origin of the Family*.

To know Marx meant also to be invited to Engels's on Sunday evenings. Engels had inherited considerable property in Manchester, where he owned a factory, and he liked to have in his house the members of Marx's family and also outside visitors, preferably German.

Marx himself was discriminate in his associations. Many European writers of note, including Laveleye, vainly expressed the desire to be introduced to him. He kept aloof from them and complained of the indiscretion of newspaper and journal reporters if they were ideologically opposed to him.

He had good, though distant relations at the time with some members of an English positivist society, particularly Professor Beesley who at that time helped to run the democratic paper *Beehive*. I also met the famous English socialist Hyndman at Marx's several times.[4] He was then a supporter of the Tories and greatly sympathised with Disraeli. . . .

Marx worked a long time in the British Museum and this to a certain extent undermined his health. He got used to reading official reports like the English Blue Books and therefore he willingly received official publications from Russia on railways, credit operations, etc. Nikolai-on and I sent him what we could, and his wife, who was anxious that he should finish his work as soon as possible, jokingly threatened not to give me any more mutton chops if I prevented him from completing it by sending him material. Marx rewrote the second and third books of *Capital* several times. He intended to crown the work with a 'critical history of economic doctrines'[5] but that intention was never fulfilled.

Marx's weekdays were taken up with work. He reserved relatively few hours for his correspondence for the New York *Tribune*. The rest of the time he worked at home, revising and correcting the parts of his work that he had already written.

His library, which was in a room with three windows, was composed exclusively of books for his work. They frequently lay in disorder on his desk or armchairs. I sometimes found him at work when I arrived. He was so engrossed that he was not able at once to engage in conversation on a subject other than the one immediately interesting him.

On Sundays he liked to go to a park with his family, but even during his walks the conversation was often on subjects far removed from actuality.

This does not mean, however, that he was not keen on politics. He would sit for hours reading newspapers, and not only the English ones, but papers from all over the world. I once found him reading *Romanûl* (Rumanian) and was able to convince myself that he managed very well with Rumanian, a language few people know.

During all the time of my association with him he only once left London for a few weeks in Karlsbad. He was allowed to pass through Germany only on condition that he would not be there any longer than required for transit. He had been forbidden to enter Paris since Guizot came to power. Thiers and MacMahon would hardly have been willing to allow him into France after publication of his *Civil*

War in France, which was an attempt to defend the Commune that had just been drowned in blood by the Versailles Government. What was most astounding in Marx was the way in which he took up passionate positions on all political questions. This was difficult to reconcile with the calm objective method which he recommended to his followers and which should investigate the economic prerequisites of all phenomena.

If we take a question such as that of Polish independence, we should not be surprised to find in Marx its energetic advocate who leaves completely unnoticed the customary account according to which the Polish question is simultaneously a question which gives support to the social feud between the Pans and the Schljachta on one side and the alien plebs on the other.

In spite of the enthusiasm that Russian youth manifested for his work and in spite of the fact that nowhere, with the exception of Germany, has he enjoyed such success as in our midst, his attitude to Russia was not essentially different from the anti-Russian prejudice of the revolutionaries of 1848, who saw in Russia only a bulwark of every type of reaction, a stranger to all democratic and liberal revolts. Marx himself was not averse to admitting that the recognition he had found among my fellow-countrymen had to a certain extent amazed him. . . .

From the letters of Nikolai-on and Kaufmann's and Sieber's articles Marx could see that the young economists in Russia were enthusiastic over his views and were ready to follow him in his criticism of the prevailing economic doctrines. This comforting impression of Russia was to be intensified by contrast with the way in which English economists systematically ignored his works up to the very last. Hyndman informed Marx of the following fact in my presence. After a popular lecture by Levi, a well-known English economist, on the 'harmony of interests' a talk was arranged at which Hyndman expressed doubts about agreement, harmony, between the interests of all classes of society. He backed his scepticism with references to Marx's *Capital*. 'I know of no such work', Levi retorted. . . . *Capital* was translated into English only after the death of its author and penetrated little into English economic circles. . . .

In the years during which I attended the Sunday evenings at Marx's in Maitland Park or met Marx at Engels's, the author of *Capital* devoted himself entirely to scientific work, to which he attributed extensive tasks. He was often obliged to devote weeks and months to the reading of works on the history of economics, especially of land-ownership, which had but an indirect bearing on his main theme. He also resumed his studies in mathematics, including differential and integral calculus, in order to be better informed of the mathematical trend in political economy of the time.

The head of the movement in Marx's time was Jevons, now it is Edgeworth.

Marx was surprisingly well versed in literature on economics, especially in English. But his was nothing like the *Belesenheit* for which German professors were so 'distinguished', especially Roscher, Marx's *bête noire*. The author of *Capital* often made remarks in his work like the following: 'Herr Roscher was eager to support the quoted banality with his authority.' Marx knew how to find in his remote predecessors vital principles admitting of further development. If of late economists have shown an interest in *Political Arithmetic* and other works by William Petty, a contemporary of King Charles II, if we have not only had a new collection of his works but also a number of memoirs on him, and in nearly all languages of the civilised world at that, it is to a certain extent to Marx that we owe it.

People habitually imagine Marx as a grim and proud negator of bourgeois science and culture. But in reality Marx was a most highly cultivated Anglo-German gentleman who from his association with Heine derived a mirth resulting from a capacity for witty satire. He was full of the joy of life because his personal affairs were as good as they possibly could be. Marx, more than anybody else I have ever met, not excluding Turgenev, had the right to say of himself that he was a man of one love.

Few people could entertain so cheerfully as Jenny Marx in such modest circumstances or combine a simple life with the manners and outward appearance of what the French call *une grande dame*. Even when his beard was grey Marx loved to bring in the new year dancing with his wife or with Engels's friend.[6] I myself once saw him smartly leading his ladies in step to a solemn march. . . .

Another family dinner at the Marxes' occurs to me. They were entertaining Karl's sister who had come from the Cape Colony with her two sons. She could not countenance her brother being the leader of the socialists and insisted in my presence that they both belonged to the respected family of a lawyer who had the sympathy of everybody in Trier. Marx took it joking and burst into youth-like laughter. . . .

Also at variance with his supposed arrogance, was Marx's unwillingness to come to lunch of his own accord: not infrequently he stipulated that his much too garrulous son-in-law should not be invited at the same time.

Marx liked to go to the theatre with his friends to see Salvini playing Hamlet, or again Irving, whom he appreciated incomparably more. I also remember how in the Egyptian Hall Marx and I enjoyed the exact reproduction of all the tricks of the spiritists by a man who said he had been in their society and was repeating all he had learned. But he was not so naive as to say how he did them, for

MAXIM KOVALEVSKY 131

then people would not have come to see his performances any more. Marx shared his affection between the families of his two married daughters and his old friend Engels, from whom he got ample return, and devoted all his spare time to them. The whole day he was engaged in serious absorbing scientific work but he still found time to show a keen interest in every question that had anything to do with the working-class party generally and German social democracy in particular. The German leader he most esteemed was Bebel, and after him Liebknecht. He frequently complained that the latter had been spoiled by Lassalle, adding with angry humour that it was hard to put a new thought into the head of a German *Privatdozent* (which was the way Marx qualified Liebknecht).

The following fact will show the passionate attitude which Marx adopted, even when he was advanced in years, towards any attempt to check the advance of the working-class party. I happened to be in Marx's library when he got news of Nobiling's unsuccessful attempt on the life of the aged Kaiser Wilhelm. Marx's reaction was to curse the terrorist, explaining that only one thing could be expected from his attempt to accelerate the course of events, namely, new persecutions of the socialists. His prophecy was unfortunately not long in coming true: Bismarck published laws which considerably delayed the successful development of German social democracy.[7]

I cannot remember anything during the two years of my fairly close association with the author of *Capital* that in any way approximated the treatment an older man gives to a younger one, which was the impression I got of Chicherin and Lev Tolstoi in my casual meetings with them. Karl Marx was very much a European and although he had perhaps not a very high opinion of his 'scientific friends' and preferred his friends in the class struggle of the proletariat, he did not manifest that bias in his conduct. For twenty-five years I have kept a grateful memory of him as of a dear teacher, my association with whom largely determined the direction of my scientific work. Close to this idea is another one: I was fortunate to meet in him one of the intellectual and moral leaders of mankind who are entitled to be called great because they are the truest mouthpieces of the progressive tendencies of their time.

SOURCE: editor's translations and *RME*, pp. 292 ff.; from M. Kovalevsky, 'Moe naučnoe i literaturnoe skital'čestvo', *Russkie sovremenniki o K. Markse i F. Engelse* (Moscow, 1969) pp. 59 ff., and, *Vestnik Evropy*, July 1909, pp. 5 ff.

NOTES

1. In fact, Darwin wrote a short and highly non-committal reply –

understandably, since the pages of his complimentary copy of *Capital* remained uncut.

2. Paul Curier, co-author of *Histoire de la Revolution du 18 Mars* (Paris, 1871).
3. The pseudonym of the Russian populist economist N. F. Danielson.
4. On Hyndman and his views, see below, no. 38.
5. This is the *Theories of Surplus Value*, edited and published subsequently by Kautsky.
6. Lizzie Burns.
7. The anti-socialist laws which were brought in in 1878.

36 Interview with the Chicago *Tribune*

The following interview, which seems to have been put together from several meetings in early December 1878, was published in the Chicago *Tribune* on 5 January 1879. The *Tribune* tended to support the Republicans and had a wide circulation. Interest in socialism was growing in the United States at this time, owing both to the prolonged American economic crisis of the 1870s and to the anti-socialist laws in Germany which Bismarck had got the *Reichstag* to pass in 1878.

London, 18 December. – In a little villa at Haverstock Hill, in the northwest portion of London, lives Karl Marx, the corner-stone of modern socialism. He was exiled from his native country – Germany – in 1844, for propagating revolutionary theories. In 1848 he returned, but in a few months was again exiled. He then took up his abode in Paris, but his political theories procured his expulsion from that city in 1849, and since that year his headquarters have been in London. His convictions have caused him trouble from the beginning. Judging from the appearance of his home, they certainly have not brought him affluence. Persistently during all these years he has advocated his views with an earnestness which undoubtedly springs from a firm belief in them, and, however much we may deprecate their propagation, we cannot but respect to a certain extent the self-denial of the now venerated exile.

Your correspondent has called upon him twice or thrice, and each time the Doctor was found in his library, with a book in one hand and a cigarette in the other. He must be over seventy years of age.[1] His physique is well-knit, massive, and erect. He has the head of a man of intellect, and the features of a cultivated Jew. His hair and beard are long, and iron-gray in color. His eyes are glittering black, shaded by a pair of bushy eyebrows. To a stranger he shows extreme caution. A foreigner can generally gain admission: but the ancient-looking German woman[2] who waits upon visitors has instructions to admit none who hail from the Fatherland, unless they bring letters of introduction. Once into his library, however, and, having fixed his one eye-glass in the corner of his eye, in order to take your intellectual breadth and depth, so to speak, he loses that self-restraint, and unfolds to you a knowledge of men and things throughout the world apt to interest one. And his conversation does not run in one groove, but is as varied as are the volumes upon his library shelves. A man can generally be judged by the books he reads, and you can form your own conclusions when I tell you a casual glance revealed Shakespeare, Dickens, Thackeray, Molière, Racine, Montaigne, Bacon, Goethe, Voltaire, Paine; English, American, French Blue Books; works political and philosophical in Russian, German, Spanish, Italian, etc., etc. During my conversations I was struck with his intimacy with American questions, which have been uppermost during the past twenty years. His knowledge of them, and the surprising accuracy with which he criticised our national and state legislation, impressed upon my mind the fact that he must have derived his information from inside sources. But, indeed, this knowledge is not confined to America, but is spread over the face of Europe. When speaking of his hobby – socialism – he does not indulge in those melodramatic flights generally attributed to him, but dwells upon his utopian plans for 'the emancipation of the human race' with a firm conviction in the realisation of his theories, if not in this century, at least in the next.

Perhaps Dr Karl Marx is better known in America as the author of *Capital*, and the founder of the International Association, or at least its most prominent pillar. In the interview which follows, you will see what he says of this association as it at the present time exists.

During my visit to Dr Marx I alluded to the platform given by C. Bancroft Davis in his official report of 1877,[3] as the clearest and most concise exposition of socialism that I had seen. He said it was taken from the report of the socialist reunion at Gotha, Germany, in May 1875.[4] The translation was incorrect, he said, and he volunteered a correction, which I append as he dictated:

First – Universal, direct, and secret suffrage for all males over twenty years, for all elections, municipal and state.

Second – Direct legislation by the people. War and peace to be made by direct popular vote.

Third – Universal obligation to militia duty. No standing army.

Fourth – Abolition of all special legislation regarding press laws and public meetings.

Fifth – Legal remedies free of expense. Legal proceedings to be conducted by the people.

Sixth – Education to be by the state, – general, obligatory, and free. Freedom of science and religion.

Seventh – All indirect taxes to be abolished. Money to be raised for state and municipal purposes by direct progressive income tax.

Eighth – Freedom of combination among the working classes.

Ninth – The legal day of labour for men to be defined. The work of women to be limited, and that of children to be abolished.

Tenth – Sanitary laws for the protection of life and health of labourers, and regulation of their dwellings and places of labour, to be enforced by persons selected by them.

Eleventh – Suitable provision respecting prison labour.

In Mr Bancroft Davis's report there is a *Twelfth Clause*, the most important of all, which reads, 'State aid and credit for industrial societies, under democratic direction.' I asked the Doctor why he omitted this, and he replied, 'When the reunion took place at Gotha, in 1875, there existed a division among the social democrats. The one wing were partisans of Lassalle; the others, those who had accepted in general the programme of the International organisations, and were called the Eisenach party. That twelfth point was not placed on the platform but placed in the general introduction by way of concession to the Lassallians. Afterwards it was never spoken of. Mr Davis does not say that it was placed in the programme as a compromise having no particular significance, but gravely puts it in as one of the cardinal principles of the programme.'

'But', I said, 'socialists generally look upon the transformation of the means of labour into the common property of society as the grand climax of the movement.'

'Yes; we say that this will be the outcome of the movement, but it will be a question of time, of education, and the institution of a higher social status.'

'This platform', I remarked, 'applies only to Germany and one or two other countries.'

'Ah!' he returned, 'if you draw your conclusions from nothing but this, you know nothing of the activity of the party. Many of its points have no significance outside of Germany. Spain, Russia, England, and America have platforms suited to their peculiar difficulties. The only similarity in them is the end to be attained.'

'And that is the supremacy of labour?'

'That is the emancipation of labour.'

'Do European socialists look upon the movement in America as a serious one?'

'Yes; it is the natural outcome of the country's development. It has been said that the movement has been imported by foreigners.

When labour movements became disagreeable in England, fifty years ago, the same thing was said; and that was long before socialism was spoken of. In America, since 1857 only, has the labour movement become conspicuous. Then trades unions began to flourish; then trades assemblies were formed, in which the workers in different industries united; and after that came national labour unions. If you consider this chronological progress, you will see that socialism has sprung up in that country without the aid of foreigners, and was merely caused by the concentration of capital and the changed relations between the workmen and their employers.'

'Now,' asked your correspondent, 'what has socialism done so far?'

'Two things', he returned. 'Socialists have shown the general universal struggle between capital and labour, – the cosmopolitan character, in one word, – and consequently tried to bring about an understanding between the workmen in the different countries, which became more necessary as the capitalists became more cosmopolitan in hiring labour, pitting foreign against native labour not only in America, but in England, France and Germany. International relations sprang up at once between the working men in the different countries, showing that socialism was not merely a local, but an international problem, to be solved by the international action of workmen. The working class moved spontaneously, without knowing what the ends of the movement will be. The socialists invent no movement, but merely tell the workmen what its character and its ends will be.'

'Which means the overthrowing of the present social system, I understand.'

'This system of land and capital in the hands of employers, on the one hand,' he continued, 'and the mere working power in the hands of the labourers to sell as a commodity, we claim is merely an historical phase, which will pass away and give place to a higher social condition. We see everywhere a division of society. The antagonism of the two classes goes hand in hand with the development of the industrial resources of modern countries. From a socialistic standpoint the means already exist to revolutionise the present historical phase. Upon trades unions, in many countries, have been built political organisations. In America the need of an independent working men's party has been made manifest. They can no longer trust politicians. Rings and cliques have seized upon the legislature, and politics has been made a trade. But America is not alone in this, only its people are more decisive than Europeans. Things come to the surface quicker. There is less cant and hypocrisy than there is on this side of the ocean.'

I asked him to give me a reason for the rapid growth of the socialist party in Germany, when he replied, 'The present socialistic party came last. Theirs was not the utopian scheme which made some headway in France and England. The German mind is given to theorising, more than that of other peoples. From previous experience the Germans evolved something practical. This modern capitalistic system, you must recollect, is quite new in Germany in comparison to other states. Questions were raised which had become almost antiquated in France and England, and political influences to which these states had yielded sprang into life when the working classes of Germany had become imbued with socialistic theories. Therefore, from the beginning almost of modern industrial development, they have formed an independent political party. They had their own representatives in the German Parliament. There was no party to oppose the policy of the Government, and this devolved upon them. To trace the course of the party would take a long time; but I may say this: that, if the middle classes of Germany were not the greatest cowards, distinct from the middle classes of America and England, all the political work against the Government should have been done by them.'

I asked him a question regarding the numerical strength of the Lassallians in the ranks of the Internationalists.

'The party of Lassalle', he replied, 'does not exist. Of course there are some believers in our ranks, but the number is small. Lassalle anticipated our general principles. When he commenced to move after the reaction of 1848, he fancied that he could more successfully revive the movement by advocating co-operation of the working men in industrial enterprises. It was to stir them into activity. He looked upon this merely as a means to the real end of the movement. I have letters from him to this effect.'

'You would call it his nostrum.'

'Exactly. He called upon Bismarck, told him what he designed, and Bismarck encouraged Lassalle's course at that time in every possible way.'

'What was his object?'

'He wished to use the working classes as a set-off against the middle classes who instigated the troubles of 1848.'

'It is said that you are the head and front of socialism, Doctor, and from your villa here pull the wires of all the associations, revolutions, etc., now going on. What do you say about it?'

The old gentleman smiled: 'I know it. It is very absurd, yet it has a comic side. For two months previous to the attempt of Hoedet, Bismarck complained in his *North German Gazette* that I was in league with Father Beck, the leader of the Jesuit movement, and that we were keeping the socialist movement in such a condition that he could do nothing with it.'

'But your International Association in London directs the movement!'

'The International Association has outlived its usefulness and exists no longer.[5] It did exist and direct the movement; but the growth of socialism of late years has been so great that its existence has become unnecessary. Newspapers have been started in the various countries. These are interchanged. That is about the only connection the parties in the different countries have with one another. The International Association, in the first instance, was created to bring the workmen together, and show the advisability of effecting organisation among their various nationalities. The interests of each party in the different countries have no similarity. The spectre of the Internationalist leaders sitting at London is a mere invention. It is true that we dictated to foreign societies when the Internationalist organisation was first accomplished. We were forced to exclude some sections in New York, among them one in which Madam Woodhull was conspicuous.[6] That was in 1871. There are several American politicans – I will not name them – who wish to trade in the movement. They are well known to American socialists.'

'You and your followers, Dr Marx, have been credited with all sorts of incendiary speeches against religion. Of course you would like to see the whole system destroyed, root and branch.'

'We know', he replied after a moment's hesitation, 'that violent measures against religion are nonsense; but this is an opinion: as socialism grows, religion will disappear. Its disappearance must be done by social development, in which education must play a great part.'

'The Rev. Joseph Cook, of Boston, – you know him –'

'We heard of him; a very badly informed man upon the subject of socialism.'

'In a lecture lately upon the subject, he said, "Karl Marx is credited now with saying that, in the United States, and in Great Britain, and perhaps in France, a reform of labour will occur without bloody revolution, but that blood must be shed in Germany, and in Russia, and in Italy, and in Austria." '

'No socialist', remarked the Doctor, smiling, 'need predict that there will be a bloody revolution in Russia, Germany, Austria, and possibly in Italy if the Italians keep on in the policy they are now pursuing.[7] The deeds of the French Revolution may be enacted again in those countries. That is apparent to any political student. But those revolutions will be made by the majority. No revolution can be made by a party, but by a nation.'

'The reverend gentleman alluded to', I remarked, 'gave an extract from a letter which he said you addressed to the communists of Paris in 1871. Here it is: "We are as yet but 3 million at most. In twenty years we shall be 50 million – 100 million perhaps. Then the world will belong to us, for it will be not only Paris, Lyons, Marseilles, which will rise against odious capital, but Berlin, Munich, Dresden, London, Liverpool, Manchester, Brussels, St Petersburg, New York, – in short, the whole world. And before this new insurrection, such as history has not yet known, the past will disappear like a hideous nightmare; for the popular conflagration, kindled at a hundred points at once, will destroy even its memory!" Now, Doctor, I suppose you admit the authorship of the extract?'

'I never wrote a word of it. I never write such melodramatic nonsense. I am very careful what I do write. That was put in *Le Figaro*, over my signature, about that time. There were hundreds of the same kind of letters flying about then. I wrote to the London *Times* and declared they were forgeries; but, if I denied everything that has been said and written of me, I would require a score of secretaries.'

'But you have written in sympathy with the Paris communists?'

'Certainly I have, in consideration of what was written of them in leading articles; but the correspondence from Paris in English papers is quite sufficient to refute the blunders propagated in editorials. The Commune killed only about sixty people; Marshal MacMahon and his slaughtering army killed over 60,000.[8] There has never been a movement so slandered as that of the Commune.'

'Well, then, to carry out the principles of socialism do its believers advocate assassination and bloodshed?'

'No great movement', Karl Marx answered, 'has ever been inaugurated without bloodshed. The independence of America was won by bloodshed. Napoleon captured France through a bloody process, and he was overthrown by the same means. Italy, England, Germany, and every other country gives proof of this, and as for assassination', he went on to say, 'it is not a new thing, I need scarcely say. Orsini tried to kill Napoleon; kings have killed more than anybody else; the Jesuits have killed; the Puritans killed at the time of Cromwell. These deeds were all done or attempted before socialism was known. Every attempt, however, now made upon a royal or state individual is attributed to socialism. The socialist would regret very much the death of the German Emperor at the present time. He is very useful where he is; and Bismarck has done more for the cause than any other statesman, by driving things to extremes.'

I asked Dr Marx what he thought of Bismarck.

He replied that 'Napoleon was considered a genius until he fell; then he was called a fool. Bismarck will follow in his wake. He began by building up a despotism under the plea of unification. His course has been plain to all. The last move is but an attempted imitation of a *coup d'état*; but it will fail. The socialists of Germany, as of France, protested against the war of 1870 as merely dynastic. They issued manifestos telling the German people that, if they allowed the pretended war of defence to be turned into a war of conquest, they would be punished by the establishment of military despotism and the ruthless oppression of the productive masses. The Social Democratic Party in Germany, thereupon holding meetings and publishing manifestos for an honourable peace with France, were at once prosecuted by the Prussian Government, and many of the leaders imprisoned. Still their deputies alone dared to protest, and very vigorously too, in the German *Reichstag*, against the forcible annexation of French provinces. However, Bismarck carried his policy by force, and people spoke of the genius of a Bismarck. The war was fought, and, when he could make no more conquests, he was called upon for original ideas, and he has signally failed. The people began to lose faith in him. His popularity was on the wane. He needs money, and the state needs it. Under a sham constitution he has taxed the people for his military and unification plans until he can tax them no longer, and now he seeks to do it with no constitution at all. For the purpose of levying as he chooses, he has raised the ghost of socialism, and has done everything in his power to create an *émeute*.'[9]

'You have continual advices from Berlin?'

'Yes', he said; 'my friends keep me well advised. It is in a perfectly quiet state, and Bismarck is disappointed. He has expelled forty-eight prominent men, – among them Deputies Hasselman and Fritsche, and Rakow, Bauman, and Auer, of the *Freie Presse*.[10] These men kept the workmen of Berlin quiet. Bismarck knew this. He also knew that there were 75,000 workmen in that city upon the verge of starvation. Once those leaders were gone, he was confident that the mob would rise, and that would be the cue for a carnival of slaughter. The screws would then be put upon the whole German Empire; his pet theory of blood and iron would then have full sway, and taxation could be levied to any extent. So far no *émeute* has occurred, and he stands to-day confounded at the situation and the ridicule of all statesmen.'

NOTES

1. Marx was sixty at the time.
2. Helene Demuth.
3. This refers to the official report of Bancroft Davis, US ambassador to Germany, to Hamilton Fish, Secretary of State under President Grant. The report included extensive reference to socialism in Germany and was published in 1877.
4. The Congress at Gotha in May 1875 united the followers of Lassalle

with those of Marx's disciples Liebknecht and Bebel. Marx's dictation here omits the demand for religion to be declared a private matter and the demand that all the workers' social funds should be managed by the workers themselves and no one else.

5. The International was formally dissolved in Philadelphia in 1876.
6. Victoria Woodhull with her sister Tennessee Claflin was the leader of Section 12 of the International in the United States. She was an advocate of women's rights, free love, proportional representation and many other radical causes. She ran for President of the United States in 1872.
7. This refers to the effort of the Italian monarchy to restore the power of the Church.
8. MacMahon commanded the government troops which put down the Paris Commune. Present-day historians estimate the number of those killed at between 20,000 and 30,000.
9. That is, 'uprising'.
10. The anti-socialist law introduced by Bismarck in October 1878 proscribed socialist organisations and publications with severe penalties for transgressors.

37 Grant Duff

Sir Mountstuart Elphinstone Grant Duff was Liberal MP for Elgin Burghs from 1857 to 1881 and Under-Secretary for India in Gladstone's first administration. The following is the major part of a letter written on 1 February 1879 to the Empress Victoria, eldest daughter of Queen Victoria and wife of the German Emperor Friedrich III. It tells of a lunch at the Devonshire Club the previous day.

Your Imperial Highness, when I last had the honour of seeing you, chanced to express some curiosity about Karl Marx and to ask me if I knew him. I resolved accordingly to take the first opportunity of making his acquaintance, but that opportunity did not arise till yesterday when I met him at luncheon and spent three hours in his company.

He is a short, rather small man with grey hair and beard which contrasts strangely with a still dark moustache. The face is somewhat round; the forehead well shaped and filled up – the eye rather hard but the whole expression rather pleasant than not, by no means that of a gentleman who is in the habit of eating babies in their cradles – which is I daresay the view which the police takes of him.

His talk was that of a well-informed, nay learned man – much interested in comparative grammar which had led him into the Old Slavonic and other out-of-the-way studies and was varied by many quaint turns and little bits of dry humour, as when speaking of Hezechiell's *Life of Prince Bismarck*, he always referred to it, by way of contrast to Dr Busch's book, as the *Old* Testament. It was all very *positif*, slightly cynical – without any appearance of enthusiasm – interesting and often, as I thought, showing very correct ideas when he was conversing of the past and the present, but vague and unsatisfactory when he turned to the future.

He looks, not unreasonably, for a great and not distant crash in Russia, thinks it will begin by reforms from above which the old bad edifice will not be able to bear and which will lead to its tumbling down altogether. As to what would take its place he had evidently no clear idea, except that for a long time Russia would be unable to exercise any influence in Europe.

Next he thinks that the movement will spread to Germany taking there the form of a revolt against the existing military system.

To my question, 'But how can you expect the army to rise against its commanders', he replied, 'You forget that in Germany now the army and the nation are nearly identical. These socialists you hear about are trained soldiers like anybody else. You must not think of the standing army only. You must think of the *Landwehr* – and even in the standing army there is much discontent. Never was an army in which the severity of the discipline led to so many suicides. The step from shooting oneself to shooting one's officer is not long and an example of the kind once set is soon followed.'

'But supposing', I said, 'the rulers of Europe came to an understanding amongst themselves for a reduction of armaments which might greatly relieve the burden on the people, what would become of the Revolution which you expect it one day to bring about?'

'Ah', was his answer, 'they can't do that. All sorts of fears and jealousies will make that impossible. The burden will grow worse and worse as science advances for the improvements in the art of destruction will keep pace with its advance and every year more and more will have to be devoted to costly engines of war. It is a vicious circle – there is no escape from it.' 'But', I said, 'you have never yet had a serious popular rising unless there was really great misery. You have no idea', he rejoined, 'how terrible has been the crisis through which Germany has been passing in these last five years.'

'Well,' I said, 'supposing that your Revolution has taken place and that you have your republican form of government – it is still a long long way to the realisation of the special ideas of yourself and your friends.' 'Doubtless,' he answered, 'but all great movements are slow. It would merely be a step to better things as your Revolution of 1688 was – a mere step on the road.'

The above will give Your Imperial Highness a fair idea of the kind of ideas about the near future of Europe which are working in his mind.

They are too dreamy to be dangerous, except just in so far as the situation with its mad expenditure on armaments is obviously and undoubtedly dangerous.

If however within the next decade the rulers of Europe have not found means of dealing with this evil without any warning from attempted revolution I for one shall despair of the future of humanity at least on this continent.

In the course of conversation Karl Marx spoke several times both of Your Imperial Highness and of the Crown Prince and invariably with due respect and propriety. Even in the case of eminent individuals of whom he by no means spoke with respect there was no trace of bitterness or savagery – plenty acrid and dissolvent criticism but nothing of the Marat tone.

Of the horrible things that have been connected with the International he spoke as any respectable man would have done.

One thing which he mentioned showed the dangers to which exiles who have got a revolutionary name are exposed. The wretched man Nobiling, he had learned, had when in England intended to come to see him. 'If he had done so,' he said, 'I should certainly have admitted him for he would have sent in his card as an *employe* of the Dresden Bureau of Statistics and as I occupy myself with statistics, it would have interested me to talk with him – What a pleasant position I should have been in', he added, 'if he *had* come to see me!!'

Altogether my impression of Marx, allowing for his being at the opposite pole of opinion from oneself was not at all unfavourable and I would gladly meet him again. It will not be he who, whether he wishes it or not, will turn the world upside down.

SOURCE: quoted from A. Rothstein, 'A Meeting with Karl Marx', *Times Literary Supplement*, 15 July 1949.

38 Henry Hyndman

Hyndman, upper-class by birth and advocating a curious blend of radical social reform and jingoistic nationalism, was the moving spirit behind the Social Democratic Federation founded in 1884. From mid 1880 to mid 1881 he paid frequent visits to Marx. Their association was broken off by Marx, who accused Hyndman of plagiarising his work.

It was natural as I drove with Karl Hirsch to make the acquaintance of Karl Marx in his modest dwelling on Haverstock Hill that my mind should go back to the visit I paid to Mazzini in the Fulham Road years before. Different and even antagonistic as the two men were in many respects, and bitter as was their struggle for control in the International, where Marx was in the long run completely successful, they were alike in that they both had given up their lives entirely to an ideal, had remained in poor circumstances when power and ease and comfort were at their disposal and had exercised a personal and intellectual effect on the youth of their generation quite unequalled, I think, by any two other men of their time. That Marx's was far the more powerful mind cannot be disputed. Writing now more than a quarter of a century after his death, it is clear to all the world not only that his analysis of the capitalist system of production stands alone, as the sole exhaustive work on the subject in existence, but that his theories in regard to the materialist basis of history are steadily supplanting in the main all other views and that his general influence is increasing every day. In fact, no economic or sociologic contributions to the science of human development can be complete at the present time without taking full account of Marx's profound investigations. Mazzini, on the other hand, who during his life enjoyed a far greater popular reputation, has ceased to produce any vivifying effect on current thought. Having known both men well I should say that while Mazzini's influence on those around him was personal and individually ethical, Marx's was almost wholly intellectual and scientific. I should not venture, however, to compare two great men of such widely different personalities and race so long after death had they not been actual rivals during life. My own view is that I approached Mazzini with admiration for his character and remained devoted to him for his elevation of thought and conduct, and that I went to Marx compelled to recognise a supreme analytic genius and eager to learn as a student.

And so I found myself with Hirsch at 41, Maitland Park Road and, ushered in by their old and trusty servant, saw Marx in the large room, on the first floor facing the gardens, which he used as his study. I wonder whether any great man fully bears out the conception you have formed of him before meeting him. I presume not. The first impression of Marx as I saw him was that of a powerful, shaggy, untamed old man, ready, not to say eager, to enter into conflict and rather suspicious himself of immediate attack. Yet his greeting to us was cordial and his first remarks to me, after I had told him what a great pleasure and honour I felt it to be to shake hands with the author of the *Capital*, were agreeable enough; for he told me he had read my articles on India with pleasure and had commented on them favourably in his newspaper correspondence. We were with him at that time for fully two hours and it did not take me long to appreciate that Marx's conversation was quite on a level with his writing.

When speaking with fierce indignation of the policy of the Liberal Party, especially in regard to Ireland, the old warrior's small deep-sunk eyes lighted up, his heavy brows wrinkled, the broad, strong nose and face were obviously moved by passion, and he poured out a stream of vigorous denunciation, which displayed alike the heat of his temperament and the marvellous command he possessed over our language. The contrast between his manner and utterance when thus deeply stirred by anger and his attitude when giving his views on the economic events of the period was very marked. He turned from the rôle of prophet and vehement denunciator to that of the calm philosopher without any apparent effort, and I felt from the first that on this latter ground many a long year might pass before I ceased to be a student in the presence of a master.

I had been surprised in reading the *Capital* and still more when perusing his smaller works, such as his pronouncement on the Commune of Paris and his *Eighteenth Brumaire*, how he combined the ablest and coolest examination of economic causes and social effects with the most bitter hatred of classes and even of individual men such as Napoleon III and M Thiers, who, according to his own theories, were little more than flies upon the wheels of the great Juggernaut car of capitalist development. Marx, of course, was a Jew, and to me it seemed that he combined in his own person and nature, with his commanding forehead and great overhanging brow, his fierce glittering eyes, broad sensitive nose and mobile mouth, all surrounded by a setting of untrimmed hair and beard, the righteous fury of the great seers of his race, with the cold analytical powers of Spinoza and the Jewish doctors. It was an extraordinary combination of qualities, the like of which I have known in no other man.

As I went out with Hirsch deeply impressed by the great personality we had left, Hirsch asked me what I thought of him. 'Well,' I replied, 'I think he is the Aristotle of the nineteenth century.' And yet as I said it I knew that this did not cover the ground. For one thing it was quite impossible to think of Marx as acting the courtier to Alexander while carrying on the profound studies which have so deeply influenced later generations, and besides he never so wholly segregated himself from immediate human interests – notwithstanding much that has been said to the contrary – as to be able to consider facts and their surroundings in the cold hard light of the greatest philosopher of antiquity. There can be no doubt whatever that his hatred of the system of exploitation and wage-slavery by which he was surrounded was not only intellectual and philosophic but bitterly personal. I remember saying to him once that as I grew older I thought I became more tolerant. 'Do you,' he said, '*do* you?' It was quite certain he didn't. It has been, I think, Marx's deep animosity to the existing order of things and his scathing criticism of his opponents which has prevented many of the educated well-to-do class from appreciating his masterly life-work at its full value, and has rendered third-rate sciolists and logomachers, like Böhm-Bawerk, such heroes in their eyes, merely because they have misrepresented and attempted to 'refute' him. Accustomed as we are nowadays, especially in England, to fence always with big soft buttons on the point of our rapiers, Marx's terrible onslaughts with naked steel upon his adversaries appeared so improper that it was impossible for our gentlemanly sham-fighters and mental gymnasium men to believe that this unsparing controversialist and furious assailant of capital and capitalists was really the deepest thinker of modern times. A very superficial acquaintance with the controversial writings of Thomas More or John Milton would have enabled them to understand Marx from this point of view a great deal better. He was fighting to a finish all through his life, and that finish will be protracted, I venture to predict, until his greatness is universally recognised.

But in 1880 it is scarcely too much to say that Marx was practically unknown to the English public, except as a dangerous and even desperate advocate of revolution, whose organisation of the International had been one of the causes of the horrible Commune of Paris, which all decent respectable people shuddered at and thought of with horror. Very few well-known Englishmen ever saw him, and of those who were well acquainted with him, I think my old friend Professor Beesly is the only one whose name would be generally recognised as that of a leader of opinion. I consider myself fortunate, therefore, that I was at this time able to get to know him as well as I did.

Marx's health was now failing. His more than Herculean labours on his great book had sapped his marvellously strong constitution. No wonder. He would be at the British Museum when the doors opened in the morning and would leave only when they closed at night. Then, after his return home, he would again work on, giving himself only a short rest and time for food, until the early hours of the morning. Sixteen hours a day was quite an ordinary day's work for him, and not unfrequently he put in an hour or two more. And such work as it was too! It was not surprising that he was now forbidden to do any writing or thinking after his evening meal. This was a serious privation to him but it gave me for a few months the opportunity of calling upon him, when I knew he would be disengaged, and of learning from him more directly and more personally than I could have done in any other way. Thus it came about that, at the close of 1880 and the beginning of 1881, I had the advantage of very frequent conversations with the Doctor, and gained a view of himself and his genius, his vast erudition and his masterly survey of human life which I think was accessible to very few outside his immediate family circle.

Our method of talking was peculiar. Marx had a habit when at all interested in the discussion of walking actively up and down the room, as if he were pacing the deck of a schooner for exercise. I had acquired, on my long voyages, the same tendency to pacing to and fro when my mind was much occupied. Consequently, master and student could have been seen walking up and down on opposite sides of the table for two or three hours in succession, engaged in discussing the affairs of the past and the present. I frequently spoke with him about the Chartist movement, whose leaders he had known well and by whom, as their writings show, he was greatly esteemed. He was entirely sympathetic with my idea of reviving the Chartist organisation, but doubted its possibility; and when speaking of the likelihood of bringing about a great economic and social transformation in Great Britain politically and peacefully he said, 'England is the one country in which a peaceful revolution is possible; but', he added after a pause, 'history does not tell us so.' 'You English,' he said on another occasion, 'like the Romans in many things are most like them in your ignorance of your own history.'

Great improvements have been made in this respect since Marx uttered this dictum; but even now it is humiliating to compare a clever educated Englishman's knowledge of the history of his country with the knowledge which nearly all Irishmen have of the history of Ireland.

On the Eastern Question Marx was anti-Russian to the highest degree. This constituted a link between us. He regarded Russia under Czardom as inevitably the great support of reaction all over Europe, as she had been in 1848, and he could not understand how it was possible for any considerable portion of the people of this island, apart from the politicians, to regard the increase of Muscovite power and influence as other than a serious danger to Western civilisation. He carried this justifiable antagonism, unconsciously intensified may be by his hereditary begettings and belongings and the atrocious treatment of his race in Russia, to an abnormal extent, and even accepted David Urquhart's views on the East with a lack of direct investigation that surprised me in a man of so critical a mind. But all must be weak somewhere, and the weaknesses of this great thinker lay in his judgement of current events and practical measures, as well as in his estimate of men.

The exquisitely funny mistakes made by himself and Engels during the most successful period of the International, and their singularly autocratic view as to the rightful management of what was supposed to be a democratic body, have never been fully recorded. Members of the International, such as Hermann Jung, Adolphe Smith, Cremer, Vésinier, and others, have had too much respect for the magnificent work done by these men in the domain of theory to enlarge upon their defects or shortcomings in the region of practice. Those, however, who were behind the scenes and knew all that was going on might reasonably wonder how so strangely composed a set of people should ever have had the influence and exercised the terrorising effect on society that at one period the International unquestionably did. The ideas were sound enough and the very possibility of their being accepted by the people occasioned the alarm. Marx, as has been wittily said, introduced the great industry into the field of international social revolution. But nearly fifty years later that system is scarcely yet an actual fact.

As to his judgement of men, it is enough to say that he was too tolerant in his estimates on one side and too bitter on the other; whilst even in the affairs of Germany he and Engels opposed Liebknecht's policy of conciliation and consolidation with the Lassalle party, when this was absolutely essential to the success of our movement in that country. It only shows what marvellous and unforgettable services he rendered to the cause of humanity and socialism that all these minor errors have faded from memory, and only his splendid work in political economy, history and internationalism is remembered.

I asked him once how the conception of social surplus value and the social basis of exchange in social labour value occurred to him. He told me that the whole idea came upon him, as he was studying in Paris, like a flash, and that he believed the illuminating notion of the social economic forces of the time, working themselves out quite unconsciously and uncontrolled into monopoly and socialism, beneath the anarchist competitions and antagonisms of the capitalist system, first arose in a co-ordinated shape from his perusal of the works of the early English economists, socialists and Chartists. The conception once clearly formed in his mind and the materialist view of the development of history thoroughly grasped and verified, all the rest became merely a matter of the exposition of the theory and the piecing together of facts in accordance with, or in apparent opposition to, that theory. It is a great mistake to imagine that Marx had any desire to belittle his obligations to his predecessors, or to deprive them of any credit that was their due. He himself called my attention to books and pamphlets, other than those cited by himself in his works, which proved that the revolt against capitalist profit-making in its modern shape had not always been by any means wholly unconscious or ignorant of the real causes at work. Any new investigation of freshly put thought on his own subject he welcomed with delight; nor was he much concerned about the wholesale plagiarisms from himself of which he might have reasonably complained.

In these matters, as in some others, Engels was far more exacting and arrogant than Marx was himself. Marx's readiness to change his views when sufficient evidence was adduced against his own opinion was also much greater than is commonly supposed. Thus, when Lewis H. Morgan proved to Marx's satisfaction in his *Ancient Society* that the gens and not the family was the social unit of the old tribal system and ancient society generally, Marx at once abandoned his previous opinions based upon Neibuhr and others, and accepted Morgan's views. In other questions of less importance he was equally open, as indeed a man of his exceptional intellectual power could scarcely fail to be.

My close acquaintance with Marx at this period naturally brought my wife and myself into contact also with Mrs Marx and their daughter Eleanor. Marx and Eleanor dined with us more than once in Devonshire Street, but Mrs Marx was already too ill to leave the house. Mrs Marx was a refined and highly intelligent woman of great charm of manner and conversation. Come of an aristocratic family, her father being a statesman of the highest distinction in Hanover, she had committed an unforgivable offence against her caste by marrying the man of genius who was now her husband. From Mrs Marx my wife heard much about Marx which brought him into far closer touch in our minds with the common life of common mortals.

They had suffered much for their opinions and had undergone many vicissitudes of fortune. On one occasion Marx himself being in great need went out to pawn some household silver. He was not particularly well dressed and his knowledge of English was not so good as it became later. The silver, unfortunately, as it turned out, bore the crest of the Duke of Argyll's family, the Campbells, with which house Mrs Marx was directly connected. Marx arrived at the Bank of the Three Balls and produced his spoons and forks. Saturday night, foreign Jew, dress untidy, hair and beard roughly combed, handsome silver, noble crest – evidently a very suspicious transaction indeed. So thought the pawnbroker to whom Marx applied. He therefore detained Marx, on some pretext, while he sent for the police. The policeman took the same view as the pawnbroker and also took poor Marx to the police station. There again appearances were strongly against him. 'Saturday night, foreign Jew, handsome silver, noble crest, etc.': the case was already decided before the investigation began. In vain Marx explained, in vain expostulated. His explanations were futile, his expostulations useless. To whom could he refer as to his respectability? Whence had he this handsome silver he was so anxious to get rid of? Why did he wait until dark to pledge the plate? There was nobody he could call in at the time. His truthful statement as to the origin of the spoons and forks was received with laughing incredulity. The number of the house where they lodged was not considered sufficient.

So Marx received the unpleasant hospitality of a police cell, while his anxious family mourned his disappearance, and awaited in trepidation the husband and father who did not come and the cash that they so badly needed. So Saturday night passed. So Sunday. Not until Monday was the founder of scientific socialism able to show conclusively, by the evidence of quite 'respectable' friends resident in London, that he was not a thief and a burglar, and that the Campbell-crested silver was honestly his property. This story, which Mrs Marx told us, half-laughingly, half-sorrowfully, has been told more than once before; but I tell it again here, as showing the sort of dangers to which the unwary foreigner is exposed in London from suspicious pawnbrokers, and even from our much-belauded police; and also as a hint to other refugees whose necessities compel them to resort to their 'uncle', to enter upon the conference in daylight and not on a Saturday night when people are out of town.

But Marx's poverty led him into more trouble than the temporary inconvenience of being locked up for thirty-six hours. Possibly I should not refer to this but for the serious effect it had upon my own relations with Marx himself. Engels, differing in this respect from Marx, had the money-getting faculty fairly well developed; and, having secured for himself a reasonable fortune by cotton-spinning in Lancashire at a comparatively early age, retired, had money at command, and devoted himself to studies in which he showed he was second, and second only, to Marx. I do not myself believe that Engels, whom I never spoke to, nor even saw, was a bad man, though certainly I have no reason personally to take other than a most unfavourable view of his character; but he was exacting, suspicious, jealous, and not disinclined to give full weight to the exchange value of his ready cash in his relations with those whom he helped.

Marx was, to put it in the common form, 'under considerable pecuniary obligations' to Engels. This, Mrs Marx could not bear to think of. Not that she did not recognise Engels's services to her husband, but that she resented and deplored his influence over his great friend. She spoke of him to my wife more than once as Marx's 'evil genius', and wished that she could relieve her husband from any dependence upon this able and loyal but scarcely sympathetic coadjutor. I was myself possessed at that time of good means, and though I am quite sure that neither Marx nor Mrs Marx had the slightest idea that I either could or would take the place of Engels if need arose, I am equally certain that Engels thought I might do so, and, annoyed at the friendship and even intimacy which was growing up between Marx and myself in the winter and spring of 1880–1, made up his mind to break down what he thought might be a rival influence to his own. The effect of all this came later. Meanwhile, as I say, my friendship and regard for Marx grew rapidly. He told me much about Heine, with whom he had a long correspondence which has never even yet been published; about Lassalle, his appearance, his vigour, his curious spluttering utterance when excited; of his own struggle against Bakunin and the sad downfall of the International – all of which was of course of the greatest interest to me. I took up my friends Boyd Kinnear and Butler Johnstone and introduced them to him; and one evening I recall when discussing Freligrath, Heine, Herwegh and other great German men of letters of the modern era, he insisted upon my reading out to himself and Butler Johnstone, Thompson's (B.V.'s) translation of some of Heine's smaller pieces, which he said were the best that had ever been done in any language.

I became, indeed, so much in the habit of calling upon him and talking with him that visitors were not unfrequently shown in as if I had not been there. It was in this way that I met the desperate Russian anarchist Hartmann, who had only that very day sought refuge in this country. The servant brought in his name, and Marx directed he should be shown up at once. I confess I disliked the appearance of the man very much indeed, and told Marx so. His reply to this, after Hartmann had gone, was pretty much what has passed into a proverb on the turf, 'They run in all shapes.' So they do; but I should certainly pick my trusted 'remover' of another shape than Hartmann's. And yet I did the man an injustice. He did his work thoroughly, and feeling unsafe from the Muscovite *mouchards* sent to kidnap him even in London, this Jew conspirator betook himself to the Argentine Republic, where it is said he was followed by the Czar's myrmidons and hounded on to destitution and death.

About this time Henry George's *Progress and Poverty* began to produce a great effect upon the public mind, partly in consequence of the land question in Ireland, and even in Great Britain, being more to the front than it has been before or since in our day; partly because of the active manner in which it was pushed first in the *Radical* by William Webster and afterwards in the Liberal press; and partly on account of the bright journalistic merit of the book itself. Marx looked it through and spoke of it with a sort of friendly contempt: 'The Capitalists' last ditch', he said. This view I scarcely shared. I saw the really extraordinary gaps in the work and its egregious blunderings in economics, but I also recognised, to an extent that Marx either could not or would not admit, the seductive attractiveness for the sympathetic, half-educated mob of its brilliant high-class journalese. I understood, as I thought, that it would induce people to think about economic problems who never could have been brought to read economic books pure and simple; and although I saw quite as clearly then as I do now that taxation of land values can be no solution whatever of the social question, I felt that agitation against any form of private property was better than the stereotyped apathy which prevailed all round us.

There was another opinion which I held and put to Marx, which also I repeated when I wrote a notice on George in the *Saturday Review* shortly after his lamented death. There is such a thing as teaching by error. It was, or so it seemed to be to me, quite impossible for any intelligent person to read through *Progress and Poverty* without detecting its gross economic mistakes. The glittering super-ficiality of George's attacks upon private ownership of land must surely, I thought, lead the least observant to reflect upon the drawbacks to the private ownership of capital. When George stated that all which was not wages was rent, it seemed incredible that any one should fail to inquire who then takes profit and interest? What had become of them? Therefore, I argued, George will teach more by inculcating error than other men can impart by complete exposition of the truth. Marx would not hear of this as a sound contention. The promulgation of error could never be of any good to the people, that was his view, 'To leave error unrefuted is to encourage intellectual immorality. For ten who go farther, a hundred may very easily stop with George, and the danger of this is too great to run.' So far Marx. Nevertheless, I still hold that George's temporary success with his agitatory fallacies greatly facilitated the promulgation of Marx's own theories in Great Britain, owing to the fact that the public mind had been stirred up to consider the social question, and political economy generally, by George's easily read book. But that George's fluent inconsequence should be uncongenial to Marx's scientific mind is not surprising. George was a boy with a bright farthing dip fooling around within the radius of a man using an electric search-light.

The longer I knew Marx the more my admiration and regard for him increased, and the more I could appreciate the human side of his character. This modification of my view of him is, I think, unintentionally apparent in what I have written about him above. At first the aggressive, intolerant, and intellectually dominant side of him preponderated; only later did the sympathy and good-nature which underlay his rugged exterior become apparent. Children liked him, and he played with them as friends. As I comprehended

Marx's views more and more thoroughly, and appreciated not only their accuracy and depth, but their vast width and scope, I determined I would do my utmost to spread a knowledge of his works and theories in the English-speaking world; while endeavouring at the same time to ally his bolder conceptions to a more immediate policy of my own. It never occurred to me, I confess, that the result of my first effort in this direction would be that I should have a serious breach with Marx himself, and that he would, misunderstanding my action entirely, enter upon a series of attacks upon myself of the most vindictive character, followed up by Engels with even more of vitriolic fervour for years. But our friendship remained, so far as I know, undisturbed up to the middle of 1881.

SOURCE: H. Hyndman, *The Record of an Adventurous Life* (London, 1911) pp. 268 ff.

39 Edward Bernstein

Bernstein was to become one of the intellectual leaders of the German social democrats and, after Engels's death, the leading proponent of revisionism. The visit to London he talks of here was made in the company of Bebel in order to patch up a quarrel with Marx and Engels, who considered Bernstein's journalism to be too conciliatory.

Marx was very short-sighted, and on returning from his excursions was always in doubt as to whether he was in front of his own house or a neighbour's and often noticed his mistake only when his key would not work. . . .

Marx's house was smaller than Engels's and the rooms in the basement were correspondingly less elaborate. Nevertheless, the Marx family took their meals in the breakfast room, whereas in Engels's house, which had a very spacious basement, the eating took place in one of the parlours. On one of the days of our visit, Bebel and I were treated to a fairly extensive and well-laden table in the basement room of Marx's house.

Marx's study was in the first storey at the back of the house. We were received there by Marx on the first day of our visit. He greeted Bebel extremely warmly and proposed immediately, as Engels had done, that they treat each other as brothers. He was very friendly to me too, and the conversation flowed much more easily than at Engels's because it turned on questions that lay outside our disagreement. Although Marx was only two years older than Engels, he seemed much older. He spoke in the quietly detached tone of a patriarch, quite the opposite of the picture I had formed of him. From descriptions that originated, I must admit, from his enemies, I had expected to meet a fairly morose and very irritable old gentleman; yet now I saw opposite me a white-haired man whose laughing dark eyes spoke of friendship and whose words contained much that was mild. When a few days later I expressed to Engels my surprise at having found Marx so very different from my expectations, he asserted, 'Well, Marx can nevertheless get most awfully stormy', which I was soon to have the opportunity of observing.

SOURCE: trs. by the editor from E. Benstein, *Aus den Jahren meines Exils. Erinnerungen eines Sozialisten* (Berlin, 1918) pp. 212 ff.

40 Karl Kautsky

Kautsky became active as a journalist in the German socialist movement in the late 1870s. He was later to be the most influential thinker of German social democracy. The visits to Marx recorded below were paid in the spring of 1881. Marx did not have as favourable an opinion of Kautsky as Kautsky did of Marx. In a letter to his eldest daughter, Jenny, in April 1881, he described Kautsky as 'a small-minded mediocrity, too clever by half, industrious in a certain way, busying himself with statistics from which he does not derive anything intelligent, belonging by nature to the tribe of Philistines'.

Engels was certainly more imaginative and broader in his intellectual interests, though Marx's breadth, too, attained legendary dimensions. Marx was more critical and circumspect and so worked more slowly and with greater difficulty, whereas Engels worked with the greatest of ease. Engels himself said to me that his worst fault had been his hastiness. Marx had cured him of it. He would not let go of a thought until he had tested it rigorously from all sides and pursued all its roots and branches. Their political practice was as different as their research. It was particularly important here that, as far as I could tell from my experience, Marx understood the art of handling men better than Engels. And this art is extraordinarily important for success in practical politics.

Neither seems to have been a very good judge of men. This is corroborated by the fact that Engels failed for so long to see through Edward Aveling, a bad lot who shared Eleanor's life and eventually destroyed her; indeed, for almost a decade he preferred him to all other English socialists, to the great detriment of the Marxist cause in England.

However different Marx and Engels might have been in their natures, that had little to do with the contrasting atmosphere in the two houses in the year 1881. The quiet which ruled in the Marx house, in contrast to the liveliness at Engels's, stemmed above all from the fact that Frau Jenny Marx was already in the grip of the frightful disease which was to terminate her life in the same year that I made her acquaintance. She died on 2 December 1881. Of course, it would be a mistake to imagine that the form of her illness was such as to confine her to bed during my London stay. The condition of the patient was highly changeable . . . and there was no talk of permanent illness. But illness was present, together with its pain and weakness that, in general, increased. Of necessity, this made the deepest of impressions on all the members of the family. . . .

Considering that this was the situation in the Marx house, of which of course I had only an incomplete knowledge, I must consider it in fact as a high honour that Marx received me at all. At all events, Liebknecht had warned me that I would have a great deal of trouble with the Londoners; and party gossip has many stories of Marx's harsh venom. My heart was therefore beating fast when I entered Marx's room. I was also seized by the fear that I would make a fool of myself like the young Heine on meeting Goethe, to whom (as he himself relates) he could find nothing better to say than to praise the sweet plums that were to be found on the road from Jena to Weimar.

Yet Marx did not receive me in any way as distantly as Goethe did his young colleague, who was then (1824) about as old as I in 1881. Marx's outward appearance inspired me with awe but was not intimidating. He received me with friendly laughter that struck me as almost paternal.

To my surprise, the first subject of conversation that Marx raised was not theoretical or political but personal. He asked after my mother.

She was then more widely respected than I in the German Party and in the Marx household. Encouraged by me and in my company she had made her way to socialism. Since 1876 she had begun to give expression to her opinions in novels. . . . Frau Marx was very enthusiastic about my mother and Marx himself spoke appreciatively of her. . . .

A further subject of conversation between Marx and myself was provided by his question as to what subject I was then working on. I have already mentioned the remarkable circumstance that Marx and Engels had turned to the study of primitive history at the same time as Höchberg and then myself, and that it was occupying them then in 1881. Naturally this afforded matter for lively discussions.

But whoever was talking to the author of *Capital* could not avoid speaking about this work. I permitted myself the remark that we younger ones were ardently awaiting the speedy appearance of the second volume of *Capital*.

'Me too', Marx answered curtly. It seemed to me as though I had touched a raw spot there.

When I then later asked him whether the time had not arrived to proceed to an edition of Marx's complete works, he said that they would first have to be completely written. Neither of us suspected that in fact they had come to an end.

An hour quickly passed in animated dialogue. When I took my leave, Marx invited me to return soon. . . .

Whatever Marx might have thought of me, he nowhere betrayed the slightest sign of ill-will. I left him highly satisfied. And this feeling grew even stronger with my subsequent visits. He was always alone when I spoke with him; only once were Schorlemmer and Tussy also with us.

On my first visit Marx had avoided the field of politics. On the next occasion he chose to discuss the policies of the Party in Germany. He was severely critical of many of its leaders, but by contrast full of praise for the attitude of the German workers. And he praised August Bebel no less highly. But he also expressed himself very satisfied with Bernstein, in particular with *Sozialdemokrat*, of which he was the editor. Bernstein was the right man for the job, fearless but still conscious of his responsibilities and avoiding any provocation that would make the struggle of the comrades in Germany more difficult. Marx also liked Bernstein's tendency to let facts speak for themselves and avoid empty phrases.

Marx's behaviour in my later visit was not so calm as in the earlier ones. He demonstrated his capacity for caustic criticism and bursts of passionate indignation. Yet I have never known him to be a real god of thunder. Like Engels, he too could flare up frightfully when he came across cowardice, falsehood or black ignorance, so his friends assured me. And yet he could laugh as heartily as anyone else about harmless human weaknesses or comic events, and his wife no less. Unfortunately, I did not have the opportunity of observing this penchant for merriment. Their physical state would not permit it. Nevertheless, Frau Marx did once laugh aloud when talking to me – the only laugh I got to hear in the Marx house.

I got to know the two Marx daughters and they were never tired of relating the often irrepressible merriment of their parents; and also the infinite kindness of their father, not only towards members of the family but also towards all the helpless and unprotected, small children, proletarians, and comrades in distress. This goodness was the foundation of his being; I too sensed it in my conversations with him and it made as strong an impression on me as the enormous compass of his knowledge and the sharpness of his mind. Even the few hours that I spent with Marx were sufficient to make me clearly conscious of the force of this mighty personality which overpowered at the same time as it enchanted.

SOURCE: trs. by the editor from K. Kautsky, *Aus den Frühzeit des Marxismus* (Prague, 1935) pp. 45 ff.

41 Virginia Bateman

Later Mrs Edward Compton, Virginia Bateman visited the Marx household in the early 1880s as an actress friend of Eleanor. She wrote the following reminiscences in 1935, at the age of eighty-two, at the request of her son Compton Mackenzie.

We used to go to see Mr and Mrs Marx on Sunday afternoons, taking that awful vehicle, a four-wheel cab. They lived in a horrid little house (I thought) with a high flight of steps to the front door – a dull small street in the St John's Wood neighbourhood. I don't remember any garden at the back. Nor do I remember having tea with them, but tea wasn't by any means universal in those days. I remember as an innovation five o'clock tea as we always called it.

Distinctly I can see Mr and Mrs Marx. I thought of him as a big man in every way, with a very large head and hair rather like 'shock-headed Peter's' way of wearing his. Mr Marx was always very kind and apparently liked us to come; he used to make fun with us. There was certainly one cat to whom he was devoted, and I think there were more than one.

Mrs Marx was most gentle, motherly and kind, but I don't think anything much in the way of looks. Eleanor who was always called Tussy, pronounced like Pussy, was very like her father and had exactly the same frizzy hair – a sort of dust-coloured hair. She was very fond of me, and I used to be at their house more often and more intimately. Her father and mother liked me too – I expect probably because I had no notion Mr Marx was a great person and was not in the least in awe of him. I am sure he was very fond of young people.

Eleanor was most anxious to make me take Shakespeare seriously, indeed she used to drag me to Furnivall's Shakespeare Society meetings. I was shockingly volatile and insisted on making fun of everything and everybody. Karl Marx sent his books to my mother, all of them inscribed. No doubt they were all sold at her death with everything else. Eleanor Marx never married, but when your father produced *Twelfth Night* at the Strand Theatre in 1886 she came to see me as Viola and was delighted to find me in Shakespeare at last. She was living then with Edward Aveling (he was called Doctor, *not* of medicine). He had deserted his wife. After a time he deserted Eleanor Marx, and she committed suicide. I don't think any of them had any religion at all. At the time we first knew Karl Marx we had very little religion ourselves. At any rate we did very little church-going. Aunt Isabel and I never left off going to church, but nobody else in the family did.

I wish I could remember more, but I'm going back to the 1880s. I do remember what a pathetic figure Mrs Marx was, of course *devoted* to her husband and daughter, the only one left of a large family; and I do remember a sort of weight one felt in being with them which I expect caused me to be utterly flippant. Indeed, at that time of my life it was the only way I managed to get through and help Aunt Isabel through also. One looks back and thinks how different one might have been, but one did not see how, and I still doubt what else one could have been.

SOURCE: in Compton Mackenzie, *My Life and Times. Octave VII: 1931–1938* (London, 1968) pp. 181 f.

42 Marian Comyn

Marian Skinner, as she then was, formed part of Eleanor's circle of acting friends in the early 1880s. She married, in 1884, Henry Comyn, who became Assistant Solicitor to the Treasury. The following reminiscences were written some forty years later.

I have a vivid recollection of my first meeting with Dr Karl Marx, whose name has recently been so much on men's lips, whose gospel has, through the action of its Russian exponents, acquired such a sinister significance.

Of his political creed, and the tremendous issues that have resulted from it, I have nothing to say. Much indeed has already been said, and the last word is not spoken. It is of his home that I would speak – the man as I saw him in the midst of his family and friends, to whom I talked in the intimacies of every-day life during his last years, and to whom I owe many memories of kindly words and generous hospitality.

This was in the early 1880s, when as a political refugee, he had found a home in England, and lived in Maitland Park Road, NW. My introduction to him took place in his own drawing-room at a meeting of a Shakespeare Reading Club, called the 'Dogberry', of which his youngest daughter Eleanor ('Tussy' to her friends) was the leading spirit. Amongst the members of this club were Edward Rose, the dramatist, Mrs Theodore Wright, whose acting in Ibsen's *Ghosts* will still be remembered, pretty Dollie Radford, the poet, Sir Henry Juta, Frederick Engels, and others to whom some measure of fame has come. I had been asked to read the Juvenile part of Prince Arthur in *King John*, but the part was an exceedingly small one, and my attention was riveted less on my princely words than on the figure of our host, who sat at the end of the long double room – an extraordinarily forceful and dominating personality.

His head was large, covered with longish grey hair that matched a shaggy beard and moustache; the black eyes, though small, were keen, piercing, sarcastic, with glints of humour in them. The nose nondescript and not in the least of semitic type. In figure he was of medium height, but rather broadly built. Behind him, on a pedestal in the corner, was a bust of Jupiter Olympus – which he was supposed to resemble.

Near him sat his wife – a lovable and charming woman. She was said to have been beautiful in her youth, but ill-health, and perhaps turbulent times, had taken their toll. Her skin had faded to a waxen pallor, there were purplish brown stains under her eyes, yet there was still an air of breeding about her and a certain distinction of manner. Her maiden name had been Jenny von Westphalen, and there was Scotch blood in her veins – through her mother, I think, who had been a Campbell.

These Shakespearean readings were supposed to take place once a fortnight at different members' houses, but as a matter of fact they were held more frequently at the Marxes' than anywhere else. Karl Marx, in common with the rest of his family, was a devoted admirer of the poet and loved to listen to his plays. As he very rarely went out at night, the only place he could hear them was in his own house. He never read a part which, for the sake of the play, was perhaps quite as well, for he had a guttural voice and a decided German accent. He was interested in talking of Shakespeare's popularity in Germany and of how it had come about; Eleanor always maintained that the German dramatic ideal approximated much more closely to the English than the French, and waxed eloquent over Lessing and Wieland, who had both done so much to make Shakespeare known in their own country. And, indeed, the 'Swan of Avon' can hardly have had a more passionate devotee than Wieland, who wrote to one of his correspondents, 'I tremble with the deepest, holiest veneration when I only speak his name: I bow down to the earth and pray when I feel the presence of Shakespeare's spirit.'

I think this fervent declaration embodies something of the sentiments of Eleanor Marx, if not of her father, though it is not likely that either would have formulated their ideas exactly in these words.

It migtt have struck an unprejudiced person as a little incongruous that after the Dogberry-ites had concluded their serious reading they should finish up the evening with games and such pastimes as charades and dumb-crambo, chiefly – as it would seem from his extreme enjoyment of them – for the delectation of Dr Marx. As an audience he was delightful, never criticising, always entering into the spirit of any fun that was going, laughing when anything struck him as particularly comic, until the tears ran down his cheeks – the oldest in years, but in spirit as young as any of us. And his friend, the faithful Frederick Engels, was equally spontaneous.

Engels looked much younger than Marx, and probably was. He was a pleasant man, not yet grey, with a trick of twitching back a lock of lank black hair that sometimes strayed over his forehead. He had a house in Regent's Park Road, where he lived with a niece, and was, I believe, a widower. For this niece he once gave a dance.

'Will you come?' he said to the Doctor. 'All these' – indicating a little group of girls round him – 'will be there.'

Dr Marx glanced at the group whimsically, and shook his head.

'I will not come. Your guests are too old.'

'Too old at seventeen?'

'I like them young – really young,' said the doctor, seriously.

'Ah! I understand. The age of your grandchildren!'

Dr Marx nodded, and they both laughed as at a thoroughly enjoyable joke.

(The dance took place, and was delightful. As a host Herr Engels was also delightful.)

Dr Marx held that old age was greatly a matter of will. He must himself have been a strong man, for he worked incessantly in his study – a good-sized, well-lighted front room on the first floor of the house, lined with plain wooden bookshelves and having a large writing-table set at right angles to the window. Here he read and wrote all day, and took his exercise in the evening, just as dusk began to fall. Many times, when Eleanor Marx and I were sitting on the rug in front of the drawing-room fire, talking in the twilight, we would hear the front door gently close, and immediately afterwards the Doctor's figure, clad in a black cloak and soft felt hat (and looking, as his daughter remarked, for all the world like a conspirators' chorus), would pass along by the window, and not return until darkness closed in.

At this time, I imagine his work must have involved tremendous responsibilities. He held in his hands the threads of that vast network of European socialism, of which he was the acknowledged leader. But, in spite of all this, he found time for the study of Russian – which language he did not essay to learn until he was past sixty. Before he died, I understood from Eleanor, he knew it fairly well.

So far as outward semblance went, no. 41, Maitland Park Road, was a very ordinary suburban villa; the charm of the household, however, was by no means ordinary. I suppose it was bohemian in its open-handed hospitality, its gracious welcome, to the strangers within its gates. And the strangers were numerous and shared the classic charm of great variety. There was one point of resemblance between them – for the most part they were impecunious. Shabby as to clothes, furtive in movement, but interesting, always interesting.

A goodly number had no doubt found their native land too hot to hold them – clever conspirators to whom London was a chosen centre, political prisoners who had contrived to shake the shackles from their limbs, young adventurers whose creed was of the 'if-there's-a-government-I'm-agen-it' order.

Amongst them was a courtly young Russian, who had attempted to blow up the Czar, and who was certainly one of the mildest mannered men that ever cut his country. He warbled Russian love songs delightfully, and punctuated them with languishing glances, and he told us that he had spent over a year in a Petersburg prison cell where there was not room to stand up, or to lie down at full length, and that the snow drifted in through the paneless window until it was chest high. He was accused of being an anarchist – which accusation was probably not true at the beginning of his incarceration, but pretty correct at its end.

Another stranger whom I chanced to see was a queer, foreign-looking man wearing a frock coat, a wonderful scarf pin, and a big beard and moustache. His name ended in 'ski,' and I was given to understand he had come from Poland, or some other restless region, on a mission to Karl Marx. A week later Eleanor alluded to this person, and I asked whether he had gone back to the land of his fathers.

'Why, no', she answered; 'since that first visit of his, a week ago, we have never set eyes on him. We have inquired at the lodgings that were taken for him, and tried every means in our power to find him. But it's no good. Not a trace of him. And the awkward part is that the business he came about is at a standstill.'

I was horrified. Visions of robbery, crime – even *murder* – rushed through my brain.

'Why not communicate with the police?' I queried.

She looked at me whimsically.

'That's just the very thing we wish to avoid.'

'What does Dr Marx say?' was my next inquiry, and she responded drily, *'Cherchez la femme!'* – adding, 'He'll turn up when he's tired of her' – and sure enough, he did.

Sunday was the Marx's official 'At Home' day, on which they kept 'open house,' and the doctor occasionally forsook his study for a while in order to entertain visitors. He usually came down to meals, which were served in the semi-basement dining-room, and seemed to be going on more or less all the Sabbath day. He had a good appetite, and thoroughly enjoyed his food, which was prepared by Helene, the nice-looking old German cook–housekeeper, who followed the fortunes of the Marx family until the death of the Doctor. After that she went into Frederick Engels's household. Helene was an excellent cook – her jam tarts are a sweet and abiding memory to this day. She was a fresh complexioned old woman, who wore gold earrings, and a chenille net over her hair, and who reserved to herself the right of 'speaking her mind' even to the august Doctor. Her mind was respectfully, even meekly, received by all the family, except Eleanor, who frequently challenged it.

Apropos of luncheon, I remember arriving late for this function one Sunday, and being pretty severely hauled over the coals by my host in consequence. He wagged his head gravely at my apologies.

'It's waste of breath to tell people of their faults, in the hope that the telling will cure them,' he muttered, in his guttural tones. 'If they would only *think* – but that is just what they won't do. What is man's greatest asset, the most precious thing that is given him? *Time.* And see how it is wasted. Your own time – well, that does not matter. But other people's – *mine* – *Himmel!* what a responsibility.' I looked as I felt – abject. His ferocity disappeared in a charming smile.

'Come, come, you shall be forgiven. Sit down, and I will tell you stories of the days when I was in Paris, and did not know French as well as I know it now.'

One story was to the effect that on getting out of an omnibus – or train – he accidentally trod on a lady's foot. She glowered at him. Sweeping off his hat, he said, with great *empressement* – 'Madame, *permettez-moi.'*

She glowered all the more, and he went on his way with the hackneyed conviction that women were queer creatures. Later on, it flashed upon him like an inspiration that *'Pardonnez-moi'* might have been more appropriate.

Another family legend was of Madame Marx going to an auction with the intention of buying a certain book, but getting confused between *livre* and *lièvre*. She returned in triumph with a *stuffed hare*.

I think the first story was absolutely true. In the second I suspected imagination.

Karl Marx was fond of dogs, and three small animals of no particular breed – of a mixture of many breeds indeed – formed important members of the household. One was called Toddy, another Whisky – the name of the third I forget, but I fancy that, too, was alcoholic. They were all three sociable little beasts, ever ready for a romp, and very affectionate. One day, after an absence of six weeks in Scotland, I went to see Eleanor and found her with her father in the drawing-room, playing with Whisky. Whisky at once transferred his attentions to me, greeting me with ebullient friendliness, but almost immediately he ran to the door and whined to have it opened for him.

Eleanor said, 'He has gone down to Toddy, who has just presented him with some puppies.'

She had hardly finished speaking before there was a scratching and scrambling in the hall, and in bounded Whisky, shepherding Toddy. The little mother made straight for me, exchanged affabilities in friendly fashion, then hurried back to her family. Whisky meanwhile stood on the rug, wagging a proudly contented tail, and looking from one to the other, as who should say, 'See how well I know to do the right thing.'

Dr Marx was much impressed by this exhibition of canine intelligence. He observed that it was clear the dog had gone downstairs to tell his little mate an old friend had arrived, and it was her bounden duty to come and pay her respects without delay. Toddy, like an exemplary wife, had torn herself away from her squealing babies, in order to do his bidding.

Judging from the books on the closely packed study shelves, Dr Marx must have had a wide and varied knowledge of English literature – not forgetting novels. I once observed on his table a book of Sir Charles Lyell, and near it one of Bulwer Lytton's, *Pelham, or the Adventures of a Gentleman*. And I remember a discussion at luncheon on Victorian authors, and the admiration expressed by the whole family for Charlotte and Emily Bronte, both of whom they placed far above George Eliot.

Dr Marx's manners to his family were altogether delightful. He was tender and considerate to his wife, whose death, I think, hastened his own. Eleanor he treated with the indulgent affection one bestows on a beloved but very wilful child.

SOURCE: M. Comyn 'My Recollections of Karl Marx', *Nineteenth Century and After*, XCI (1922) pp. 161 ff.

43 Eleanor Marx (iv)

The following is from a letter by Eleanor Marx to Wilhelm Liebknecht. Liebknecht had asked her for an account of Marx's last years and included her letter *verbatim* in his memoirs.

You asked some questions about our good Helene, or 'Nym', as we called her towards the end, Johnny Longuet having given her the name for some reason unknown to me when he was a baby. She entered the service of my grandmother von Westphalen when she was a girl of eight or nine and grew up with Moor, Mother and Edgar von Westphalen. She always had a great affection for the old von Westphalen. So did Moor. He never tired of telling us of the old Baron von Westphalen and his surprising knowledge of Shakespeare and Homer. The baron could recite some of Homer's songs by heart from beginning to end and he knew most of Shakespeare's dramas by heart in both German and English. In contrast to him, Moor's father – for whom Moor had great admiration – was a real eighteenth-century 'Frenchman'. He knew Voltaire and Rousseau by heart just as the old Westphalen did Homer and Shakespeare. Moore's astonishing versatility was due without doubt to these 'hereditary' influences.

To come back to Lenchen, I cannot say whether she came to my parents before or after they went to Paris (which was soon after their marriage). All I know is that Grandmother sent the girl to Mother 'as the best she could send, the faithful and loving Lenchen'. And the faithful and loving Lenchen remained with my parents and later her younger sister Marianne joined her. You will hardly remember this, for it was after your time. . . .

A few more words about our dear Mother. She was dying for months, bearing the appalling tortures that cancer brings with it. And yet her good humour, her inexhaustible wit that you know so well never left her a minute. She asked with the impatience of a child about the results of the elections in Germany (1881). And how she rejoiced at the victory! She was cheerful to her very death, trying to dispel our anxiety for her with jokes. Yes, she who was suffering so terribly actually joked and laughed at the doctor and all of us because we were so serious. She was conscious almost till the last minute, and when she could no longer speak – her last words were for 'Karl' – she squeezed our hands and tried to smile.

As far as Moor is concerned, you know that he went out of his bedroom to his study in Maitland Park, sat down in his armchair and calmly passed away. The 'General' had that armchair until he died. Now I have got it. When you write about Moor do not forget Lenchen. I know you will not forget Mother. Helene was in a way the axis on which everything in the house revolved. She was the best and most faithful friend. So do not forget Helene when you write about Moor.

I shall now give you some details about Moor's stay in the south as you asked me to. At the beginning of 1882 he and I stayed a few weeks with Jenny at Argenteuil. In March and April Moor was in Algiers, in May in Monte Carlo, Nice and Cannes. He was at Jenny's again about the end of June and the whole of July. Lenchen was also at Argenteuil then. From there he went to Switzerland, Vevey and so on, with Laura. Towards the end of September or beginning of October, he returned to England and went straight to Ventnor, where Johnny and I went to see him.

Now for a few notes in answer to your questions. Our little Edgar ('Mush') was born in 1847, I think, and died in April 1855. Little Fawkes (Heinrich) was born on 5 November 1849, and died when he was about two. My sister Franzisca was born in 1851 and died while still a baby, at about eleven months.

All I can tell you about Moor's stay in Mustapha (Algiers) is that the weather was shocking, that Moor found a very nice and capable doctor there and that everybody in the hotel was friendly and attentive towards him.

During the autumn and winter of 1881–2 Moor first stayed with Jenny at Argenteuil, near Paris. We met him there and stayed a few weeks. Then he went to the south of France and to Algiers, but he was not well when he came back. He spent the autumn and winter of 1882–3 in Ventnor, Isle of Wight, returning in January 1883 after Jenny's death.

Now about Karlsbad. We went there for the first time in 1874, when Moor was sent there because of liver trouble and sleeplessness. As his first stay there did him extraordinary good he went again by himself in 1875. In the following year, 1876, I went with him again because he said he had missed me too much the preceding year. In Karlsbad he was most conscientious about his cure, scrupulously doing everything prescribed for him. We made many friends there. Moor was a charming travelling companion. He was always in a good humour and ready to take pleasure at everything – a beautiful landscape or a glass of beer. And his immense knowledge of history made everyplace we went to more living and present in the past than in the present itself.

I think a certain amount has been written on Moor's stay in

Karlsbad. I heard, among other things, of a fairly long article but I cannot remember what paper it was in.

In 1874 we saw you in Leipzig. On our return we made a detour to Bingen, which Moor wanted to show me becasuse he was there with my mother on their honeymoon. On these two journeys we also visited Dresden, Berlin, Prague, Hamburg and Nuremberg.

In 1877 Moor was to go to Karlsbad again but we were informed that the German and Austrian authorities intended to expel him, and as the journey was too long and expensive to risk an expulsion he did not go there any more. This was a great disadvantage for him, for after his cure he always felt rejuvenated.

Our main reason for going to Berlin was to see my father's faithful friend, my dear Uncle Edgar von Westphalen. We only stayed there a couple of days. Moor was greatly amused to hear that the police went to our hotel on the third day, just an hour after we had left.

By autumn 1881 our dear *Mömchen* (mother) was so ill that she could rarely leave her sick bed. Moor had a severe attack of pleurisy, the result of his having neglected his ailments. The doctor, our good friend Donkin, considered his case almost hopeless. That was a terrible time. Our dear Mother lay in the big front room, Moor in the small room next to it. They who were so used to each other, whose lives had come to form part of each other, could not even be together in the same room any longer.

Our good old Lenchen – you know what she was to us – and I had to nurse them both. The doctor said it was our nursing that saved Moor. However that may be, I only know that neither Lenchen nor I went to bed for three weeks. We were on our feet day and night and when we were too exhausted we would rest an hour in turns.

Moor got the better of his illness again. Never shall I forget the morning he felt himself strong enough to go into Mother's room. When they were together they were young again – she a young girl and he a loving youth, both on life's threshold, not an old disease-ridden man and an old dying woman parting from each other for life.

Moor got better, and although he was not yet strong, he seemed to be regaining strength.

Then Mother died on 2 December 1881. Her last words – a remarkable thing was that they were in English – were addressed to her 'Karl'.

When our dear General (Engels) came he said something that nearly made me wild at him:'Moor is dead too'.

And it was true.

When our dear Mother passed away, so did Moor. He fought hard to hang on to life, for he was a fighter to the end – but he was a broken man. His general condition got worse and worse. Had he been selfish he would have let things go as they wished. But for him one thing was above everything else – his devotedness to the cause. He tried to complete his great work and that was why he agreed to another journey for his health.

In spring 1882 he went to Paris and Argenteuil, where I met him. We spent a few really happy days with Jenny and her children. Then Moor went to the south of France and finally to Algiers.

During the whole of his stay in Algiers, Nice and Cannes the weather was bad. He wrote me long letters from Algiers. I lost many of them because I sent them to Jenny at his wish and she did not send me many back.

When Moor finally returned home he was very poorly and we began to fear the worst. On the advice of the doctors he spent the autumn and winter in Ventor on the isle of Wight. Here I must mention that at Moor's wish I spent three months at that time in Italy with Jenny's eldest son, Jean (Johnny). At the beginning of 1883 I went to Moor, taking Johnny with me, for he was his favourite grandson. I was obliged to return because I had lessons to give.

Then came the last terrible blow: the news of Jenny's death. Jenny, Moor's first-born, the daughter he loved the most, died suddenly (on 11 January). We had had letters from Moor – I have them in front of me now – telling us that Jenny's health was improving and that we (Helene and I) need not be anxious. The telegram informing us of her death arrived an hour after that letter of Moor. I immediately left for Ventnor.

I have lived many a sad hour, but none so sad as that. I felt that I was bringing my father his death sentence. I racked my brain all the long anxious way to find how I could break the news to him. But I did not need to, my face gave me away. Moor said at once, 'Our Jennychen is dead.' Then he urged me to go to Paris at once and help with the children. I wanted to stay with him but he brooked no resistance. I had hardly been half an hour at Ventnor when I set out again on the sad journey to London. From there I left for Paris. I was doing what Moor wanted me to do for the sake of the children.

I shall not say anything about my return home. I can only think with a shudder of that time, the anguish, the torment. But enough of that. I came back and Moor returned home, to die.

SOURCE: *RME*, pp. 126 ff.; from the German original in W. Liebknecht, 'Karl Marx zum Gedächtnis', *Mohr und General* (Berlin, 1970) pp. 150 ff.

44 Karl Marx's Confession

The following is Marx's version of a common Victorian parlour game, taken from a Confessions Book belonging to his daughter Laura. They were written (in English) in the mid 1860s.

Your favourite virtue	Simplicity
Your favourite virtue in man	Strength
Your favourite virtue in woman	Weakness
Your chief characteristic	Singleness of purpose
Your idea of happiness	To fight
Your idea of misery	Submission
The vice you excuse most	Gullibility
The vice you detest most	Servility
Your aversion	Martin Tupper[1]
Favourite occupation	Book-worming
Favourite poet	Shakespeare, Aeschylus, Goethe
Favourite prose-writer	Diderot
Favourite hero	Spartacus, Kepler
Favourite heroine	Gretchen
Favourite flower	Daphne
Favourite colour	Red
Favourite name	Laura, Jenny
Favourite dish	Fish
Favourite Maxim	*Nihil humani a me alienum puto*[2]
Favourite motto	*De omnibus dubitandum*[3]

SOURCE: *RME*, p. 266.

NOTES

1. Victorian popular writer
2. 'I consider that nothing human is alien to me.'
3. 'You must have doubts about everything.'

Critical Bibliography

Beer, M., *The Life and Teaching of Karl Marx* (London and Manchester, 1921). A small book; necessarily dated.

Berlin, I., *Karl Marx. His Life and Environment* (Oxford, 1939). A very readable short biography.

Blumenberg, W., *Karl Marx* (London, 1971). An excellent brief biography mainly using Marx's own words, with a varied selection of photographs.

Carmichael, J., *Karl Marx. The Passionate Logician* (London, 1968). A shortish, undistinguished biography.

Carr, E. H., *Karl Marx. A Study in Fanaticism* (London 1943). A well-written critical biography of medium length.

Gemkow, H., *et al.*, *Karl Marx. A Biography* (Berlin, 1970). A well-documented, but quite uncritical, piece of hagiography.

Kapp, Y., *Eleanor Marx*, vol. I: *Family Life 1855–1883* (London, 1972). A fascinating mine of information on the Marx household.

Kettle, A. C., *Karl Marx, Founder of Modern Communism* (London, 1963). A good short biography by a communist.

Korsch, K., *Karl Marx* (New York, 1936). An insightful biography by an ex-communist.

Lewis, J., *The Life and Teaching of Karl Marx* (London, 1965). A good medium-length biography presenting Marx in a favourable light.

McLellan, D., *Karl Marx: His Life and Thought*, 2nd edn (London, 1976). A comprehensive and detailed account.

Mehring, F., *Karl Marx* (London, 1936). The classical biography of Marx; somewhat out of date and slightly hagiographical.

Nicolaievski, B., and Maenchen-Helfen, O., *Karl Marx, Man and Fighter* (London 1933; 3rd edn 1973). An excellent biography emphasising Marx's political activities.

Padova, S., *Karl Marx. An Intimate Biography* (New York, 1978). An extensive and well-researched account of Marx's private life.

Payne, R., *Marx, a Biography* (London, 1968). A lot of information on Marx's private life, though the author's understanding of Marx's ideas is extremely deficient.

Raddatz, F., *Karl Marx. A Political Biography* (London, 1979) A readable, rather racy account of Marx's private life, emphasising its bourgeois aspects.

Ryazanov, D., *Karl Marx, Man, Thinker and Revolutionist* (New York, 1927). A well-informed series of lectures of Marx's life.

Schwartzchild, L., *Karl Marx. The Red Prussian* (New York, 1948). A strongly critical biography.

Seigel, J., *Marx's Fate* (Princeton, NJ, 1978). A perceptive, detailed and scholarly portrait of Marx from a neo-Freudian angle.

Spargo, J., *Karl Marx. His Life and Works* (New York, 1910). The first biography of Marx in English.

Sprigge, C. J. S., *Karl Marx* (London, 1938; New York, 1962). A short biography.

Stepanova, Elena A., *Karl Marx* (Moscow, 1962). A short piece of pure hagiography.

Biographical Index

AESCHYLUS (525–456 BC): Greek playwright of classic tragedies; author of *The Oresteian Trilogy* and *Prometheus Bound*, 45, 69, 167

ALEXANDER THE GREAT (Alexander III of Macedon) (356–23 BC): conqueror of the Persian Empire, 144

AMADEO, FERDINANDO MARIA (DUKE OF AOSTA) (1845–90): King of Spain (1870–3), 87

ANNEKE, FRIEDRICH (1818–72): Prussian artillery officer; member of Communist League and participant in Revolution of 1848–9; his arrest was mentioned in the *Neue Rheinische Zeitung*, 18

ANNENKOV, PAVEL VASILYEVICH (1812–87): Russian liberal and landowner; friend of Marx, 11 ff., 19

ARISTOTLE (384–22 BC): Greek philosopher, metaphysician, logician; compromised between idealism and materialism; author of *Ethics* and *Politics*, 45, 144

AUER, IGNAZ (1846–1907): German social democrat and journalist; *Reichstag* deputy, 139

AUERBACH, BERTHOLD (1812–82): friend of Moses Hess; novelist of peasant life, 2

AVELING, EDWARD (1851–98): English socialist and publicist; common-law husband of Eleanor Marx in 1884; member of Social Democratic Federation and helped found the Socialist League; co-translator into English of Marx's *Capital* and Engels's *Socialism: Utopian and Scientific*, 120, 153, 157

BACH, JOHANN SEBASTIAN (1685–1750): German baroque composer, 80

BACON, FRANCIS (1561–1626): English philosopher and scientist; Lord Chancellor of England; developed experimental method; author of *Essays* (1597–1623) and *Magna Iustauratio* (1603–24), 133

BAKUNIN, MIKHAIL ALEXANDROVICH (1814–76): Russian anarchist and publicist; participant in Revolution of 1848–9; member of First International, later expelled, xii, 11, 19, 89, 114, 116 ff., 125, 127, 150

BALZAC, HONORÉ DE (1799–1850): French novelist noted for character development; author of *La Comédie Humaine* (1828–50), 70, 73, 101

BANNER, HENRY: singing teacher of Jenny and Laura Marx, 28 f.

BATEMAN, VIRGINIA (MRS EDWARD COMPTON) (1853–1940): actress friend of Eleanor Marx; mother of Sir Compton Mackenzie, 156 f.

BAUER, BRUNO (1809–82): German idealist philosopher; leading Young Hegelian; friend of Marx during student days; later became a democrat, 88

BAUER, EDGAR (1820–86): German writer and Young Hegelian; brother of Bruno Bauer and friend of Marx, 63 ff., 88

BAUMAN, F.: German socialist and co-editor of *Freie Presse*, 139

GEORGE, HENRY (1839–97): American economist and publicist; founded the Single Tax movement; author of *Progress and Poverty* (1879), 150 f.

GIGOT, PHILIPPE CHARLES (1820–90): Belgian Communist; member of Communist League; friend of Marx and Engels, 20 f.

GLADSTONE, WILLIAM EWART (1809–98): leader of the Liberal Party and Prime Minister four times (1868–74, 1880–5, 1886 and 1892–4), 140

GOETHE, JOHANN WOLFGANG VON (1749–1832): German romantic poet, writer and man of letters; author of *The Sorrows of Young Werther* (1774), *Wilhelm Meister's Apprenticeship and Travels* (1793–5) and *Faust* (1808), 49, 69, 81, 84, 133, 154, 167

GOGOL, NIKOLAI VASILIEVICH (1809–52): Russian writer; author of *Diary of a Madman* (1835), 70

GONCOURT, EDMOND (1822–96): French realist writer on social history; collaborated with his brother Jules, 73

GONCOURT, JULES (1830–70): French realist writer on social history; collaborated with his brother Edmond, 73

GÖTZ, PETER OTTO VON (1793–1880): Russian writer; friend of Marx in London, 24

GRANT, ULYSSES SIMPSON (1822–85): eighteenth President of the United States, 139

GRIMM, JACOB (1785–1863): German philologist; historian of German culture, language, literature and mythology; collaborated with his brother Wilhelm, 39, 46

GRIMM, WILHELM (1786–1859): German philologist; historian of German culture, language, literature and mythology; collaborated with his brother Jacob, 39, 46

GUIZOT, FRANCOIS PIERRE GUILLAUME (1787–1874): French historian and statesman; Orleanist and director of French domestic and foreign policy (1840–8); author of *The History of European Civilisation* (1845), *The History of French Civilisation* (1845) and *The History of the English Revolution* (1826–56), 19, 128

HANDEL, GEORGE FREDERICK (*né* GEORG FRIEDRICH HÄNDEL) (1685–1759): German baroque composer; lived in England, 64

HARIRI, ABU MUHAMMAD AL-QASIM AL (1054–1122): Arab scholar and poet, author of several philological works, 84, 93

HARNEY, GEORGE JULIAN (1817–97): English Chartist and editor of the *Northern Star* and *Red Republican*; founder of Society of Fraternal Democrats, 27

HARTMANN, LEV NIKOLAYEVICH (1850–1913): Russian anarchist, populist and Narodnik; emigrated to America in 1879, 150

HASSELMAN, W. (1844–?): Prussian deputy expelled by Bismarck from *Reichstag*, 139

HATZFELDT, SOPHIE VON (1805–81): German countess; friend and follower of Lassalle, 28

HAYDN, JOSEPH (1733–1809): Austrian classical composer and teacher of Beethoven, 64

HECKER, P. (1811–81): German publisher; editor of *Volksfreund*, 43

HEGEL, GEORG WILHELM FRIEDRICH (1770–1831): German objective idealist philosopher; principal advocate of idealist dialectics and major influence on Marx; author of *The Phenomenology of Spirit* (1807); *The Science of Logic* (1812) and *The Philosophy of Right* (1821), 3, 6, 9, 69, 71, 81, 115

HEINE, HEINRICH (1797–1856): German poet and friend of Marx; author of travel poems on Germany and France and *The History of Religion and Philosophy in Germany* (1834), 3, 10, 19, 34, 69, 76, 81 f., 125, 130, 150, 154

HEINZEN, KARL (1809–80): German radical journalist; critic of Marx and Engels; emigrated to Switzerland, England and finally (in 1850) to America, xi, 5 f., 20

HERWEGH, EMMA (1817–1904): wife of Georg Herwegh, 7, 19

HERWEGH, GEORG (1817–75): German poet and democrat; friend of Marx, 6 ff., 19, 150

HERWEGH, MARCEL: son of Georg Herwegh, 6 f.

HERZEN, ALEXANDRE IVANOVICH (1812–70): Russian materialist philosopher and democrat; lived in exile in London, where he published for Russian émigrés; author of *Dilettantism in Science* (1843), *Letters on the Study of Nature* (1845–6), *From the Other Shore* (1850) and *The Russian People and Socialism* (1852), 125

HESS, MOSES (1812–75): German communist; introduced communism to the Young Hegelians; close friend and collaborator with Marx on *Rheinische Zeitung*; participant in early congresses of the International, 2 f., 19 f., 20

HIRSCH, KARL (1841–1900): German social democrat and journalist for SPD newspapers, 143 f.

HÖCHBERG, KARL (1853–85): German social democrat; financed various socialist journals and newspapers, 154

HOFFMANN, ERNST THEODOR AMADEUS (1776–1882): German romantic writer; later became a reactionary, 93, 101

HOLBACH, PAUL HENRI DIETRICH (BARON D') (1723–89): French materialist philosopher and a theist of the Enlightenment; author of *The System of Nature* (1770), 3

HOMER (? 8th cent. BC): Greek epic poet; author of the *Iliad* and *Odyssey*, 101, 163

HUXLEY, THOMAS HENRY (1825–95): English naturalist and biologist; sympathetic to Darwin's theory of evolution; author of *Evolution and Ethics* (1893), 52

HYNDMAN, HENRY MAYERS (1842–1921): English socialist; founded the Democratic Federation (1881) and its successor, the Social Democratic Federation (1884); author of *England for All* (1881) and *The Historical Basis of Socialism in England* (1883), 126, 128 f., 132, 142 ff.

IBSEN, HENRIK (1828–1906): Norwegian dramatist; father of modern drama, 158

IMANDT, PETER: German communist, teacher and later, democrat; member of Communist League; participant in Revolution of 1848–9; friend of Marx in London, 24

IRVING, SIR HENRY (1838–1905): English stage producer and Shakespearean actor, 127, 130